The Awakened Life
Spiritual Knowledge from India's Sacred Traditions

Jayaram V

Published by
Pure Life Vision LLC
New Albany, Ohio

The Awakened Life: Spiritual Knowledge from India's Sacred Traditions
Copyright © 2024 by Jayaram V. All rights reserved.
Published and Distributed Worldwide by Pure Life Vision LLC., USA.
Second Edition 2024

No part of this publication may be reproduced, stored in a retrieval system, or transmitted in any form or by any means, electronic, mechanical, photocopying, recording, scanning, or otherwise, now known or hereinafter invented, except for quotations in printed reviews, without the prior written, express permission of the publisher or the author. Requests to the publisher for permission to print portions of this book or for bulk purchase of the book should be addressed to Pure Life Vision LLC, PO Box 1003, 102 W Main St, New Albany, OH 43054.

Pure Life Vision LLC is a registered company in the U.S.A. Pure Life Vision books and products are available through many bookstores and online websites. For inquiries, please visit https://www.PureLifeVision.com.

NO AI TRAINING: Without in any way limiting the author's [and publisher's] exclusive rights under copyright, any use of this publication to "train" generative artificial intelligence (AI) technologies to generate text is expressly prohibited. The author reserves all rights to license uses of this work for generative AI training and development of machine learning language models.

Limit of Liability/Disclaimer of Warranty: While the publisher and the author have used their best efforts in preparing this book, they make no representation or warranties with respect to the accuracy or completeness of the contents of this book and specifically disclaim any implied warranties of merchantability or fitness for any particular purpose. No warranty may be created or extended by sales representatives or written sales materials. The advice and strategies contained herein may not be suitable for your situation. You should consult with a professional where appropriate. Neither the publisher nor the author shall be liable for any loss of profit or any other commercial damages, including but not limited to special, incidental, consequential, or other damages

Publisher Cataloging-in-Publication Data

V, Jayaram
The Awakened Life: Spiritual Knowledge from India's Sacred Traditions
A Catalog record for this title is available from the Library of Congress.
LCCN: 2010928818
ISBN- 13: 978-1-935760-13-9
ISBN- 10: 1-935760-13-0
Printed in the United States of America
10 9 8 7 6 5 4 3 2
Second Edition

The Bodhisattva vow

Though the many beings are numberless,
I vow to save them.
Though greed, hatred, and ignorance rise endlessly,
I vow to end them.
Though the path is vast and fathomless,
I vow to understand it.
Though enlightenment is beyond attainment
I vow to embody it fully.

To

My Teachers and Parents

Books By Jayaram V

1. The Bhagavadgita: Unveiling the Gita's Secrets
2. Shiva Sutras: Mystic Knowledge Explained
3. Sadhana Panchakam - The Fivefold Spiritual Practice
4. Brahman
5. Essays on the Bhagavadgita
6. The Bhagavadgita: A Complete Translation
7. The Bhagavadgita: A Simple Translation
8. Introduction to Hinduism
9. Selected Upanishads
10. Brihadaranyaka Upanishad
11. Chandogya Upanishad
12. Think Success: Essays on Self-help
13. Being the Best: Practical Advice for Peace and Happiness
14. Thoughts and Quotations
15. The Awakened Life: Spiritual Knowledge from India's Sacred Traditions

About the Author

Jayaram V, a renowned author with a unique perspective, has penned 15 books, including Brahman, The Awakened Life, An Introduction to Hinduism, Bhagavadgita: Unveiling the Gita's Secrets, Essays on the Bhagavadgita, Selected Upanishads, Brihadaranyaka and Chandogya Upanishads, and Shiva Sutras: Mystic Knowledge Explained. Jayaram's insightful writings, appreciated worldwide, delve into Hinduism, Buddhism, Jainism, Sikhism, Zoroastrianism, Spirituality and Self-improvement. He is the Founder and President of Hinduwebsite.com, a comprehensive website on Hinduism and related religions, where most of his writings can be found. To learn more about Jayaram V, please visit https://www.jayaramv.com.

Contents

Preface to the Second Edition 11
Author's Note.. 13
Introduction.. 15
Look For God in Everything 22
Cultivate Friendship with God... 27
Let God be Your Role Model 31
Think of God Constantly 35
The Ego and Its Challenge.. 38
Triple Means of Making Sense... 52
Avoiding the Extremes by The Middle Path 58
Letting Go of Your Fears 70
The Hidden Symphony of Life 79
The Four Faces of Suffering.. 83
Manifesting With the Right Intentions 94
Being True to Yourself 99
Understanding Desires and Intentions............................... 101
Manifesting Abundance for the Common Good 105
Understanding the Real Person in You 109
The Problem with Your Extended Identities 113
Cultivating Sameness and Tolerance................................... 118
The Importance of Faith... 124
Spirituality For Worldly People 132
Unity and Diversity of the Human Body 145
Seeing Things as They Are 157
The Spiritual Aspects of Food... 165
Purification, Transformation, and Liberation.................... 174
The Spiritual Laws That Govern Our Lives....................... 184
The Bhagavadgita on Suffering and Its Causes................. 190
The Purpose and Value of Spiritual Practice 200
Living Like a Lotus Leaf in the Waters of Life 206
Morality and Spirituality 218
Ten Important Spiritual Truths for Reflection................... 227
Finding the Right Teachers for Guidance 239
The Glossary of Sanskrit Terms.. 255
Recommended Reading... 264

Preface to the Second Edition

The first edition of this book, titled The Awakened Life, A Collection of Writings on Spiritual Life, was published in September 2010. It primarily consisted of the content from the author's previous writings, which were published at Hinduwebsite.com between 2000 and 2010. These writings were edited, rewritten, and compiled into the first edition. After nearly 14 years, we felt the need to republish them with further improvements. The first edition was well received, but many developments took place in these 14 years, both in the way the knowledge has improved and the way content is presented in multiple formats. Therefore, we decided to republish the earlier edition as a second edition and in different formats. Jayaram made significant changes to the previous edition, revising and updating the content wherever necessary. Some chapter titles have also been changed.

Spirituality associated with the philosophies and religions that originated in India is the main focus of Jayaram's spiritual writings. They reflect his familiarity and authority on these subjects. Since he spent his early life in that country and imbibed its ethos, they shaped his spiritual knowledge, beliefs, and practices. India is essentially the land of spirituality where some of the world's profound ideas developed. According to some historians, the Indian subcontinent and adjoining areas comprise the cradle of human civilization. Unfortunately, the people in this region did not maintain any records of their achievements or explorations. Therefore, we cannot validate such claims definitively, although we have circumstantial evidence. Spiritual ideas and practices have flourished in the region since the earliest times. Many of the beliefs and practices that grew in its soil are deeply ingrained in the consciousness of its people even today. Many ideas that require time and effort to understand by outsiders are known to many people who live there, even if they may possess a minimum literacy. No one needs to explain to them the meaning of karma, Dharma, or rebirth.

Jayaram has been drawn to the spiritual knowledge of this land from an early age. He studied it extensively in the last 45 years and assimilated the essential knowledge. His familiarity with Indian spirituality is well reflected in most of his writings, including this work. Because of the ease with which he writes, we are confident that his writings can be understood and appreciated by all, regardless of their knowledge of Eastern religions and philosophies. We hope you will find them useful for your practice, irrespective of your cultural or spiritual background.

Publisher
July15, 2024

Author's Note

These articles were written a long time ago with a certain frame of mind. In these 25 years, I have grown older, and my perspectives on many aspects of life have changed. However, these writings are still relevant to those who are going through different phases of their learning and transformation. Please do not judge them as the ramblings of an unknown author. I am indeed unknown by choice. They are relevant to all types of people who are drawn to spirituality and spiritual practice. They are useful to those who have advanced on the path, to the novices who started their journey, and to those who have not yet overcome their fascination with the world but are willing to experiment with spirituality. Their emphasis is on lay practice and how to reconcile and balance our worldly and spiritual aspirations and find peace and fulfillment. They are especially relevant to householders who are primarily worldly people engaged in various occupations but practice some form of spirituality while still living their worldly lives. They are meant to draw lay practitioners or novices, engage them in spiritual thoughts, let them think about themselves, and explore the possibilities that are available to them beyond their ordinary and mundane lives, irrespective of their beliefs, age, or gender.

Jayaram V

Jayaram V

Introduction

If my memory serves me correctly, in the summer of 1993, I went to Mount Abu in Rajasthan, India, to attend a three-day seminar organized by Brahma Kumaris, an organization run by the female followers of Brahma Baba (Lekhraj Kripalani), who founded it in 1930 in the Sindh region of present-day Pakistan. During my stay in their ashram, I met many people who seemed to be fully dedicated to their mission and their ideals. I enjoyed their simple food, which they prepared lovingly and served with great attention and hospitality. When I was staying in the ashram complex, I went through déjà vu type spiritual experience. I felt an expansive state of awareness when I was in my bed and relaxing in a room they allotted to me on their campus, reminiscing about the day's events. Suddenly and unexpectedly, I felt disconnected from myself and felt connected to everything. I saw the world around me filled with an indistinguishable sense of Self or the feeling of "I" or "I am only." I began seeing everything from a subjective state of the same subjective awareness. In that expansive and unified state of awareness, I realized that in the universal consciousness, there was no duality, no second, no otherness, no you, and no this. Everything was one endless feeling or experience of "I am-ness." I realized what the Self meant and why Upanishads and most Indian texts use the term to refer to Brahman or Atman instead of the word soul.

Everything in that space surrounding me, and as far as I could sense, was filled with the same sense of Self. There was no feeling of separation. Self-awareness extended from me into everything. I was watching myself, seeing myself, perceiving and experiencing all that outside me as myself. Perhaps it was God's consciousness that enveloped briefly and showed what it meant to be. I felt how foolish it was to blame God for our problems or treat him like he was a separate entity. Our problems are his. Our experiences are his. He experiences all that we experience simultaneously. Through multiple bodies, countless eyes, hands, legs, and bodily parts, he goes through Samsara. When he gives something, he does not give it to anyone but to himself. When he answers our prayers, he answers but to his prayers only. Our pain is his pain. Our exhilarating journey, with all its ups and downs in this world, is his journey only. It is sheer ignorance to assume them as ours. I also realized the full import of the Bhagavadgita's teachings and why Lord Krishna repeatedly advises us not to assume ownership, doership, or agency of any actions.

The feeling of universality that enveloped me was not of this world. I was fortunate to experience it not in a reverie or dream-like state but in wakeful consciousness. I was well aware of my surroundings and where I was, but at the same time, I was going through that expansive state of awareness. Years later, I realized that it was the state of Turya or Shiva consciousness experienced by the Shiva yogis when they attained perfection and saw the whole world as an extension or projection of their minds. Indeed, what I felt in those moments was the touch of God (Brahma Sparsh) and Shiva's affectionate hug. It was perhaps his way of telling me that I should not think of him as a separate Being and that I should not approach him with a feeling of separation, doubt, or duality. He wanted me to see the world the way he always sees it and how he keeps no differences, no barriers, no high and law, superior and inferior. It was the state of sameness or equality (samatvam), which Lord Krishna defines in the Bhagavadgita as the highest Yoga and which is the goal of all yogis and the state of liberation. That one central state of "I am" pervades the whole universe and manifests in every form. You will experience it as your essential nature on a regular basis only when you dissolve your limited egoism, delusion, agency, doership, and ownership of things and actions and become one with it. Such a state exists perhaps in the realm of Brahman and all those liberated souls who attain him. They suffer from no limitations, divisions, distinctions, wants, desires, or complements because they are completed and perfect in all respects. They are self-existent, self-knowing, and self-aware.

The feeling of oneness persisted in me for a few days, though not with the same intensity, but as a strong memory or recollection. Wherever I went, it followed me like perfume and showed me what it was like to watch the world with God's eyes as a universal witness. However, gradually, as I returned to my daily routine and resumed my normal it, it disappeared. I had several strange experiences in my early life and later, after I completed my post-graduation. One strange experience was when I was about eight years old. I was suddenly overwhelmed with utter sadness at the thought all the people I knew, my parents, grandparents, relations, friends, and all the people around would die someday, and I would never see them again. I did not know why that came and persisted for a long time. It scared me and filled me with a lot of despair and hopelessness. Maybe they were flashes of memories from my past lives. However, fortunately, they never lasted long. I consider them as small openings, little cracks, through which you often get a glimpse of your connection to God or to the universe itself.

I consider myself a worldly person in the sense that my interests are rooted in the world, and I am bound to certain worldly goals. I prefer to be a Bodhisattva and return to the earth repeatedly rather than seek enlightenment and disappear forever. I do meditation, but not regularly, like the people I know who are serious about their practice. Meditative and contemplative states come to me naturally in moments of profound silence and attentive observation, during which, sometimes, it occurs to me that we do not pay attention to that which observes us all the time. I believe that we all are connected to the universal consciousness at a deeper level, and it does try to speak to us in its mysterious ways. We do not receive the communication because we do not believe in the "here and now" possibility of God's universal presence. We envision Him as a heavenly being seated somewhere in the stratosphere. Such preconceived notions prevent us from seeing Him wherever we are.

The universe is always eager to speak to you. You are one of its faces, voices, names, and forms. You are one of the channels through which it speaks to itself. You are not aware of it because you are lost in your little play called your life, with you as the center of attraction, and you do not let go of the numerous identities you build and the little circles you draw around yourself. In your mind, you see only the separation and duality you constantly experience. You are like a king, lost and forlorn in a castle that is under seize from hostile forces intent on breaking through those walls and destroying your very existence. Therefore, even if you are a living and breathing face of God, you are content with your status as a limited being in an infinite universe ruled by a remote God with a rule book that you cannot truly follow. Perhaps, if you open your heart to his universal presence in you and around you and open yourself with faith and conviction, he may fill it with his sublime love and give you a glimpse of that eternal and absolute state. Hanuman, the supreme devotee of Lord Rama, epitomized such love and devotion. He exemplified the kind of exclusive devotion Lord Krishna mentioned in the Bhagavadgita. Through his devotion, he also proved to us that God never forsakes his dearest devotees whose minds are always absorbed in him and who do not see him with any distinction or duality. If you ever felt the sublime love experienced by Hanuman in your heart, you know what I mean.

Spiritual experiences may be real or self-induced. I do not know where and how we can draw the line. But I know that the universe is alive with the same feeling of subjectiveness or selfness everywhere. If you compare it with the sky, you can compare the clouds and the stars with the little individualities that glitter and flutter against the backdrop of a mysterious and indistinguishable consciousness, which does not treat you and me separately but as itself. We feel the duality and the distinctions because we cannot accept the notion that we are an inseparable part of the same reality.

This book is about cultivating a deeper awareness of life and the world around you from a spiritual perspective and dealing with the problems and situations in your life accordingly. I believe spirituality is living with a deeper awareness about yourself and your existence, transcending the petty concerns of your limited Self without being unduly disturbed by what life offers to you. You accept them and endure them with certain stoical resignation that they are not under your control and you should not let them control you.

In today's world, I do not think that you have to renounce everything and live like an ascetic to be a spiritual person or practice spirituality. It is not necessary that you have to give up everything and retire to some secluded place unless your aim is liberation. If you aim to find peace and stability within yourself, you can find it even amidst this world despite all the distractions and disturbances. You can create your sanctuary, a place of peace and comfort, to which you can retire whenever you desire. In the past, people resorted to traditional renunciation (sannyasa) or retired to monasteries when they were dissatisfied with themselves, their circumstances, or their suffering. They went to forests, leaving behind all comforts and relationships in search of answers to their suffering or the problems that vexed them. Some practiced extreme austerities and literally tortured themselves to gain control over their minds. Some starved their bodies slowly to death, thinking that their bodies were the last vestiges of their sinful karmas and impurities and that by sacrificing them, they could be free. Maybe the traditional sannyasa or monkhood is still the best option, without the extreme methods people practiced in ancient times. However, it may not be necessary if you know how to grow beyond your limited self and selfish desires and relate to the world around you through empathy, knowledge, awareness, and understanding.

Today, we think about spiritualism in moderate terms. We aim to live holistically, trying to satisfy both our spiritual and material needs, accepting what is being given to us by Nature or God, and improving what we can within our limitations, but, at the same time, without subjecting ourselves to the extremities and dualities of life. Spirituality has wider connotations in today's world. Even caring for the plants in your backyard or feeding the birds and little creatures constitutes spirituality. They indicate that you are growing spirituality as a human being and developing a deeper level of connection with the life around you. You are personifying the idea of oneness with the rest of creation by outgrowing your selfish mindset and your narrow thinking.

For some, this is more or less a compromise of sorts, what we may call spiritual materialism. It means you are not yet ready to outgrow all your desires and attachments. You are not willing to give up your comforts, wealth, or your way of life. Yet, you are willing to become a lay spiritual practitioner, bring some of the ideas you learned from the scriptures or spiritual people, and give them a try. Many ancient spiritual traditions like Buddhism and Jainism allow this two-tier spiritual practice as a compromise of sorts or as a starting point for those whose karma has not fructified enough to let them become full-fledged renunciants.

It does not guarantee liberation but gives the enthusiasts enough motivation to withstand the pressures of their lives and circumstances with greater understanding and endurance. At least, it will not crush them beyond hope or let them surrender to the forces that torment their minds and lives. It is better than letting oneself fall into the depths of baser instincts and animal nature or succumbing to self-destructive habits that permanently put out the light inside.

In today's world, you may consider yourself a spiritual person if you go beyond the immediate needs and concerns of your mind and body and think about others or their well-being or your role and place in the world or if you spend time thinking about your essential nature or your true purpose of your life. You are spiritual if you outgrow your attachment to your body and physical pleasures, pay attention to your other identities, spend time practicing yoga or meditation, or outgrow your selfishness and help others without abandoning your personal, social, and family duties and responsibilities. You are spiritual if you believe in God and develop a personal relationship with him or consider yourself a spiritual entity and identify yourself primarily with your spiritual nature, soul, or Self instead of giving free rein to your mind, body, and senses.

It is also my conviction that belief in the soul or God is not necessarily a primary condition to live spiritually or practice spirituality. God is perhaps an inadequate term to express the immensity and universality of the power that pervades this world, which is both personal and impersonal and knowable and unknowable. It is impersonal when you look upon him as vast as the sky or space that stretches into eternity, containing within itself vast and unfathomable mysteries. It is personal when you see him in someone or an object or form that you love dearly or that uplifts you and fills you with wonder, such as a child, a pet, a flowing river, a majestic mountain, a sprawling tree, the image of a deity, the beauty and symmetry of things, or an enlightened master.

The Buddhists do not believe in the existence of an individual soul or Self. Yet, it does not make them less spiritual. The Jains also do not believe in the existence of a creator God, but Jain monks are known to pursue one of the most rigorous and austere spiritual practices in the world. They also revere Tirthankaras, whom they consider absolute and infinite beings. It is perhaps time we turn our attention from the externalities of religious rituals and primitive notions of God in a human form to the universal vision of him as a universal being, as described in some of our scriptures, to know him and relate to him without the mind's distortions.

Coming back to the contents of this book, I have to say that some of the topics in it are intended for serious aspirants, while some are for everyone who wants to dabble with spirituality out of curiosity or to experiment. I am not sure where to draw the line. So, I leave it to your judgment. In the following pages, I have tried to present spiritual lessons primarily in familiar terms without minimizing or compromising their value or importance. In them, you will find enough opportunities to grow mentally and spiritually or develop a newer understanding.

Spiritual awakening comes from self-transformation after years of study, inquiry, contemplation, persistence, faith, and devotion. Through practice, we develop a newer understanding and vision. We become self-aware, compassionate, sensitive, responsive, thoughtful, and insightful. Through that awakening, we learn to see the world differently, as an extension of ourselves, and accept its inherent contradictions and anomalies without judgment.

Look For God in Everything

There is a Spirit who is hidden in all things, as the cream is in milk, and who is the source of all knowledge and self-sacrifice. This is Brahman, the spirit Supreme. This is Brahman, the spirit Supreme. Svetasvatara Upanishad

Where there is light, there is God, a divine presence that fills the world with wonder. In the darkness, His hidden presence is a mystery waiting to be revealed. In the light, He fills us with wonder and awe at His manifestations. Where there is love, there is God, a force that transcends all. In the beauty of a flower, in the innocence of a child, in the radiance of the sun, in the generosity of the earth, in the harmony of the universe, in the beauty of the heavens, in the waters of the rivers and oceans, in the intelligence of man and the vastness of the universe, His sacred and dynamic presence is a source of awe and mystery. This recognition has the power to transform your relationship with the world, your attitude towards life, and your interactions with all beings. You will see His invisible force behind all creations and find His benign presence hidden in everything and enveloping everything.

When one develops that vision and understanding and comprehends His omnipresence in all things you perceive and experience, the entire universe becomes His huge temple, and the Seer, who is his reflection in you, becomes his earnest devotee and true worshipper. For that, seeing one who is filled with an intense devotion for him, every moment becomes an opportunity to worship Him and draw himself closer to Him. In their devotional affinity with Him, those who reach these spiritual heights find their true purpose, love, and duty. When they establish with Him a bond of love and devotion that transcends time and stretches into eternity, their lives become symbols of hope and encouragement for others to follow.

When you realize that God is the pure consciousness and intelligence in you, in others, and in all of creation, including your mind and intelligence, you will feel a deep, personal connection to Him. You do not have to envision God as a mysterious being who lives in faraway heaven but as a pervasive presence that is with you always, right here and right now. This presence is not limited by space or time but is a part of your very consciousness and liveliness. If God is a Being, he is limited. If He is a presence, he is unlimited and with you always, a part of your very being. You may envision him as a Being if you are

Look For God in Everything

not drawn to abstract notions and prefer to relate to him through his names and forms. At the same time, you must remember that He is not exclusive to you or limited to a name or form. This is necessary to acknowledge his universality and not to become lost in your attachment to particular forms and prevent your spiritual growth.

Therefore, look for the signs of God everywhere and in everything, as far as your mind and senses go, and feel His presence in your mind and body. Accept everything you perceive as an aspect of Him only. Change the way you view the world and relate to it, accepting it as His living manifestation, a direct result of His consciousness working in tandem with his forcefield. Feel His presence in the silence of your heart and in the clamor of your longing for the things you cherish and the fulfillment you seek, knowing that your desire for things is your desire for completeness. You are attracted to them because you cannot live in isolation forever.

Continue the thought process until it becomes your second nature. When your senses fall asleep, when your thoughts are purified, and your desires are subdued, your mind will rest in its void and let you find him in your true Self. If you persist on the path, you will cross all the barriers and enter His world of light and delight, filled with an awareness that is not of your mundane mind. When you find that center of stability and pure awareness without duality and division, you will experience equanimity and stability, overcoming the limitations and vulnerabilities that are part of your ordinary and precarious existence.

When you believe that you are inseparable from God and all that he pervades, fear will cease to bother you. When you have the conviction that you live in His care, you will let go of your worries and anxieties and experience true freedom. When you accept Him as your guide and the real doer, you will not incur sin because he becomes the agent and source of your actions and drinks the poison of your life. When you replace your ordinary self with Himself, you will be freed from the darkness of ignorance and the weight of your sins. If you act on his behalf or in his name, with total surrender and exclusive devotion, His power will be bestowed on you, and you will enjoy immunity from wrongdoing.

The seers and saints translate such exalted ideals into practical wisdom. They perceive the oneness of the whole existence as they silence their egos and discipline their minds. With that awareness and realization, they allow the Supreme Lord to live through them and express his will. For such self-realized yogis, everything in the universe is sacred because they feel His hidden presence in every manifestation. For them, nothing is abominable or detestable because even the darkest of things are his manifestations only and exist for a reason. They, the enlightened ones, suffer neither from the conflicts of life nor from the pairs of opposites nor from the duality that is perceptible in creation. In their integrated awareness, all conflicts and divisions resolve themselves into a harmonious whole.

When God's holistic vision becomes an indistinguishable part of your consciousness, you let Him take over your life's reins. In his care and protection, you become an observer of your life's continuing saga, filled with mindful curiosity. You seek nothing except His ongoing presence in your being and his continued attention. Filled with gratitude and impassionate reverence for all existence, you become unassuming and nonjudgmental, enduring everything and accepting what you endure as His play and an extension of your consciousness filled with him. In that expansive state of awareness and feeling, you cease to fight for your selfish interests.

This is the path of the radiant masters and the eternal souls, who are permanently freed from the bondage of earthly life and ready to enter God's supreme abode, never to be born again. It is not easy for ordinary people to reach such an exalted state of unity and remain divine-centered all the time, especially when they are deeply involved with the world and have a craving for things or fulfillment. To attain him and be one with his consciousness, you must remove the barriers that stand in your way, cultivate virtues, and purify your mind and body. You must empty and silence your surface consciousness and make it stable and pure to the extent you can, setting aside your cares and concerns so that He will fill that emptiness with his consciousness and energy and shape it according to his will and wisdom. Those who want to find him within themselves and absorb themselves find these suggestions useful.

When you use your heart rather than your intellectual mind, you have better chances of feeling His presence in you. You will find him first in your heart and then in your whole being. Our scriptures say the heart is His primary abode in humans.

1. If you live mindfully, treating your spare moments to relate to Him in diverse ways, you will find Him in the simple aspects of life, in moments of exaltation and devotional outpouring, and experience the world differently.

Jayaram V

2. When you slow down occasionally amidst a busy life or hectic activity, take a deep breath, and observe yourself, you will become aware of your current state. You can then find a moment to reset yourself and connect to the silence hidden in all the noise that is inherent to all existence and yourself, which we do not usually notice.

3. If you replace your ego with God, offer him everything you have and do, and acknowledge him as the true owner of everything you own and doer of all your actions, you will become an offering in His sacrifice, and you will live freely, untroubled by fear, want, and scarcity. This is the essence of true surrender and renunciation.

4. Whenever you have an opportunity, step outside your ego-self and your preoccupation with yourself, your worries and anxieties, pursuits, and desires. Think of others. See how you may outgrow your selfishness and relate to the world around you as God's true Self. One way to do it is by overcoming your limited self-awareness and attachment to your mind and body or your name and form and seeing the world as an extension of the same consciousness that exists in you and everywhere.

5. Your body is a temple Nature builds to house your identity and consciousness. It keeps you preoccupied with your surface consciousness while hiding your pure consciousness beneath, beyond your mind and senses, so that you remain ignorant and a part of her Play. To find it and experience it, you must dissolve the barriers of egoism, desires, ignorance, and delusion that prevent you from reaching it and becoming one with it.

6. If you think you are distinct and separate from the rest of creation and you have to fend for yourself, you will experience loneliness, negativity, desires, and passions such as anger, envy, pride, greed, etc. If you want to experience life differently from a broader perspective, you must step out of the circle. You must renounce the limited field of experience you build around yourself in your anxiety for stability, security, peace, and happiness. By transcending your ordinary thinking, egoism, and selfishness with faith in God's universal presence, you can connect to Him through your consciousness and divine nature.

7. See all that you see and experience as an extension of your reality and the play of the same consciousness that exists in you, others,

and everywhere. See them with compassion as different versions of yourself, going through their lives and experiencing the same reality differently from different perspectives, as if they are stuck in their little worlds and lost with their problems, attachments, and suffering.

8. If you truly surrender to God, accept Him as your inseparable Self, and invite Him into your life to be the center of your consciousness and the upholder of your life and actions, you will have a different perspective on life and whatever you experience. You will let Him live in you and through you and become your eyes and ears.

9. The best way to elevate your consciousness is through devotion and sameness. When you become his ardent devotee and fill your mind with his thoughts, He becomes your true companion, guardian, and support. When you cultivate virtues and exemplify his qualities and consciousness, you will become his true embodiment and bring God into your life and wakeful consciousness.

Cultivate Friendship with God

All the gods in the heaven of Brahman adore in contemplation their Infinite Supreme Spirit. This is why they have all joy, and all the worlds, and all desires. And the man who on this earth finds and knows Atman, his own Self, has all his holy desires and all the worlds and all joy. – The Chandogya Upanishad

Those who worship me fixing their minds always upon me, with unflinching sincerity and supreme faith, I consider them to be the most perfect in Yoga. - The Bhagavadgita

If any man is in Christ, there is a new creation; behold, all things have become new. – St. Paul

I think of Agni as Father, as Kinsman, as Brother, as a Friend forever. - The Rig Veda, 10.7.3

Make God your intuitive companion, a source of comfort and security. Pray to Him to be with you, your protector and benefactor at all times, guiding you in the right direction and aiding you in all your efforts and undertakings. Make Him your trusted companion and mentor, a confidant to whom you can share your wishes, secrets, worries, and anxieties, seeking his help to realize or resolve them. Let Him be the One you cannot part with, cannot do without, and who is always by your side, no matter where you are and what you do or think.

God may not speak to us directly in a human voice that we can hear, but He communicates with us in various ways. If you have faith and devotion and if you are receptive, he reciprocates with abundant love. If you keep an open mind, you will receive his disguised messages and discern them. You can establish a direct relationship with Him by sharing your thoughts and opinions, your secrets and weaknesses, your pain and laughter, your goals and dreams, your doubts and fears, and your losses and gains. You can communicate with Him even through silence. As you prepare yourself to rest, you can let Him enter your heart through silence, manifest in your dreams, and stir your mind.

It is through friendship with God that we realize the meaning of a true relationship, which rests upon the values of trust, faith, appreciation, understanding, and unconditional love and is free from desires and attachments. It is through our friendship with Him that we become aware of our essential nature and our oneness with Him. That friendship with Him may begin as an offshoot of our imagination or exhilaration. However, with faith and devotion, we can pour life into it and actualize it, establishing Him in our minds and believing that He is responding to our requests and listening to our thoughts and prayers.

Know that imagination is the creative power of God bestowed upon us by Nature. Through that, she has incorporated a whole universe into our consciousness and given it unlimited powers to recreate mentally whatever we can see or remember. Its strength may be diluted by the frailties of our minds and the desires of our hearts but it can be enriched with the brilliance of our vision and intelligence. If you persevere with the strength and certainty of faith, you will realize that what you envision and seek in your imagination with clarity and firm belief becomes a living reality, bringing God right into the center of your world and your life.

In the early stages of your friendship with God, you may have many expectations, and at times, you may even feel disappointed with the responses, for He does not think the way we think and does not act the way we expect Him to act. We may not think of Him all the time, but his attention is undivided. We may not clearly fathom the purpose behind His actions, but He knows what is good for us and what we really deserve. Whatever reality He may cause to manifest in your life is a part of His mysterious plan, in which the outcome can only be your good and your welfare.

He who spends his entire day in God's company is never lost to Him. God will take care of his worries and concerns and look after his needs. This is the message we find in all religions. It is an assurance that God has given to all humankind through his prophets, messengers, and masters whom he sent and with whom He spoke to his devotees in the past.

In the company of God, we have nothing to lose except our pettiness and partial vision. With Him as our friend and benefactor, we have all the riches of the world at our disposal. In the light of His love and the power of His Truth, we are freed from the aberrations of the human mind and the limitations of our egoistic consciousness. He imparts to us such qualities that are only heard but not experienced. He develops in us a vision that is rarely achieved by ordinary mortals.

Jayaram V

Cultivate Friendship with God

He pours into our lives such delight and depth of experience that we can hardly even imagine, filling us with joy and fulfillment.

In your friendship with God, do not be a mere passive receiver of favors and blessings. Reciprocate sincerely with your heart and mind, like a true friend, and offer Him whatever you have in total surrender, loyalty, and devotion. Instead of seeking favors from Him, give Him what you believe is truly yours. Offer Him everything that comes to you as a reward or punishment. Set aside all ideas of ownership and make Him the true owner of your life and your wealth. In the spirit of true friendship, abide by the values and the laws which He upholds. Lead your life according to the values and teachings that are enshrined in our scriptures. It is by giving and through self-denial that you subject yourself to the will of God and become His dear companion, not by seeking His favors or using Him to further your egoistic ambitions. Your sincerity and devotion are valued and significant in this relationship.

When we do not seek God for our ends, we establish a true relationship with Him. When we erase the circles that we create around ourselves, we transcend our wants and desires and become closer to Him. When we set aside our cares and concerns in complete trust, we find in Him a reliable and attentive companion who would answer our prayers and requests. Exclusive devotion to God may not be possible for everyone. Although devotion without desires is the highest goal, everyone cannot practice it. Yet, worldly people with spiritual aspirations should not lose heart. Even a little devotion, tinged with some desire, is better than having no faith or devotion. These suggestions will strengthen your resolve in that direction.

1. Meditate on the thought that God is an infinite Being whose capacity for love and compassion is unlimited and who is detached and impartial.

2. Meditate on the thought that you are immersed and enveloped by His universal presence all the time and that you are never separate from Him or different from Him at any point of time in your entire existence, just as you are not separate from the space in which you live.

3. If you believe in the possibility that God listens to your prayers when you seek Him earnestly, you enhance the power of your prayers and imagination. When you ask repeatedly and

perseveringly, not as a test of your faith or His prowess, but out of your conviction, you will be heard eventually.

4. You represent an aspect of God. You are one of the little worlds that exist in Him through which He speaks to Himself. You are an eternal being, not very different from Him in essence. It is where you may find Him in your meditative and contemplative states of self-absorption.

5. When you are pure and detached, have faith and reverence, express gratitude and devotion, and think of Him constantly as your very Self, His will becomes your will in pure devotion and guides you consistently. With Him guiding you and acting as yourself, you will face the difficulties of your life with stoical tolerance and understanding.

6. Do not let your friendship with God be one-sided. See Him in others, just as you see Him in yourself, and help them without desires and expectations and taking any credit, as if you are serving Him and His numerous manifestations.

7. The best way to worship God and show Him your devotion is to cultivate the divine qualities that are mentioned in various scriptures. They bring you closer to Him and His essential nature and purify your consciousness.

8. Develop an expansive and all-encompassing vision as part of your spiritual practice to feel God's presence in every aspect of your life and in everything you perceive.

Jayaram V

Let God be Your Role Model

And so the only thing to do is to enter into contact with it- not to give a name or describe it. In fact, there is hardly any use giving it a name or describing it. One must try to enter into contact, to concentrate upon it, live it, live that reality, and whatever the name you give it is not at all important once you have the experience. The experience alone counts. The Mother

In truth, who knows God becomes God. - Mundaka Upanishad

Let the mind be in you, which was also in Jesus Christ. St. Paul.

The Knower and the known are one. Simple people imagine that they should see God, as if he stood there and they here. This is not so, God and I, we are one in knowledge. Eckhart.

Imagine a scenario where God, in all His divine glory, takes on a human form, retaining His divine qualities but suppressing his unlimited divine or supernatural powers. Picture Him living among us, just like an ordinary human being, pure and divine but very human-like and ordinary with his divinity concealed. Now, visualize how he would navigate His day-to-day life, communicate with others, and conduct Himself in his personal and public life. Consider how he would work for His physical and material well-being or salvation, resist evil thoughts, cultivate virtues, fight against injustice and inequality, or practice virtue and morality in a world of temptations and distractions.

Imagine and live that way. Imagine that you are a divine being in human form and learn to live and experience life that way. See the world the way He would have seen, experience it the way he would have experienced, feel it the way he would have felt, dealing with the dualities such as pain and pleasure or joys and sorrows the way he would have dealt. Visualize yourself as a pure Self, a being of pure light, inside a human body, living an ordinary human life with God's awesome powers and his absolute concealed but otherwise, virtuous, pious, and generous in every possible manner.

Make Him that image you build in your mind as your role model and live like Him. Engage with the world and conduct yourself diligently, with your mind focused upon Him and thinking whether He would approve your actions and intentions in specific situations or in dealing with your problems or difficulties. This is not an impossible or unachievable task. With a little imagination, anyone can practice it. If we can choose other people as our role models despite their weaknesses and shortcomings, we can also choose God as our role model, who is complete and perfect in all respects. Millions of people waste their lives imitating or modeling themselves on the celebrities they admire or worship. If they can do it, they can replace them with God. They may not succeed completely in that since it requires near perfection. However, they can at least try because there is no loss in that, even in failure. Living like God in our minds and bodies and emulating him, we can bring His awesome power, purity, and vision into our lives, hearts, and minds and mold our lives accordingly.

If you believe in God's incarnation, you can perhaps guess why he incarnates and what ultimate purpose He serves. If God comes to the earth as a human being, He will live here in an exemplary manner, radiating His divine qualities and setting an example for the world to follow. Because He is not bound to any tradition or custom, He would perhaps live in many different ways. But if He chooses to retain His essential purity and divinity, He would epitomize the human character, giving expression to the highest of human virtues such as patience, compassion, generosity, intelligence, truthfulness, wisdom, tolerance, contentment, detachment, dispassion, and equanimity. His expansive vision would transform everything it touches.

If you are aspiring for spiritual liberation, you should let God enter your life and guide you every step of the way. You should cease to live for your selfish needs and spend your life doing good works, exemplifying His virtues. With humility, trust, and unassuming sincerity, you should allow God to manifest His will and vision through you as your inner Self. You should perform your obligatory duties without expectation as a part of your self-purification and inner transformation, practicing virtues and personifying the best of human values. It is even better if you can give expression to a holistic life in which you treat contradictions of life and human nature with tolerance and compassion.

From a spiritual perspective, you are a divine Self in a human form. You are an embodied Self who is caught in the whirlpool of life. You may not have the purity to express the divine in you or free yourself from the limitations of your mind and body due to your attachment to your name and form and due to your desires and deep involvement with the material world. In the course of your existence on earth, you become entangled with a center of awareness that will

Let God be Your Role Model

not let you see yourself or the world as they are. You cannot discern the reality of you from the false illusion of you. You cannot see your divine nature or your invisible and hidden connection with God or your pure Self. In God's consciousness, there is no fixed center of awareness and no definite center of being. If you weaken your ego through detachment, surrender, devotion, and sacrifice and diffuse the center of awareness that deludes you into believing that you are a physical being, you will move closer to the expansive, unified, and non-dualistic state of consciousness that is not of your mind or body but rooted in the deepest core of your being as a remnant of God himself. Established in that, you will feel connected to everything and experience profound peace and oneness.

In each of us, there is an ideal vision of life, a higher aspiration, which whispers to us, in moments of silence, awe, and wonder, about the possibilities and opportunities with which we can transcend our lower nature and return to our pristine state of purity and divinity. Concealed within us and hidden beneath all our desires and self-promoting behavior is our deepest yearning for freedom and unbound awareness. You will become aware of it only when you withdraw from the outer layers of your surface consciousness that has its roots in your mind and body and pay attention to the consciousness that is hidden beyond it. Your wakeful consciousness is a replica of the world. Your hidden consciousness is a replica of the divinity that stems from God.

It is not that God has never visited the earth or tried to serve as a role model. He incarnated on earth several times, communicated with enlightened minds, and revealed to us the right knowledge and wisdom to dispel our ignorance and open our eyes to many transcendental truths. He established norms for righteous conduct and norms and values that are essential for peace and stability on earth. His incarnations teach us a lot about righteous conduct and moral responsibility. We can learn from them to cultivate virtue, practice restraints, and purify ourselves.

Therefore, if you are intent on your transformation and spiritual journey, make God your role model. Bring Him into your life and let him become your ideal guide and teacher. Exemplify Him and His qualities to become an example to others. Follow Him in word and deed, practicing the moral percepts and the divine wisdom that He has revealed to the world through various scriptures. With the richness of your imagination and the strength of your devotion, you can bring him into your life and express him through your thoughts, speech, words, and actions. You can cultivate the divine qualities enumerated in the scriptures and express the divine in you. In oneness with him in thoughts and deeds, you can live on earth as a divine entity, practicing detachment, purifying yourself, overcoming your impurities such as egoism and delusion, and developing an expansive and holistic vision and consciousness in which you see yourself as a manifestation of the one eternal Supreme Lord.

Think of God Constantly

"T" stands for transcendence, timeless awareness, talent bank, and tithing. My personal experience is that without transcendence, life has no beauty. In order to live a full life, it is necessary to go beyond all boundaries. Deepak Chopra

There are other realities that exist besides the reality you can see, touch and hear with your physical senses. These are the higher dimensions that your Higher Self lives in. These realities are very real; your Higher Self, other people's Higher Selves, and many high beings live there. Orin

Well, if suddenly you become conscious within of something very different and much higher, then whatever it may be, this will be a spiritual experience. The Mother

The mind is free only when it is no longer conditioned by its own experiences, by knowledge, by vanity, envy; and meditation is the freeing of the mind from all these things, form all self-centered activities and influences. JK

Yes, it is possible to develop a God-centric consciousness, which means to be aware of God all the time, remain divine-centered, think like Him, and think of Him constantly, even while engaged in mundane actions. It is possible when we step out of our limited individualities and thinking selves and identify ourselves with the Universal Supreme Self. Although many spiritual aspirants want to live this way, most of them do not succeed despite their best efforts and intentions. It is especially true when we are busily engaged in performing our daily tasks or dealing with our daily problems and anxieties.

Our minds are fickle and unstable. Due to desires and attachments, and passions such as fear and anger, we are easily distracted by myriad things. Although we think of God and engage in spiritual thoughts occasionally when we are in the company of holy men or holy places, most of us do not think of Him or remember Him when life goes on normally and when we are not challenged by adverse situations or difficulties. We believe salvation can wait compared to the other problems and needs we have and we can postpone our spiritual aspirations into the future and address them later when the time is convenient. For most people, that time rarely arrives.

Due to the force of habit or nature, our minds are mostly drawn to worldly pursuits, desires, and attachments. We forget about God and

His teachings in the face of reality and when we have to deal with the practicalities of life or attend to the immediate and most pressing problems. Unfortunately, it does not prepare us well to face the world or our problems adequately or let us experience peace and happiness with inner strength and better awareness and discernment. Most people live for themselves, paying only as much attention to others as is necessary for their survival and self-promotion. If they do not see any personal gain or apparent value, they will not undertake any action to help others or engage in God's work. If they like someone or help someone, it may be because they see in them a reflection of themselves or feel some connection. With God-centric awareness, we can overcome these limitations, overcome self-centeredness, and change the way we think and act.

A mind that is filled with the thoughts of God is divine. It radiates His glory and declares His greatness. A mind that is saturated with the thoughts of God speaks the language of God. It expresses His thoughts all the time. To think of God continuously is to invite Him into your mind. To invite God into your mind is to make your life divine-centered, blessed, and uplifted. God is the best companion we can have in our lives. We can make Him our silent, invisible, loving, and ever-forgiving companion, to whom we can willingly express our true feelings and our fears without any hesitation. We can confide in Him our most cherished thoughts, our deepest yearnings, and private feelings. We can seek His help and guidance to remain on the path of righteousness and protect ourselves from the negative consequences of our actions.

Make God your invisible and inseparable partner and facilitator. Even when performing the most ordinary tasks, seek His approval and offer Him your actions. Seek Him everywhere through your longing, prayers, meditation, and surrender. Find Him deep in your own heart, silencing the cravings and the desires of your seeking and striving mind. Imagine Him to be with you, as your silent partner, in whatever you do, guiding you and showing you the way. Give Him a place of Honor and respect in your mind and your life.

A mind that is filled with the thoughts of God is a doorway to salvation. By repeating His name, thinking of Him, concentrating upon Him, visualizing Him, looking for Him everywhere and in everything, and attributing to Him all your successes and failures, you manifest the power and wisdom of God in your life. By surrendering to Him with love and devotion and by offering Him

Think of God Constantly

your life and your possessions, you draw Him into your being and make Him the center of your life, feeling His dynamic presence in your consciousness and every aspect of your life. When you fill your mind with the thoughts of God, using every opportunity to think of Him only, your life becomes holy, and your very consciousness becomes suffused with pure intelligence and rare wisdom.

So, remember God on every possible occasion. Give Him all the credit for your successes and failures, and cultivate a sensitive heart to feel gratitude, appreciation, love, devotion, and admiration for Him. Let Him speak to you in moments of silence, when you are alone or in contemplation. In the beginning, your thoughts of God may be mere thoughts, but over time, you will feel His dynamic presence in your consciousness and realize the true value of His friendship and support. The easiest way to realize God is to become His true devotee in thought and deed. Repeatedly, we have been told by the Masters of Wisdom who experienced oneness with God that the best way to reach Him is by surrendering to Him and offering Him all your actions.

You will reach Him when you are empty inside and let Him fill that void. You will reach Him if you let go of your rigid mindset and allow God to shape your life with His awesome power and magic. You will reach Him when your mind naturally rests upon the thoughts of God instead of the thoughts of selfishness. You will reach Him when you invite Him into your life and let Him sit on the throne instead of occupying it. If you focus on material success and if you cannot get over your attachments, you will return to this world repeatedly to repeat similar mistakes and suffer from similar problems. You will be running on the wheel of life under the illusion of making progress. However, if you discipline your mind to think of God constantly, you will let His power manifest in your life and lead you towards your liberation.

The Ego and Its Challenge

Whether we are asleep or awake, everything that exists in our surface consciousness belongs to the domain of the ego-self. By ego-self, we mean the awareness that creates your distinct identities, individuality, and feelings of separation. The mind and its faculties, knowledge, awareness, intelligence, reason, thoughts, emotions, and feelings, and the entire body, with its constituent parts, belong to your individuality or, in spiritual terms, your personality shaped by your egoism. When two people meet, what they see in each other is their respective ego-selves because the ego-self, distinguished by its names and forms, is the most visible, physical, and relatable part of each of human being. Even if we resolve to see an abstract concept of ourselves or others as God's numerous forms or aspects of consciousness, with our minds and senses, we can relate to others through our ego-selves and interact with their ego-selves only. Hence, in whatever spiritual phases we may be, our reality is driven mostly by our egos and is reinforced repeatedly by our egos. Hence, spiritually, it is the toughest obstacle.

The ego-self is a formation around the soul or the Self. It is a false personality or a formation that veils the real Self and assumes its identity. In the physical and the objective world, it represents the individuality and identity of each person and stands for him. It cannot be done away with since one's very existence in the physical world depends upon it, and the relationships it builds with things and others cannot be wished away. Even if you withdraw entirely from the world, your ego remains active and alive. It represents what belongs to you and what you presume yourself to be in your physical consciousness. It is so pervasive in your consciousness that you cannot distinguish it from your real Self, which lies beneath all surface activity as the supporting substratum in its pure and unadulterated state. In spiritual life, it becomes a real problem because we do not distinguish the ego or the apparent Self from the real or the hidden Self. When initiates begin their spiritual practice, overcoming their egos becomes a major problem as they wage a constant battle within them to assert themselves and prevent their dissolution. The ego in you is not a separate entity, although, for the sake of discussion, we may describe it so. It is you, as you know

The Ego and Its Challenge

yourself to be. To deny it or silence it means to negate yourself and make yourself inconsequential, a nobody.

In worldly life, your egoistic personality is a facilitator and an essential component of your existence and consciousness. But in spiritual life, it becomes an obstacle and a major problem. For this discussion, it is important to remember that the ego-self is not the real Self, and it will never be. It is not the one that is in bondage to samsara or the one that needs to be rescued from it. It is a temporary formation that is subject to change and impermanence. At the time of death, it disintegrates and returns to Nature, leaving a little residue of its consciousness with the soul consisting of its dominant thoughts and desires as a record of its karma. They become a part of one karma and act as the seed for the next life.

From a spiritual and theological perspective, your ego personality is just a vehicle. This physical casing facilitates the journey of the soul from bondage to freedom, sacrificing itself in the end on the altar of life. Our scriptures confirm repeatedly that our souls are immutable, pure, and self-absorbed even when they are held in bondage by Nature. On the other hand, the ego personality is subject to constant transformation. It is the most unstable, mutable, and unpredictable part of the consciousness. Therefore, there should be no confusion in our minds about the distinction between the ego-self and the real Self. They are different components, although they may coexist in the same space. Understanding this distinction is crucial for our spiritual and worldly contexts, as it guides our actions, decisions, and interactions.

People generally think that the ego-self represents only a few aspects of our consciousness, such as egoism and pride. But it is not true. The ego-self is not just a generic name for a few associated qualities. It represents the entire human personality, the very identity that lives, breaths, and exists as an entity by itself and forms attachments and relationships. It is everything that you think you are, including your notion of who you are, your morals, virtues, and your thoughts and opinions about yourself, others, and God himself. Anything that you create with your mind, including your imagination, opinions, and judgments, is a part of your ego-self. Since we do not regard our identities as our ego selves, we do not think that we are the problem in our liberation. If you do not know what your ego-self is, very likely, you will spend an entire lifetime, or perhaps several, chasing a mirage called liberation in which you will do everything except deal with the real problem. In your ordinary mental state, you are the ego-self, the real problem. You have to deal with it appropriately, acknowledging what it is and how it can help you or harm you before you can set your real Self free. You need to know with humility that you are a temporary structure created by Nature around the real Self, and until it is dismantled, the Self cannot be truly free. From the surface of your awareness, you cannot see the distinction. However, as you begin to empty yourself and go deeper, you begin to realize the duality that is hidden in you.

In the following paragraphs, we will examine the distinct nature of the ego-self and the way it blocks the liberation of the real Self. For lack of better expression, I have used the same word, "you," to denote the ego-self as well as the real Self. I will try to keep the distinction wherever possible, but where I cannot, I hope you will use your discretion. Many people begin spiritual practice without knowing that their individuality or identity is the main problem they have to resolve first before they see any progress. The ego keeps deluding them, creating the illusion that they are making progress. They do not progress much unless they address the main problem, which is to dismantle their identities by emptying themselves and letting go of their need for control, security, comfort, and certainty. As long as you seek these, pouring life into your ego, your inner Self will remain bound to the world.

The ego-self is the fabled villain, the enemy

To whatever religion we may belong, we are introduced to demons and devils from our early childhood as a part of our cultural conditioning. They become a part of our consciousness and influence our thinking and behavior. We hold them in our memory with fear and negativity as the forces of darkness and enemies of God who take pride in their power and abilities and who can torment us with their cruelty, pride, and arrogance. According to our scriptures, evil beings exist not only in the universe of God but also inside us as the qualities and components of our egoistic nature.

It is perhaps easier to deal with an evil entity that exists outside of you. However, what about the evil, which is part of you and which is so mixed up with your consciousness that you cannot clearly distinguish it and deal with it? From a spiritual perspective, your ego-self is vulnerable to evil influences by its very nature. For all practical purposes, it acts like a real enemy because it holds the real Self in bondage and does not give up its control of the senses and the mind. It is similar in temperament to an evil entity, disguised by your deluded nature as your identity and your very personality so that you will not know that you are standing in the way of your liberation and discernment. When we attribute all our imperfections and weaknesses to an external entity while their source lives within us, gathering strength with each step, we can imagine why it is so difficult to achieve self-transformation on the spiritual path.

Rightly, the first step in your transformation should be the realization that your egoistic individuality is the real problem. It is the cause of your suffering and your bondage because it shelters several demons in the universe of your mind and body as desires, passions, and evil intentions and lets you down whenever you try to control them. Just as the evil ones in the world act like Gods unto themselves and wage war against Him and His forces of light, your ego-self assumes the identity of the real Self and wages a battle against your good thoughts and good intentions. It tricks you into believing that your real enemy is somewhere outside, whereas it is the real one. It is the real agent of evil, which needs to be transformed and purified in the first place before you can experience peace and stability in yourself and achieve some progress on the path.

Your ego-self makes you look for God everywhere, except in yourself, because that way, it can keep you distracted and prevent you from knowing who you really are. The scriptures say that in the macrocosm of the universe, many real devils and demons inhabit the sunless worlds and constantly keep looking for an opening to attack vulnerable people. They gain strength and rule over us if we nourish their representative qualities in our consciousness and allow them to be active and alive. A big, wide world exists within you, made of both light and darkness, inhabited by diverse thoughts, desires, energies, and emotions. Although your pure Self is the Lord (Iswara) of your mind and body, your consciousness arising from them is ruled by your ego-self. If you are serious about your salvation, you must deal with this duality and the darkness that exists within you as your very personality and dispel the darkness through self-discipline, austerities, self-denial, detachment, and renunciation.

The ego pretends to know

How do we know any truth about ourselves, others, or the world? How do we know that what we think or decide is the right one? This dilemma troubled scholars and philosophers from the earliest times. Since we can know the truth only through limited means and cannot be certain whether our knowledge is perfect or complete, we cannot be sure whether what we consider true is really valid, justifiable, or universal. The problem arises because of the imperfect ways in which we gather information through our senses and process them. We are subject to many cognitive distortions. We entertain many assumptions and illusions about our knowledge and the reality surrounding us. We cling to our opinions and conclusions rather stubbornly because we consider them collectively as a part of our identities and our distinct worldviews. From a theological perspective, as egoistic individuals, we personify ignorance and delusion. We actually thrive upon them. Staying in our little cocoons, we arrive at truth rather laboriously and sometimes erroneously through speculative and intellectual means. Our knowledge is an accumulated mass of memories and perceptions shaped by the conditioning to which we are subject and which is rooted partly in our collective failure to think rationally. With limited faculties, we try to make sense of the world through a narrow tunnel of relative truths, generalizations, exaggerations, and insufficient facts and yet hold them as absolute.

Nowhere the pretensions of our egos are more evident than in our attitude towards such theological and speculative subjects as God, heaven, and hell, and the individual soul and its redemption. Except for a few rare individuals, no one really comes into direct contact with God or any divinity. Almost everyone, with no exception, relies upon scriptures to ascertain truths about Him or transcendental truths. Yet a vast majority of people believe that their beliefs about God and heaven alone are true and defend them like they are confirmed facts. In the name of God and religion, many people would bring out the worst of their behavior and try to silence those who disagree with them, disobeying and denigrating the very values that their faith proclaims. Deluded by their attachments and pride, they feed the very demons whom they want to slay through their religious observances. For many people, religion is an extension of their egoistic identities and selfish interests. Their religious passion ends there, as they feed their egos with the pride that comes from their religious identities, relying upon a few half-baked truths to defend their beliefs and their collective egos. Next time when you feel proud of the superiority of your religion or your religious identity, know that it is your ego that is trying to assert itself. Your divine nature does not participate in it. It is driven by the ego consciousness.

The egoistic religious fervor does not lead those who are driven by it to salvation but to suffering and, in some cases, to violence and bloodshed. True wisdom is to live with the humility that the knowledge assimilated by the human mind is limited, that it may not have all the answers, and that what it considers true knowledge and true scriptures may not necessarily be the only ones one can follow. As the One Supreme Lord becomes many, the One Supreme Knowledge also becomes many. Just as the material universe is mysteriously complex and can be viewed from different perspectives, our existential truths and truths about ourselves are complex and multifaceted. They can be reached through innumerable ways and means.

The ego-self thrives on divisions and duality

The mind belongs to the domain of the ego-self and serves as its playground and kingdom. The human mind is an abstract entity, part physical and part mental. From a spiritual perspective, it is a very complex receptacle of thoughts and impressions, where a great deal of churning takes place and where the human drama actually unfolds. Our minds operate within the field of the known and the boundaries of the objective world, and therefore, they are incapable of grasping the entire truth. Since we perceive the world only through physical means, we cannot comprehend the infinity or the absolute and usually draw our conclusions and our opinions in terms of dualities, divisions and categories. We bring the same attitude into our religious practice.

Although all religions speak about the underlying unity of the entire creation and its inseparable connection with God as the Lord and Supreme Ruler of all, we do not accept the spiritual unity of our existence wholeheartedly or consider ourselves as part of one indivisible and universal truth. As egoistic individuals, we only see the duality and the divisions that separate us from the rest of the world and the problems and the opportunities that arise because of it. We would rather prefer to keep the world divided and disunited because we know how to deal with divisions and make use of them to extend our influence and fulfill our desires. Each religion is but an invention of egoistic individuals who want to fight their selfish battles in the name of God and assert their identities, opinions, self-importance, and collective will through their allegiance to it.

The same attitude is reflected in our egoistic approach towards God and the way we worship Him. God is one. But we see Him in different ways and different forms, according to our inclinations, intentions, and frames of reference. Since we perceive God egoistically, we think of Him objectively as a person with names, forms, divisions, distinctions, and duality and with whom we can have attachment. Therefore, we have this God, that God, your God, my God, and many other Gods. We have God who is merciful and God who is wrathful. We have God, who speaks in Sanskrit or Latin or Hebrew or in whatever language with which we are familiar. We have God who speaks for a particular nation, tribe, race, or religion. We have God who wages wars and unleashes destruction on behalf of certain people because they think that they have been wronged and that God sides with them only. We have God, whose job, it seems, is just listening to our frivolous problems and forgiving our daily sins. Each of these deities created by the human egos is worshipped by groups of people with shared beliefs.

As egoistic individuals, we are not merely content with undermining the sanctity and purity of God; we also want to degrade Him further by making Him a partner in our petty quarrels and evil actions. We put so much of our egoism into our notions of God that He, who in reality represents the most sublime qualities of love and peace and who is the source of all, becomes the source of divisions, disunity, hatred, ill will bloodshed, and violent wars. Imagine one hand of yours trying to fight with the other to protect you from yourself. It may sound foolish, but it is what millions of people do in the world, habitually in the name of God and religion.

The world is a cauldron of conflicts and divisions, and it will always remain so as long as we are subject to Nature and to the divisions and dualities that are part of our consciousness. Even if we erase all the walls and boundaries upon earth, we will invent new ones to perpetuate our individual and collective identities. As long we are centered in our egoistic selves, we cannot escape from the divisions and dualities of life. Even if you ignore them, you cannot escape from the divisions and differences that exist within your being and that need to be resolved before you can experience peace and stability. It makes your spiritual practice all the more difficult and painful.

Jayaram V

The ego-self is the main obstacle

According to the Bhagavadgita, the Self is the friend of the Self and also the enemy of the Self. If it is confusing, let me clarify that the scripture is alluding here to the lower self and the higher Self or the ordinary egoistic self and the divine Self. The two selves are present in all of us. They are separate and distinct. They represent the two facets of creation, one temporary and transformative and the other permanent and fixed. If you remain centered in your egoistic self, you will not know the other. If you feed your ego constantly, you will become an enemy of your divine self, holding it as your hostage. However, if you transform yourself spiritually and identify yourself with your higher Self, you become your friend and improve your chances of liberation. This is what Lord Krishna meant when He said that the Self is the friend of the Self and its enemy. In its natural state, the egoistic self is the true enemy of the soul. It prevents the latter from becoming free, acting in selfish, ignorant, and perverted ways. It keeps the mind and the body in a constant state of agitation, refusing to settle down, and holds the soul in bondage, subjecting itself to the wheel of karma. Since the ego-self is not the real Self, there is no salvation for it. However, it can be enlightened and transformed. Through a series of yogic practices, you can make it a partner in your spiritual progress.

The ego is the toughest obstacle on the spiritual path. It is not amenable to spiritual transformation because it is an instrument of Nature that fights until the end to preserve itself. To accomplish such a difficult task, you have to become nothing and renounce everything that you dearly love. To let the light of the divine Self shine through you, you have to let go of all your attachments. No one really likes to be empty or nameless and faceless in this world because the world does not like empty people. It worships and follows those who are weighty, mighty, and powerful. Because of our values and conditioning, therefore many people shy away from spiritual life and try to fill their lives with some meaningful activity, even if it is not really going to make them happy or complete. To become free, we have to deconstruct our egos and empty our consciousness. We have to sacrifice ourselves without expecting reward or punishment. If we are not prepared for it, we may seek spiritual masters to assuage our fears and insecurities, but we will not be able to address them or escape from them.

The ego-self pursues morality for selfish ends

The ego's consciousness is murky. It is a mixture of light and darkness, with the predominance of negative qualities rather than positive ones. It has a propensity to use everything for its selfish and egoistic aims, including spiritual and religious matters and moral standards. The higher Self is not subject to our social and moral codes because it is an absolute and complete entity without qualities and contradictions. Morality belongs to the domain of the egoistic self, and it pursues it vigorously, using it and misusing it for its self-preservation and self-promotion. Whether we like it or not, we deal with the moral dilemmas of our lives almost every day. Sometimes we follow them, and sometimes we do not. Sometimes, we circumvent them to get things done. We also change our standards of morality according to our convenience and the people involved. The outward, superficial, and pretentious practice of morals is the hallmark of an egoistic attitude. As egoistic individuals, we make use of morality rather than practice it sincerely because it gives us an opportunity to impress the world and earn the appreciation and approval of society.

The ego cannot discern truth clearly

When we are driven by desires, our judgment becomes clouded. When we are deeply attached to things, we lose our discretion. When we are too close or too far from things, we fail to perceive them clearly. Our vision is limited. We can perceive the world from only a limited perspective and may mistakenly consider it the whole truth. However sincerely we may try, our perceptions are tainted by our egoistic expectations of how things should be. These are some of the inherent limitations to which we are subject, which stand in our way of seeing and knowing the truth correctly. The egoistic self considers itself a separate entity, unable to see its connection with the rest of the universe. In itself, it is an illusion because it is a temporary construct, and its knowledge is grounded in an unstable and impermanent reality. We may not have much difficulty in perceiving the objective reality. But when it comes to transcendental truths, we are not sure how to deal with them. Truth is multidimensional, but egoistically, we prefer to draw a straight line to it, refusing to consider other possibilities and viewpoints. Even if we broaden our vision and open our minds, we cannot still understand the whole truth. We may see some parts and mistakenly consider them the whole. We can reach neither God nor our souls through the egoistic thought process. We cannot comprehend the metaphysical truths, when we are centered in our limited selves. To understand truth, we need a different paradigm and new approach, in which, consciously and deliberately, we have to cultivate feelings of oneness with the universal body of God and become fully absorbed in it.

The ego-self prefers religious activity

The ego-self prefers to indulge in religious activity because religion serves its interests well. It is not drawn to spiritual life easily because spiritual life is hard to practice and demands unconditional surrender and sacrifice. Salvation is a great idea. But it makes no sense if you are centered on your egoistic self. You may pursue it for some egoistic reason, but in the end, you will find no material advantage in being spiritual. Spiritual life demands that you gradually weaken your ego and purify it so that your inner Self will shine through. For the ego-self, the whole process is rather suicidal because salvation means the end of its story. When it turns to spiritualism, it has to choose between the two irreconcilable goals of ending suffering and ending itself, renouncing everything, and sacrificing its very identity and existence for the sake of something which it does not understand clearly.

Many people are hesitant to turn to spirituality because they are not comfortable with the notion of losing everything and becoming nothing for the sake of the real Self, which they have not experienced yet. On the spiritual path, our lives turn upside down. We have to forego everything that we dearly seek in our lives. As we embark upon the journey, the self-transformation process throws up many difficulties and demons of pain and suffering. Therefore, although many become interested in spiritual life, only a few manage to walk the walk until the end. The rest become distracted by one thing or the other, or they will create a religion out of their spiritual beliefs and worship their gurus or their teachings without sincerely practicing them.

The ego-self loves religion and is more comfortable with it because religion is more accommodating and forgiving. It is easier to practice religion than an ascetic discipline. To practice any religion, you do not need to make many sacrifices. You can be immoral, unethical, selfish, and even evil, and yet count yourself as a religious person by observing a few rules of conduct imposed by your religion and creating the impression that you are indeed on the side of God and his teachings. You can conveniently hide the truth about yourself behind the cloak of your religion and find social acceptance.

Our religions are very forgiving towards human frailties. They do not seek to destroy human society or upset the social balance. They would prefer people to be religious rather than irreligious and abide by the word of God. In fact, they try to preserve the world and life on earth from our wickedness by instilling in us certain moral and religious values. They cater to the needs and demands of influential people who want to transform the world in their own egoistic and divisive ways, sometimes in total disregard for the very values that religions uphold. Thus, the ego-self finds a convenient ally in whatever religion to which it is drawn without attracting undue criticism or social disapproval.

The ego-self assumes many identities.

The ego-self assumes many identities in different bodies over many lives and the same body in each lifetime. It is attached to name and form and does everything to protect its distinction and identity. Take away your form and appearance, and the world does not know you. Ours is a world of egoistic beings in different stages of development and different states of transformation. Whether it acts individually or as a collective entity, the human ego is subject to many influences and continuous transformation. Attitudinally selfish, it may often act selflessly with a hidden motive. Individually, we are a mixture of opposites. It is difficult to generalize and stereotype our behavior because we live in a state of flux and do not fit into easy categories. Many aspects of our personalities are difficult to explain. We may consider the complexity of human nature both as a blessing and as a curse. It is a blessing because we can experience the world in many different ways with a rich tapestry of our emotions and feelings. It is a curse because it renders our behavior unpredictable and uncontrollable.

For the ego, religion is a tool.

The ego-self loves the drama, the mystery, and the aura associated with the religion it follows and the power and authority that stems from it. For the ego-self, religion is just another tool to propagate its identity and further its interests. It tries to balance its worldliness with the illusion of being pious. The superficial, ritualistic, and superstitious aspects of every religion are the invention of egoistic minds, who find in them a great opportunity to extend their influence and establish their authority. Religion gives them an opportunity to feel good about their religiosity without the compulsion to make major sacrifices or corresponding effort, accepting or rejecting their religious beliefs according to their convenience and personal agendas. In short, for the human ego, everything connected with religion is a means to further its ends.

Because our egos exert so much influence upon our religious beliefs and practices, no religion in this world is free from imperfections and inconsistencies. Our religions do not represent God as much as our identities and worldviews. They do not reveal the truth but the truth we want to pursue. They do not represent God but the God in whom we want to believe. Although we are not familiar with transcendental truths, we live and act as if we are certain about our religious beliefs and our notions of what God is and what He is not. We use religion to boost our egos, enhance our identities, and proclaim our authority and superiority over others. Under the influence of our religious beliefs, we take pride in our religious identities, in the scriptures we read, and in the prophets, saints, and teachers we follow. When ignorant and illiterate people usurp religious authority, you cannot expect much from them. In today's world, religion is misused for many selfish ends. In almost every religion, we find people who want to help God instead of seeking His help for their salvation. They speak for Him and try to assist Him as defenders of faith and soldiers of God as if God is some political leader who wants His people to speak for Him and defend His reputation and ideology.

Serving humanity in the name of God is one thing. However, indulging in acts of violence and destruction in the name of God is entirely different. It is ignorance and pride which makes people indulge in the most heinous acts and fight religious wars in God's name, as if God has created this world to stage His holy wars and violent crusades. Such ignorance and arrogance degrade the very aim our religions intend to serve, which is spreading the ideal of oneness and universal brotherhood. The material world is an integral and inseparable part of God's universal body. You harm it, and you are harming a part of God's body. You defile it, and you are but defiling a part of God's universal form. Some may assume that God lives only in heaven and rules it. They may tell you that all the divinity, sanctity, and morality come from heaven or some invisible and formless God.

It is profound ignorance to believe that God is not found here on earth but only in heaven or in certain holy places where you can set up your shop and do your business. When people talk to one another egoistically about God and religion, nothing much comes out of it except hatred, ill will, skepticism, anger, and violence. When religions come under the influence of our individual and collective egos, they become responsible for much of the bloodshed and violence on earth and unleash the very evil that everyone wants to avoid in the first place. Even after centuries of ill will and religious hatred, we have not learned from our past. We continue to divide humanity in the name of God and religion, denigrating the very moral and spiritual values that they preach. The concept of God, which our religions promote, is discolored and disfigured by our narrow-mindedness and social conditioning.

Although we know that God is beyond all limitations and conditioning, we impart various levels of conditionality and personality to Him and engage in endless debates to prove or disprove our respective beliefs and theories about Him. God and the ego-self have a peculiar relationship. The latter is a shadow, a formation, which can exist only in a relationship with God or Self. It cannot exist independently without Him. It cannot also coexist with Him as His equal. However, it strives to usurp His role, speak for Him, and engage in acts that defy His law. The traditional role assigned to the egoistic self is that of a follower or a devotee. However, many people act egoistically as if they are God's spokespersons and guardians. The ego-self is truly an enemy of God while it pretends to be His earnest and most loyal and obedient devotee and follower.

The ego-driven consciousness can be transformed.

The human ego is amenable to transformation, although it may take quite an effort and many sacrifices on our part to accomplish it. The ego-self never becomes the real Self because it is a temporary formation. It may willingly undergo transformation to liberate the real Self. It may become pure and transparent through discipline and radiate the light of the soul. It may gain knowledge and wisdom through study and observation and cultivate virtues by practicing devotion and divine qualities. But in the end, it just withers away and drops off into the abyss of human history.

Jayaram V

Every human being has a choice to pursue worldly desires or to live for the inner Self. According to our scriptures, if you pursue your selfish desires egoistically, you will incur karma and suffer from the consequences of your desire-ridden actions. But if you live for the sake of your real Self and work for its liberation, consecrating all your actions to God as a sacrifice, you will be free from karma and its negative consequences.

Here are a few points worth remembering about the egoistic self.

1. The egoistic self cannot be liberated, but with discipline and effort, it can be enlightened and purified.
2. As you become purer in your mind and body, you begin to reflect the beauty and the brilliance of the Self.
3. Your egoistic self may not achieve salvation, but if you purify it with determination and restraint, you will experience the illumination of the Self in you.
4. If you perform actions egoistically with selfish intent, you will incur karma. But actions performed for the sake of the Self will not taint you.
5. Your egoistic self persists even after death in the form of latent impressions, which work as the seed for your next life. But if you burn them through the practice of yoga, your ego-self will eventually dissolve into nothingness.

Your egoistic self is a temporary formation, what the Buddhists call the no-self. There is nothing eternal about it. It is an aggregation of diverse components which remain in a constant state of commotion. By understanding its true nature, you become free from all attachments and experience peace and stability.

Triple Means of Making Sense

Emotions, reason, and beliefs play an important role in our lives. They shape much of our thinking, behavior, actions, knowledge, and consciousness and make us what we are: humans. We rely upon them to make sense of the world, understand others, make choices, respond to situations, pursue goals, or form relationships. For instance, when we feel fear, our reason might tell us to avoid the source of fear, and our belief in our own abilities might give us the courage to face it. In many ways, they define our lives and personalities. They are also interlinked and mutually influence each other. Emotions impair reason and judgment. Irrational beliefs can induce irrational thinking, faulty reasoning, and emotional reactions. Therefore, we should know them and their relative importance to develop better awareness about ourselves, our actions, and our reactions. By knowing them and using them properly, we can develop a better knowledge and understanding of ourselves, our actions, mental states, and relationships.

From a spiritual perspective, emotion, reason, and belief represent the trinity of the human personality. Symbolically, they correspond to the body, the mind, and the ego, respectively. Emotions are more physical in the sense that you physically feel the sensations associated with them in various parts of your body. In contrast, your reasoning power is mental. You do not feel it physically, but you know that it exists in your consciousness and helps you in many ways to resolve problems and find solutions. Your beliefs are part of your identity and your unique individuality. While you share your emotions and reasoning power with the rest of humankind, your beliefs make you a unique individual and influence the way you make use of the other two. You hold on to your beliefs because they represent you, define you, and help you practice your religious values and relate with your innermost Self. Your life is complete only when you know how to make use of them in a balanced way. Let us examine these three faculties of our minds in some detail.

Emotions

Emotions are not just fleeting mental states but a vital part of our survival and well-being. They induce subjective experiences and specific behavioral and physiological reactions or responses.

Although we experience numerous emotional states, there are said to be six basic emotions: fear, disgust, anger, joy, sorrow, and surprise. These emotions are the very essence of humaneness that gives us the vitality and vibrancy to live and feel like and be like humans. They can be positive or negative. Positive emotions help us to feel good about ourselves, our competence, and our actions. Negative emotions produce negative feelings about ourselves, others, and our relationships and destabilize our minds. Strong emotions, especially negative ones such as fear and anger, impair our thinking, judgment, behavior, attitude, and physical and mental responses to the situations or problems we face. However, we cannot do away with negative emotions. They make us tough and resilient, prepare us for the harsh realities of life, teach us valuable lessons, and help us become aware of our strengths and weaknesses. Studies show that in difficult and emotionally disturbing situations, we react emotionally before we think rationally. It means that under their influence, we may potentially make mistakes and respond inappropriately. Hence, we should be careful when emotions sway our thoughts. Although they are problematic and difficult to control, emotions are necessary for our survival and well-being. They help us experience the world, express ourselves, detect changes and hidden dangers, read people, respond to potential threats, and safeguard ourselves.

From a spiritual perspective, emotions and feelings (vedana) are responsible for the modifications and the instability of our minds. They are induced by impurities such as egoism, ignorance, delusion, desires, and attachments. Our scriptures suggest that they arise due to delusion, egoism, desire, and attachments, produce afflictions and mental modifications (vrittis), and thereby keep us in restless and agitated states. According to classical Buddhism, negative emotions (kleshas) constitute defiled impressions of the mind (citta samskaras) and give rise to negative karma. They can be purified through mindfulness and meditation and by realizing the impermanence of the phenomenal world and our very physical constitution. According to the tenets of classical yoga, the purpose of yoga is to suppress the modifications of the mind that arise because of the contact of the sense organs with the sense objects. They are responsible for our duality, ignorance, and suffering. The best way to deal with emotions is to subject the mind and the body to intense purification through the eightfold yoga and stabilize them. It is done by practicing restraints, austerities, physical postures (asanas), breathing exercises, sense withdrawal, concentration, meditation, and self-absorption. When the mind is stabilized, one experiences transcendental states of self-absorption.

Emotions, when controlled, can be a source of inspiration and motivation. Instead of suppressing them, we can observe them mindfully and flow with them without outwardly responding, especially if the response could be negative. By labeling our emotions or using reason to calm ourselves, we can transform our emotional responses. This emotional control is a key aspect of self-control, mental stability, and detachment. Through yoga, meditation, and mindfulness, we can gain control over our emotions and learn to live with them without causing harm to ourselves or others.

Reason

Reason, or the ability to think rationally or logically to solve our problems, respond to situations, overcome obstacles, or reach our goals, is an important faculty that determines how developed we are mentally and spiritually. The ability to think, analyze, compare, evaluate ideas, and discern truths helps us know one thing from another, distinguish right from wrong, ascertain causes and their effects, find patterns, relationships, similarities, and differences in the world we perceive, solve problems, overcome difficulties, plan and execute actions, and manage our lives, behavior, emotions, and actions. Through discernment, we come to know the truths of our existence, ourselves, and others. It allows us to draw logical inferences, comprehend complex concepts, and make informed choices. Reason also helps us think creatively, draw conclusions and inferences, and synthesize information by gaining new insights or validating existing truths.

Although we tend to be emotional under stress, we rely more upon reason to perform our tasks, deal with our daily problems, and navigate through difficulties. Logical thinking is required even to perform such simple and routine tasks as cooking food, making a cup of coffee, driving a car, or visiting a friend. We take these actions for granted as routine tasks without realizing that they require logical thinking. Rationality is our biggest asset in resolving problems, surviving against the odds, and adapting to the vagaries of life. Our decision-making skills, common sense and intuition also depend upon it. From a spiritual perspective, our reasoning, analytical, and discerning power comes to us from the higher mind or intelligence (buddhi). It is considered the highest faculty (tattvas) in our bodies produced by Nature and an essential part of our thinking and perceiving brain or the internal organ. It is said to be illuminated by the brilliance of the Self or the pure consciousness that remains hidden in each of us beneath the chaotic surface consciousness. It gives us the ability to discern truth and know right from wrong so that we may live righteously, cultivate virtues and divine qualities, worship God, and pursue liberation. It is not the same in all. Its purity and perfection depend upon one's spiritual development and essential nature. Just as when the glass is pure the light in the lamp shines brightly for everyone to see, buddhi shines brightly through our words and actions when the impurities such as pride, envy, and greed are removed from us. Our minds are prone to right logic (tarka) and illogic or perverted logic (vitarka). The former arises from purity or the predominance of sattva, virtue, knowledge, and the absence of desires, delusion, egoism, and attachments. It strengthens with right conduct, devotion, and self-purification. The latter arises from ignorance, delusion, the predominance of tamas, evil desires and intentions, and lack of purity, discipline, virtue, and discernment.

Hence, although we are rational beings and possess reasoning, the faculty of intelligence or reasoning power does not develop equally in everyone. Very few people succeed in attaining perfection in logical thinking, mainly due to desires, attachments, biases, ignorance, delusion, egoism, emotional problems, mental instability, lack of knowledge, etc. The human mind is subject to several cognitive distortions that impair its ability to think logically, arrive at the right decisions, draw the right inferences, or ascertain truths without confusion or ambiguity. Therefore, every time we use reason, we cannot be sure whether we found the right solution or drew the right conclusion. Despite our best knowledge, analysis, and understanding, we may not reach the right conclusion or make the best judgment. Therefore, it is better to check and counter-check our decisions and conclusions, review the information, question our assumptions, and consult others if necessary to avoid making mistakes. Equally important is not to rush to judgment or accept your surface thoughts and popular opinions in haste without examining them. You should also cultivate the right thinking and improve your intelligence or discernment by overcoming desires, attachments, biases, emotions, logical fallacies, and distorted thinking. Cultivate an open mind with humility and the understanding that you may not have all the right answers or the right information and that there may be other possibilities and alternatives that are not immediately known to you. Rational people are also not necessarily the best people in the world. Rational people may make realistic decisions and draw the right conclusions, but they may not relate well with others, especially the way emotionally healthy people do. Overly rational people can be insensitive, intimidating, manipulative, dull, apathetic, and boring. You may also find them cold and calculated or judgmental and opinionated. A truly rational person should have the discretion to know when to rely on reason and when to use other types of intelligence.

Beliefs

We acquire knowledge in many ways: directly through observation and indirectly through inference, the testimony of scriptures, and the teachings of learned masters. Belief comes into the picture when there is no definitive way to know truths or facts, and we have to rely upon indirect sources to ascertain them or establish the correct knowledge. Of the indirect methods, the testimony of scriptures is considered the best. The ancient Indian seers accepted it as a valid method because they believed that those who came before them had already validated them through their insight and experience. The scriptures are of two types: those that are created by men of intellect and those that are revelations of God. Of the two, the latter kind is considered more reliable. The Yogasutras of Patanjali prescribes self-study (svadhyaya) to acquire knowledge and dispel the ignorance of the mind. The Isa Upanishad states that one should pursue both spiritual knowledge and worldly knowledge. Those who pursue only the higher knowledge or only the lower knowledge will not achieve liberation but actually fall into deeper ignorance because they fail to comprehend the truth, which is complete.

Beliefs have no rational basis. They are not necessarily rooted in our experience or reality. Hence, we must be careful when we act upon them and use discretion and our best judgment without falling into the trap of false and irrational beliefs that cannot be validated by experience, inference, or scriptural authority. Irrational and superstitious beliefs, assumptions, preconceived notions, prejudices, etc., hinder our progress. They cloud our judgment and prevent us from knowing ourselves or making the right decisions. Intuition, hunches, or gut feelings are partly based on reason and partly on beliefs. Even in their case, we must be discrete and act with caution.

At the same time, we cannot simply ignore them. Beliefs shape our worldviews and thinking as much as emotions, facts, and reason. They are useful when we do not have facts or when our knowledge and experience are inadequate to realize truths, ascertain facts, or deal with complex and ambiguous situations. On the positive side, they help us deal with the ambiguity, uncertainty, and complexity of our lives. They sustain our relationships by building trust and faith. In the face of difficulties and adversity, they help us persevere in our actions and reach our goals. When we believe in ourselves, we feel motivated to overcome obstacles, problems, and difficulties, reach our goals, and realize our dreams. Through beliefs and sustained actions, we can materialize our thoughts and desires and create our reality. Beliefs uplift our thoughts and fill us with positive enthusiasm. They keep us moving forward and achieve difficult goals by making possible the impossible and the most difficult worth trying. Because of them, we think positively, remain life-oriented, and work for our salvation. Therefore, with proper judgment and an open mind, we should make use of our beliefs in performing our actions and reaching our goals.

Conclusion

Your thoughts, emotions, and beliefs are windows to your consciousness. From a spiritual perspective, they are responsible for the modifications of your mind and the resulting suffering and restlessness. But they also play an important role in making your life meaningful and letting you know who you are and what you may do about your suffering and your problems. By using them appropriately, you can enrich your life and experience health and happiness. Whether we seek material comforts or spiritual truths, we cannot ignore the value and importance of these three powerful components of our consciousness. They help us in many ways to make sense of the world and deal with it effectively and definitively. Using them, we can improve the quality of our lives and expand our awareness. Knowing their weakness, we can safeguard ourselves from their negative influence.

References
1. Paul Eckman, 1975

Avoiding the Extremes by The Middle Path

The middle way discovered by the Perfect One avoids both these extremes; it gives vision, it gives knowledge, and it leads to peace, to direct acquaintance, to discovery, to nibbana. The Buddha

O Arjuna, yoga is not for the one who eats voraciously, nor for the one who does not eat at all; not for the one who sleeps for too long, nor for the one who always remains awake. The Bhagavadgita

When you keep your hands at a proper distance from the fire, it warms you, but if you put it too close, it will burn you. So is desire or any worldly pursuit, which is like fire. Based on what a Sufi saint told me.

Nature created all living beings to survive and thrive in moderate conditions. We are not designed to withstand extreme temperatures or living conditions. Our survival is best ensured when we avoid life's extremes. We are not made to endure extreme heat or cold, extreme pleasure or pain, extreme suffering, or exposure to extreme conditions, climate, or environment. The same holds true for all aspects of our lives, including spiritual practice. Extreme austerity, self-denial, or indulgence is equally detrimental to our well-being. Neither extreme asceticism nor extreme enjoyment is conducive to the development of balance, stability, harmony, and equanimity that are necessary for spiritual progress. In life, repeated failure can lead to frustration, unhappiness, and lower self-esteem. Conversely, excessive success or fame can induce pride and delusion or unlimited desires and restlessness and distance people from reality or their past relationships, friends, and well-wishers. If overeating is harmful, so is obsessive and compulsive dieting. If lack of sleep affects our physical and mental fitness, excessive sleep can result in inertia, lethargy, and mental torpor.

In the journey of life, we must follow the middle path and avoid the extremes to stay on course and stay safe. Our relationships will not survive for long if we are too close or annoyingly indifferent or aloof. Your friends may desert you if you do not give them enough space to be themselves. You will ignore them, too, if they do not honor your privacy or breach your trust. If you love your children too much or too little, they will be unhappy, feel oppressed or neglected, and may even resent you.

The world does not appreciate eccentric, abnormal, and extreme people. Even though they are often depicted in books and films as the main characters and well appreciated, in real life, people do not feel comfortable around such people and prefer to stay away. People appreciate moderation and balance in all aspects of life, including in matters of public policy or governance. For example, the most unpopular governments are those that are extremely weak or extremely authoritarian and vindictive. People disapprove of anarchy as much as a rigid monarchy. In our relationships, we do not appreciate people who are too selfish or self-centered. Whether in our personal lives, professional, or public lives, we prefer to maintain balance, live within our limits, and temper our interests with social or family responsibility. A circle is complete only when the opposite ends meet in perfect balance. Life is complete only with friendships and relationships. Nature weaves life upon earth on the principles of balance and moderation. It nurtures life according to the environment and punishes those who disregard their safety.

The principle of moderation is enshrined in the teachings of many religions, especially Hinduism, Buddhism, and Taoism. These religions draw a clear distinction between the extreme practices of uninhibited materialism and uncompromising ascetic idealism. They suggest a holistic way of life in which their adherents can pursue both material and spiritual goals without going to extremes or upsetting their lives. Those who are not ready to renounce the world are given an opportunity to become lay practitioners and continue their lives and duties until they are ready. Those who are ready for renunciation or develop a distaste for worldly life are initiated into monastic life and allowed to pursue liberation. In the following discussion, we will focus on how each of these faiths accomplishes this fine balance.

Hinduism

In Hinduism, there are many approaches to liberation, which range from one extreme to the other. On the one extreme, we have some ascetic paths that advocate self-mortification and self-denial to achieve self-realization. They rely upon painful austerities and extreme spiritual practices, including total sexual abstinence and extreme fasting, to control the mind and body and stabilize the mind in contemplation. An example is the Hatha yoga practice. On the other extreme are the left-hand tantric methods, which give a lot of freedom to the practitioners to engage in passionate activities to free themselves from mental blocks, social conditioning, and normal inhibitions. Falling in between these two extremes are the moderate paths that recommend benign spiritual and devotional practices to achieve liberation or attain a good birth in the next life. These moderate paths include Bhakti yoga, which advocates devotion to a personal god, and Karma yoga, which emphasizes selfless action without attachment to the results, which is considered a form of devotion only.

The Bhagavadgita is one of the most sacred texts of Hinduism. It analyzes the various ways in which one can pursue salvation and deal with the problems and difficulties associated with them. It identifies God as the source of all creation and the doer of all deeds, portraying all living beings as mere players in a cosmic drama produced, directed, and enacted by Him for His sole amusement. The scripture offers several alternatives or yogas to the devotees to purify themselves and achieve oneness. They may follow any path, the path of action, knowledge, or renunciation, but must secure God's grace through exclusive devotion and self-control. These approaches emphasize balance and moderation. They acknowledge the hardships of human life and the limitations to which we are subject.

Thus, Hinduism offers a broad spectrum of alternatives to its followers to pursue their liberation according to their essential nature without being dogmatic or oppressive. In its attitude towards the dualities and complexities of human life, it is neither escapist nor pessimistic, neither tortuous nor licentious, nor dogmatic nor superstitious. In matters of salvation and retribution, it lets the law of God and the wheel of karma take care of the actions and decisions of mortal beings, providing them with many opportunities to find God in their hearts in their own time and space and according to their circumstances. It aims to bring people on the path of salvation in incremental steps according to their inborn inclinations arising from their essential nature (sahaja svabhavam) and their previous efforts. It is very tolerant, lenient, flexible, and forgiving towards human frailties. It aims to release people from the samsara (births and deaths) by gently nudging them toward their deliverance instead of rushing them into it. It acknowledges the importance of social and religious institutions and our social, moral, and religious obligations to preserve them for future generations as a part of our obligatory duties. It believes in letting people choose their paths and pursue their spiritual goals according to their karma and fate within the confines of their obligations and personal responsibilities towards themselves, their families, others, the world, and God.

The concept of the middle path is well-evident and deeply interwoven in the principles and practices of Hinduism. We can find it in the descriptions and personification of various Hindu gods and goddesses, who, despite their divinity and infinity, exemplify the virtues of moderation and balance in what they do and uphold as a part of their divine responsibility. The Hindu divinities are vibrant beings who represent the positive pleasures, passions, and enjoyments of life, in contrast to the demons, who personify dark and demonic nature, evil passions, pain, and suffering. The gods live in opulence and comfort, personify material and spiritual abundance, and serve as role models for others to follow. They encourage people to practice self-restraint and moral purity on the path of righteousness and suggest a way of life that is in harmony with our highest ideals and spiritual aspirations. We see this approach evidently in the personification of several divinities like Ganesha, Vishnu, Shiva, Brahma, Rama, Krishna, etc.

Even the extreme ascetic and tantric god, Shiva, with a family of his own and a robust physique, and Lord Vishnu, with his calm demeanor and compassionate gaze, personify the ideals of moderation. The Vedic divinities, such as Indra, Varuna, and Mitra, are pleasure-loving beings. They descend all the way from the heavens to accept the offerings made by the performers of Vedic rituals. They reside in our bodies and share the food we eat and the pleasures we enjoy. If we starve our bodies excessively, they will be unhappy and highly displeased. Therefore, we are advised not to abandon our internal sacrifices of eating, sleeping, and enjoying life.

The same principles are at work in the way of life Hinduism upholds. According to its tenets, human beings must live responsibly in the four phases of their lives, from childhood to old age, performing their obligatory duties. In each stage, they must fulfill their obligations and ensure the order and regularity of the world without neglecting their salvation. An equally important concept is the four chief aims of human life (purusharthas), which they must pursue as householders.

- Dharma, the pursuit of religious study and obligatory duties
- Artham, the pursuit of wealth for practicing Dharma
- Kama, the pursuit of sensual pleasure for procreation

- Moksha, the pursuit of liberation to escape from suffering

These four goals are not obligatory for all. People may pursue liberation only by taking up sannyasa (renunciation). However, they will be better off if they pursue them all for the sake of the world and themselves, harmony and balance, fulfilling their obligations, and clearing their karma.

Buddhism

The Great Buddha arrived at the principle of moderation through his own experience, having tested the futility of extreme austerities and self-mortification. He found extreme methods disturbing, distracting, and unnecessary. Therefore, he proposed the Middle Path, also known as the Eightfold Path, as a very painless and practical approach to resolving human suffering. He prescribed cultivating morality (sila), stability (samadhi), and wisdom (prajna) by practicing these eight virtues: right thought and attitude, right intention, right speech, right conduct, right livelihood, right effort, right awareness, and right concentration.

For the Buddha, the Eightfold Path was not merely a theoretical or speculative dogma but a definitive and practical approach, based on his own experience, to resolve suffering, cultivate peace, and attain Nirvana. He defined Nirvana as neither existence nor non-existence but an indeterminate state between them. Born as Prince Siddhartha, he lived an opulent life as a crown prince and married a beautiful princess through whom he had a son. Then, seeing human suffering, he left behind all comforts, renounced worldly life, and practiced self-mortification for years in the dense forests of India to find a solution. He finally realized desires and attachments or cravings as the cause of human suffering and attained enlightenment under a bodhi tree. As the Buddha, the enlightened one, he advised his followers to shun the extreme ascetic practices and embrace the noble Middle Path as the best way to attain Nirvana or freedom from suffering. He declared the pursuit of sensual gratification as "low, vulgar, common, unworthy and useless" and self-torture as "painful, unworthy and useless. As an alternative, he presented the Middle Path, which he said would open the eyes, produce knowledge, and lead to peace, insight, enlightenment, and nirvana. (Samyutta-Nikaya 56-11).

The Buddha's Middle Path appeared on the religious scene of ancient India at a time when a great churning took place in Indian philosophical schools and established religious dogmas, beliefs, and practices faced skepticism and intense scrutiny. The Lalithavistara, a Buddhist text, speaks of the confusion and decadence that prevailed in the Indian subcontinent during the Buddha's time. In one of the dialogues, the Buddha himself enumerated 22 methods of self-mortification and thirteen types of clothing (S. Radhakrishnan, 1999) the ascetics adapted. People were so preoccupied with rites, rituals, and the superficial aspects of religious duty that they had little interest in knowing truths about themselves, solutions to their suffering, or the nature of their existence.

The Buddha's Middle Path stood in stark contrast to the prevailing religious traditions of his time. It rested on the firm foundations of individual morality and inner perfection, the pursuit of which, he believed, would lead to immutability, the ending of births and deaths, and the fruit of karma. It was a pragmatic approach that combined "ethical idealism" and moderate asceticism with unconventional atheism as a definitive solution to the existential problems of human life. Whatever truths and solutions the Buddha preached were within the realm of human experience and needed no metaphysical or transcendental realization to ascertain them. He made virtue the foundation of spiritual transformation, in which neither God, fate, nor divine intervention had any role. What mattered most was a tireless effort to resolve suffering by overcoming desires through righteous practices that could stretch across many lives or births and deaths.

The Buddha's Middle Path makes sense logically because human suffering cannot be mitigated through self-inflicted torture of the mind and body or the relentless pursuit of pleasure at the cost of one's physical, mental, and spiritual well-being. It can be resolved only by knowing and resolving the underlying causes of human suffering. The Middle Path was a logical outcome of the following Four Noble Truths the Buddha declared.

- Life is full of suffering.
- Suffering arises from cravings or desires and attachments.
- It is possible to end suffering by overcoming desires.
- The Middle Path is the best path to end suffering.

The Buddha's Middle Path was not just about right living and right conduct but also about keeping the head straight and the eyes wide open. He wanted people to be free from self-induced illusions and false expectations. He avoided speaking about God or soul because he did not want to distract people with speculative discussions. He firmly believed that speculation on abstract notions that were beyond the pale of human experience would not resolve human suffering but prolong it. He saw the human personality as the coming together of five aggregates, namely the form, feelings, perceptions, impulses, and witness consciousness, to which it returned repeatedly until its individuality was completely dissolved and nothing was left for further change. For him, liberation did not mean the release of the Self or its realization as an eternal entity through transformation but its disintegration and dissolution as an entity so that self-awareness itself became extinct, and there was neither the seer, seeing, nor the seen. He spoke against the caste system and empty rituals but respected the Brahmanas and Kshatriyas for their knowledge, wisdom, and virtue. He established a monastic order based on a strict code of conduct for the monks yet encouraged them to be lamps unto themselves and be guided by themselves.

After the Buddha passed away, Buddhism branched out into different schools, rightly so because the Buddha encouraged free inquiry and freedom from the authority of dogma and institutionalized beliefs. Schools such as the Madhyamika school of Nagarjuna or the Yogachara School differed widely in their interpretation of the teachings of the Buddha and their understanding of existential reality. But they all accepted the Middle Path as the most effective and suitable means to practice his teachings and attain nirvana. The concept of the Middle Path remained the central theme of Buddhism, even when it left the borders of India to faraway countries and branched out further into diverse paths. Justice Christmas Humphreys, a British scholar, spoke about the Middle Path in the following words:

"The way of Buddhism is Middle Way between all extremes. This is no weak compromise but a sweet reasonableness, which avoids fanaticism and laziness with equal care, and marches onward without the haste, which brings its own reaction. The Buddha called it the Noble Eightfold Path to Nirvana, and it may be regarded as the noblest course of spiritual training yet presented, in such a simple form, to man."

The Buddha exemplified the virtue of avoiding extremes and following the middle course to escape from suffering. His teachings are still relevant and popular for their realistic approach and the ease with which they can be incorporated into one's daily life.

Jayaram V

Jainism

Compared to Hinduism and Buddhism, Jainism is a more austere and ascetic religion, which recommends severe penances, self-mortification, and uncompromising moral purity as the means for salvation. According to Jainism, karma is not an invisible operational principle but a real substance made up of fine particles of karmic matter, which becomes attached to the beings as they indulge in various actions. As long as the individual souls are enveloped by the karmic accumulations, they are bound to the cycle of births and deaths and undergo suffering. They become free only if they can get rid of the karmic matter deposited on them through severe austerities and penances and by leading an uncompromising virtuous life, practicing non-violence, celibacy and fasting, speaking truth, venerating the liberated souls (jinas) and worshipping the enlightened masters (Thirthankaras).

In Jainism, the concept of non-violence is also observed in its extremes. According to its doctrines, souls reside not only in animate but also in inanimate objects such as wood and water, either individually or in clusters. Some souls are said to be so minute that we may not even notice them with the naked eye. Since souls are everywhere and sometimes invisible, one has to live with extreme care and caution and avoid hurting them through carelessness, even when performing such routine actions as walking, eating, breathing, and sleeping, to avoid hurting them and incurring karma. Because of such an extreme stance on non-violence, Jainism lays down a strict code of conduct for its followers about the professions they can choose, foods they can eat, or lifestyles they can follow.

With such uncompromising beliefs about the world, life, and liberation, Jainism presents a rather disconcerting image of the earthly life as a perilous ordeal from which one can gain freedom only through immense personal sacrifices, austerities, and even self-mortification. In Jainism, there is no place for moderation or half-hearted attempts at liberation or self-purification because karma operates inexorably, incessantly, and universally, sparing none from its gambit. It is not a religion you would like to follow normally unless you are born into it or unless you are completely disgusted with human life and want to escape from it forever. The rules are somewhat slack for the lay followers. But the dogma makes sure that they live responsibly and take no liberties with their spiritual destinies.

Jainism offers no compromises for the ardent seekers of knowledge and liberation who want to escape from the ordeals of samsara. They have to lead extremely austere lives to remove all the impurities that accumulate around their souls, like the dirt on a whirling fan. Finally, in the last stages of their lives, they have to prepare themselves for the final departure, leaving behind their bodies, the remnants of their last impurities, through a gradual process of withdrawing into themselves and limiting their movements and food intake, including water. By all standards, Jainism is an extremely difficult religion to practice. It is not for the weak and the insincere or for those who want to pursue spiritualism rather superficially. For the uncompromising Jinas, religion is not a side business or a frivolous activity. It is a serious pursuit that demands complete dedication, sacrifice, and unconditional surrender. However, it offers a middle path to the lay followers so that they can study the dogma, practice its basic percepts, and prepare themselves gradually for the more austere and difficult path reserved for advanced practitioners.

Sikhism

Sikhism originated in India, but its followers are now found in every part of the world. Among the world religions, it is the youngest, but its teachings are rooted in the most ancient spiritual values of the Indian subcontinent. A simple and straightforward religion, with its emphasis on moral conduct and unconditional devotion to an all-pervading omniscient God, Sikhism stands in stark contrast to the rigors of Jainism and similar ascetic traditions. It is unencumbered by the mechanics of ritual worship and the complexities of speculative philosophy found in other religious traditions of the Indian subcontinent. It is also opposed to the monastic and agnostic idealism of Buddhism and the atheistic approach of Jainism. In many ways, Sikhism strikes a deep chord with the mindset of Hindu devotional (bhakti) traditions, minus idol worship, rites and rituals, and blind dogma. With its emphasis on prayers, morality, exclusive devotion to God, selfless community service, reverence for the Gurus, and deep respect for their faith and Holy Scripture (Adigranth), Sikhism offers a middle ground between Hinduism and Islam.

There is no place in Sikhism for extreme penances or torturing the mind and body for the liberation of the soul. For salvation, it advocates simple acts of devotion and adherence to the teachings of the ten spiritual masters (gurus). Sikhism is free from the weight of speculative philosophies, didactical analysis of existential truths, and ritual complexity that characterize Hinduism. It is a simple and straightforward religion that aims to connect the hearts and minds of devotees with God through surrender and love. Guru Nanak, the founder of Sikhism, went to the extent of advising his followers not to waste their time arguing about speculative issues like what constituted meat and whether to eat vegetarian food or not. He wanted them to cultivate deep reverence for life, righteous conduct, and God. Sikhism is a truly moderate religion centered around human virtues, piety, and unconditional love.

Taoism

Taoism projects the vision of an ideal human life through a sublime, poetic, and mystic philosophy. Its teachings are based on the principles of unity, moderation, inner balance, heavenly aspiration, simplicity, letting go, and staying in harmony with oneself and Nature. Taoism does not believe in strenuous effort or self-torture to attain peace and balance. Instead, it advocates effortless living with the belief that in the ebb of life, things would eventually resolve themselves and join the flow. It speaks about living in accordance with the highest aspirations, which people can envisage in their moments of profound awareness and deepest tranquility, uninterrupted by the concerns of their mundane lives, overexertion, or the skepticism of their pragmatic mindset.

The Taoist practices of Tai-chi and Feng-shui and the Taoist symbols of Yin and Yang acknowledge the balance, beauty, and symmetry hidden in the creation and what we may do to resonate with life by emptying and unfettering ourselves. They affirm the ideal of living in harmony with Nature and with the unseen and mysterious process, referred to as Tao or Dao, which guides everything silently and mysteriously. Moderation is one of the three jewels of Taoism, the other two being compassion and humility. They allude to an idealism that refuses to compromise its expansive vision of an invisible force guiding silently, universally, and effortlessly all life for the sake of enjoying transient pleasures and gains or escaping from pain and loss. One of the verses in the Tao Te Ching reminds us of the impermanence of the world and the futility of our existence and the reasons why sages do not waste their time in "excessive effort, extravagance, and easy indulgence." Another verse declares that in regulating human conduct and rendering proper service to the heavens, there is nothing like moderation. The echoes of moderation are self-evident in the following verse (59) also.

It is only by this moderation that there is affected an early return (to man's normal state). That early return is what I call the repeated accumulation of the attributes (of the Tao). With that repeated accumulation of those attributes, there comes the subjugation (of every obstacle to such return). Of this subjugation, we know not what shall be the limit; and when one knows not what the limit shall be, he may be the ruler of a state.

Conclusion

If there is one lesson we can learn from Nature and our own experiences, it is to live within our limits and avoid the extremes. Life on earth is conditioned on the principle of moderation. There is an inherent balance in creation, which is reflected well in its symmetry, beauty, harmony, and rhythm. It is self-evident in the symmetry of forms and shapes, the aggregation and configuration of objects even to the level of atoms, the orderliness of life's progression from birth to death, the regularity of seasons and celestial movements, and the predictability of cosmic events and planetary events. In some intricate and inexplicable ways, the diverse components of the universe remain in equilibrium and act like the different notes of one great symphony. From the chaos emerges order. The sun is warm enough to sustain life on Earth. The seas are deep enough to support both terrestrial and marine life. Our bodies are conditioned to perform effectively within the limitations imposed by Nature. Each season plays its part in the creation, destruction, and renewal of the earth's resources. Even the natural calamities, which unleash great destruction and human tragedy, have their place in the general scheme of things. Without orderliness and inherent balance in creation, life on earth would be extremely chaotic and stressful. Following moderation and pursuing the middle path is the most practical and appropriate approach in every aspect of our lives. It is sanctioned by Nature, approved by scriptures, and prescribed by the prophets, seers, and sages for our liberation as well as self-preservation. It is the most efficient way to experience peace and harmony in our material and spiritual endeavors.

Jayaram V

Works Cited

1. Samyutta-Nikaya 56-11.
2. Indian Philosophy, Volume 1, by S.Radhakrishnan, Oxford University Press 1999.
3. Justice Christmas Humphreys commented about
4. Let good conduct be thy fasting - Guru Nanak Var Majh
5. Excerpt from Tao Te Ching by Lao-tzu, translated by J. Legge, From the Sacred Books of the East, Volume 39, 1891

Letting Go of Your Fears

Fear is an instinctive learned response that is experienced physically, mentally, situationally, or instantaneously in response to external threats that may be real or imaginary and mild or severe. It is the most dominant emotion built into our nature as a fail-safe mechanism and is experienced by both humans and animals alike. This crucial role of fear in our survival and self-preservation is often underappreciated. Both humans and animals use it to protect themselves and, importantly, to establish control and dominance over others. Fear feeds upon itself, aggravated by imagination, distrust, and irrational beliefs. Some fears are so vague and yet so persistent that it is hard to locate their exact causes and deal with them. Fear dominates our thinking and behavior and colors our perceptions, desires, and expectations. It is an inherent, instinctual, and subterfuge emotion that erupts whenever we are threatened, obstructed, or challenged. Whether we are asleep or awake, a part of our consciousness remains focused on ensuring our safety and continuity.

In fact, fear plays a significant role in shaping our lives. We spend much of our lives trying to resolve our fears or escape from them. It is also our most limiting and inhibiting factor, a major weakness that keeps us in bounds and prevents us from realizing our true potential. We are bound to it like a boat is bound to its rudder. Because of fears, we erect defensive walls around ourselves and remain prisoners within them, rarely escaping from them to experience true freedom. Fear also controls much of our thinking, behavior, and actions. It is in response to our fears that we establish relationships and accumulate things excessively, even when we do not need them, often at the cost of our own happiness and inner peace. Fear is interwoven in our consciousness because of the uncertainty and impermanence of our lives and the world in which we live. We are afraid instinctively, sometimes even without an apparent cause, because we know that the world is not a safe place and we are vulnerable to many threats.

The manifestations of fear

Fear manifests itself in various ways, influencing our personalities and mental states. Timidity, anxiety, nervousness, panic attacks, stress, anger, aggression, paranoia, depression, low self-esteem, loneliness, phobias, inferiority complex, shyness, sociopathic behavior, etc., are some of the ways in which people experience or respond to fear. It drives people to live against their wishes and compromise their values and dreams. Due to its pervasive influence, many people tend to undersell themselves, act submissively, or avoid taking risks. At times, they may feel helpless or blame others for their problems and difficulties.

Fearlessness is indeed a mythical quality. In real life, you will not find fearless people but people who act despite their fears. Fearlessness is not the absence of fear but the ability to act courageously in the face of fear. People may differ in their ability to cope with their fears, but no one is ever free from this natural emotion. In its extreme form, it is known as phobia. Phobias are the deep-rooted, persistent, irrational, absurd, unrealistic, delusional, and abnormal fears that can prevent people from living normally. People experience them due to deep-rooted subconscious or psychological causes that are difficult to resolve without ascertaining them. We discuss here the normal fears most people experience in their daily lives and how we may resolve them through self-effort. First, let us explore the causes.

The causes of our fears

Fear is inherent to life because we are constantly exposed to many known and unknown threats. Therefore, it is natural and, in some ways, healthy to be afraid and fear for our lives and survival. Our fears are caused by many factors, some of which are listed below.

1. **Intense situations:** People experience fear or panic when they are exposed to intensely dangerous, hostile, or threatening situations, such as wars, natural disasters like earthquakes or tsunamis, violence like muggings or assaults, accidents like car crashes, and life-threatening situations like medical emergencies.

2. **Unfamiliarity**: We are usually afraid of the unknown, the inexplicable, and the unfamiliar because we do not know how to deal with them. We prefer to stay in our comfort zones and stick to our daily routines, predictable situations, known relationships, and familiar places rather than venture out and take risks or expose ourselves to unknown threats.

3. **Lack of information**: When we deal with events, places, people, or situations where we do not know much about them

or cannot assess the risks involved, and if they are critical to our needs and goals, we naturally experience fear and anxiety.

4. **Uncertainty**: This is a major drive of fear. The stock markets are a good example of how uncertainty induces fear and influences people's investment decisions and trading habits. People feel secure when they are certain about their actions, decisions, and outcomes. Since the future is never certain, we are rarely comfortable about it, which forces some to seek the assistance of astrologers and fortunetellers to alleviate their fears.

5. **Experiences**: Most of our fears are learned or acquired from observation, knowledge, or experience. They may intensify or become reinforced if we repeatedly experience them. Sometimes people may experience irrational fears without an apparent cause, when they find themselves in situations that induced fear in them previously.

6. **Imagination**: Our fears need not be real. Sometimes, we imagine the worst, think negatively, and aggravate our fears. Our imagination can create scenarios that are far worse than reality, leading to heightened fear and anxiety. It is true that much of what we fear may not happen ultimately or happens differently.

The spiritual dimension of fear

From a spiritual perspective, fear is an indication of egoism and lack of trust in oneself and God. When we believe that we are alone in the universe and that we have to face our problems all by ourselves in a world where we are pitted against many opposing forces and conflicting interests, we suffer from anxiety, fear, and uncertainty. Physically as well as mentally, it makes us feel like lone warriors in a tough world facing many unknown enemies and inimical forces. This is the burden of a non-believer, which we also carry even though we presume ourselves to be believers of God. According to the Bhagavadgita, you suffer from fear if you think you are a mere physical self, presume yourself to be the real agent of your actions, pursue your desires egoistically, and do not surrender your will to God and do not perform your actions without desires and offer them to Him as a sacrifice with exclusive devotion. If you take pride in your actions and assume ownership and doership, you must take

Letting Go of Your Fears

responsibility for all your actions, take upon yourself the great karmic burden, and suffer from their painful consequences.

The greatest fear that everyone has to face ultimately is the fear of death. In the normal course of our lives, we usually do not like to think about it. However, we know that no one can escape from it. If you do not believe in God or your divine nature, you will suffer from fear and anxiety whenever you think about death. The very notion that one day you will eventually depart from this world and leave behind a void puts your ego in great grief. But if you believe in eternal life and your fundamental unity with God, you will gradually learn to accept death as a window to another world and an opportunity to correct your past mistakes and move closer to your divine nature. According to Buddhist beliefs, death is a mere dispersion of a phenomenon that never was. The identity of a being is a temporary illusion, a trick played upon our minds by our perceptions and ignorance. Therefore, there is nothing much to fear about death, but accept it as another transition in a series of transitions that characterize the phenomenal world.

Fear is also caused by our cravings, attachments and clinging. You will experience fear and anxiety if you have strong likes and dislikes. We are usually afraid of not getting what we want or getting what we do not want. We suffer from this mental polarity constantly, almost every day. We also entertain many illusions about what we love and hate. It is true. We try to run away from things we hate, even if they are not hateful. We also try to run towards things we think we love, even if they are not lovable. We are forever caught between the dualities of life and in the confusion due to the lack the wisdom and the discretion to know what is right for us. Our attachments are responsible for much of our suffering and insecurity. We carry them with us wherever we go, even though they make us unhappy, weak, and vulnerable. When we cannot let go of things, we become lost in a maze of worries and troublesome memories.

Impermanence and the irreversibility of time aggravate our fears. Fear of aging, old age, sickness, and death are common fears we experience from time to time. There was a time when old age had its charm and dignity. But in today's world, it is not advantageous to be old, look old, or act old because the world is overly preoccupied with youth and does not seem to appreciate old age, experience, or the wisdom that comes with it. If you are old, very likely you will be either bumped down or bumped out of your job. Once you become old, you and the world begin to move in different directions. You become increasingly isolated from the rest of the world and the people who matter, which in itself makes you feel worried, anxious, neglected, and lonesome.

From a spiritual perspective, you may fear if you strongly believe in ghosts, in the devil, in evil spirits, in magic, and in the possibility of you getting hurt by them. Such fears are aggravated by ignorance, superstition, and unfounded beliefs. They are also often used by institutions and vested interests to establish control and dominance over groups of people and invoke their obedience and submission. Fear may also arise from the fear associated with sin, feelings of guilt, and the expectation of punishment and condemnation from God or religious authority due to desires, lust, greed, envy, pride, and the immorality or the guilty conscience that arises from them.

Coping with fears

The good news about fears is that we can learn to cope with them. Since our fears are mostly learned through observation and experience, we can change our habitual responses to them in more empowering and creative ways and learn to cope with them. We can observe closely how fears arise in our minds and deal with the causes that produce them. Alternatively, we can learn to accept them and tolerate them with understanding and fortitude. Here are some of the strategies to deal with them or endure them.

1. Become aware of your fears

Fear is just a response, a state of mind, a habitual thought pattern that intends to protect you or alert you. It may arise for any number of reasons that you can think of. Sometimes, you may fear for no apparent reason but because of some illusion that you may entertain. Most of the time people do not pay attention to what goes on inside their minds and bodies. They are drawn so much into the outside world that they cannot just look into themselves with detachment. They may tell you how they began their careers or where they met their first love. But they do not know much about the history of their fears.

With careful observation, you can learn a lot about your fears. By observing your thoughts and habitual reactions, you can discern what triggers your fears, what sustains them, how you respond to them habitually or instinctively, and whether you accept the

Letting Go of Your Fears

responsibility for them or shift the blame to others or to an external agent to assuage your feelings of guilt and inadequacy. As you become familiar with your fears through mindful observation, you will learn to accept them without feeling guilty or unhappy and assimilate them into your system without being shaken by them. This approach will not set you free from fears since fear can never be taken out of your system permanently or completely. However, it will help you live with them and tolerate them. By extending your awareness into the depths of your consciousness, you come to acknowledge them as normal, natural, and human reactions of your mind and body, which may sometimes trouble you or help you. You will accept them with that understanding just as you accept the other facts of your life, behavior, or personality.

2. Confront your fears by being in the present

In a fearful situation, you are left with two choices: fear and run or stay and fight. They are known as the flight and fight responses. Without exception, we all use them to deal with fearful situations. There is nothing heroic or cowardly about them. They are the basic survival responses used by all humans and animals alike in difficult situations. In fact, sometimes, the flight response is a better option because the threat may be too difficult to resolve, or it may endanger your life and lead to further problems. However, if the threat can be resolved without much difficulty, but if you still want to escape from it due to some inexplicable hesitation or anxiety, that is a problem or a habit you must address. Life is all about making intelligent and appropriate choices. Whether you believe it or not, you always have a choice in every situation that warrants a decision. You may not exercise it because of fear or hesitation or some other disempowering reason. However, the choice is there, even if you do not think of it. We can respond to our fears in many different ways, depending upon what is necessary and what is appropriate in a given situation. In a fearful situation, by being in the present, we can learn to stand our ground and face our fears. Gradually and painfully, with each little victory we score against them, we can build our esteem and confidence and take control of our lives.

3. Practice visualization

Visualization practice is the best and the safest way to change your habitual response to fear. It is an ancient and reliable method used since ancient times to overcome fears, especially in ascetic and monastic schools. In Tibetan Buddhism, for example, monks use a special technique called chöd to cut off the ego and cultivate fearlessness. It is said to be originally an ancient tantric practice in which the practitioners use visualization techniques to subdue their egos, tolerate pain and suffering, overcome fears, and develop a compassionate attitude toward all sentient beings. During the practice, a monk visits a desolate place, such as a graveyard, in the middle of the night and practices the meditation, sitting alone. In the meditation, he visualizes hungry and dreadful monsters in their fiercest forms and mentally offers them the parts (skandhas) of his mind and body until nothing is left. Through its repeated practice, the monk develops a nonreactive awareness, experiences great relief from pent-up feelings, and experiences great calm. With his ego falling into silence and his mind becoming empty of all hurtful thoughts, feelings, and fears, he overcomes all disturbing thoughts and emotions, including fear. The practice is also useful to overcome the fear of death, accept death as a natural process in the coming and going of all living beings, and depart from here peacefully at the time of death into the beyond.

We can use similar techniques in the comfort of our homes, without endangering ourselves, to overcome the most troubling fears. We can visualize situations that induce them and deal with them mentally in empowering ways. Through repeated practice, imagining different scenarios creatively, and running through them with different responses until they cease to be troubling, we can learn to deal with them effectively in real-life situations.

4. Transfer the burden of your fears to God

Our fears multiply when we think we are alone and we are not going to find help from others. However, imagine if you have the help of an invisible partner, in the form of God, a deity, an angel, or your radiant Self, who is willing to help you whenever you want it. Would you still be afraid of anything? If you have faith in God or some supernatural power, you will not feel anxious about your future or your problems. Even if you are a firm believer in God but feel anxious about your life or your future, it is a sign that your faith is weak, and you do not trust God as much as you want to. It is a pity that many people readily believe in the existence of ghosts and vampires but lack the same conviction about God and divine beings. Many pray to God when they are in trouble. But once things improve, they forget

Letting Go of Your Fears

about Him. There is a lot about our lives that is mysterious and cannot be explained rationally. We do not know much about anything, which in itself is a great limitation. We cannot also see far into our future. When we know that we have limitations, it is prudent to turn to God and ask for help. If you are afraid or if a problem is bothering you and causing you sleepless nights, pray to God and seek His help. Express your gratitude for every help you receive. Keep an open mind even if your prayers are not answered because you do not know what is good for you. True surrender means you transfer the burden of your life entirely to God and let Him take care of your problems and concerns. The idea is that when you surrender to God, you will be freed from the burden of taking care of yourself, and you will let God make all the decisions for you, not necessarily in your worldly interests or as you expect them to happen, but in the interests of your salvation and spiritual well-being.

5. Let go of your fears through detachment

Our attachments are more pervasive than we think. In reality, everything that holds you back from being your radiant Self is an attachment. Your memories, your likes and dislikes, your faith, your prejudices, your thoughts, your opinions, your judgments, your relationships, your concerns, and your anxieties are but different manifestations of the same attachment, which pulls you towards the material world and keeps you entangled. It also manifests as your fears, your love, your anger, your envy, your name, your identity, your family, your wealth, your habits, your talents, your skills, your beliefs, your knowledge, your gods, your friends and relations, and myriad other things. We are afraid of losing what we love or dealing with the unexpected. There are no simple remedies to the problems such as these, which arise from our attachments. When you live in the midst of the world, you have to deal with the expectations and anxieties that arise from your interactions with it. You can either suffer from them or make use of them to deal with your fears.

You can make a beginning by renouncing your most simple attachments to develop sameness or equanimity. You may let go of what you love most and what you hold dearly as a part of your name and form. Your attachments are essentially your viewpoints, a way of looking at things with a particular mindset. You are drawn to them because you think they define your identity or give you comfort and security. You fight for them and defend them because you think you are defending yourself. However, think about it. We worry about these things because we feel lost and empty without them. Instead of feeling secure, we feel more insecure.

You will come to know a great deal about your motivation, if you withdraw from the entanglements and become more introspective. If you probe your mind attentively, you will realize why you love or hate certain things. If you persist in your efforts, you will gradually understand why you depend upon things and how you seek security, stability, and pride through your material possessions and sense of ownership. You will also realize that there are better ways to experience peace and stability in your heart without seeking things and without feeling desperate about what you may or may not get. You will also realize that your true worth lies not in having things but in being yourself.

In the Buddhist tradition, there is a beautiful concept called the heroic effort. It is not about being a warrior in the physical sense but acting with conviction and heroism in the most extenuating circumstances, without losing hope and courage. If you persist in your spiritual practice despite all the negativity, discomfort, and suffering, it is a heroic effort. If you wake up every morning with a cheer in your heart and a smile on your face, even though life is pretty depressing and difficult, it is a heroic effort. Courage is sustaining your interest and motivation to keep going and pursue your goals or persevering at your tasks despite opposing fears, negativity, and discouraging thoughts from others. On the spiritual path, this is how you must deal with your fear and negativity, confront the demons of your mind and drive them away.

The Hidden Symphony of Life

An intelligent blueprint is intricately woven into all creation, a sight that never fails to inspire awe. In God's manifestations and creations, we witness the unmistakable presence of beauty, symmetry, perfection, and intelligent patterns. From the structure and function of an atom to a living cell, the solar system, a constellation, or a galaxy, we are greeted with order and regularity, a distinctive sign of his hidden presence. While some may dismiss these marvels as the work of random events, those with discerning eyes cannot help but feel a sense of wonder towards the magnificent expansiveness of the whole material universe and its divine basis, even if they may not certainly and clearly define it.

Even in the seemingly random processes of life and evolution and our very lives, we can see definitive patterns, orderly processes, and predictable mechanisms and outcomes. The logical mind cannot be satisfied with the simple explanation that they arise from random processes and accidental happenings. Although our lives are uncertain and unpredictable, and we do not have much control over what happens to us, we can still control parts of our lives and destinies and make things happen. We may not know why we are here, but we know why we must live, perform our duties, or reach our goals. We may not fully control our lives or destinies, but we know that our minds and bodies have beauty and symmetry and have set ways of performing functions in an orderly and predictable manner.

The universal order

Our scriptures suggest that the world was chaotic before God established order and regularity or what the Vedas call Rta (rhythm). Rta is the cosmic order, the principle of natural order that regulates and coordinates the operations of the universe. The Puranas portray the whole creation as a battleground between good and evil forces. God is the protector and upholder of divine virtues and order, while evil forces try to disrupt it and spread chaos. The Vedas attribute the order, beauty, and symmetry (Rta) hidden in the creation to the universal laws, functions, and properties (Dharma) established by God. They affirm that the creation will continue and life will prevail as long as Dharma prevails and that Rhythm lasts.

Dharma is the force that moves the cycle of creation and ensures its orderly movement. They attribute all happenings and movements to his divine will and encourage people to uphold Dharma to preserve and ensure their continuity. Whenever the order is disturbed due to the decline of Dharma, God himself will incarnate on earth to restore them. Through his inviolable laws and obligatory duties, he ensures that Time and Fate move as ordained, planets move in their respective orbits, seasons happen, life goes on through births and rebirths, and the world continues its existence through the four great epochs as destined. We can see the same rhythm, order, and regularity within ourselves, the way our bodies are made, the way they function, and the way we go through different phases of life from birth to death.

The argument that God is the source of all creation becomes more convincing when we discern the intelligent patterns, perfections, and orderly processes hidden in it. The Hindu Puranas and epics revolve around this concept and extol God himself as the source of all and the supreme personification of beauty, harmony, symmetry, purity, order, balance, stability, constancy, completeness, perfection, excellence, peace, and bliss. The belief that a certain balance and order existed in the universe and God was responsible for it was not just convincing but also comforting for ancient Indians, who had to deal with the vagaries of Nature frequently and witness Death and destruction from very close. It empowered them to deal with the anxieties and uncertainties they experienced living in a hostile environment and endowed them with faith to establish the same order, harmony, and discipline in their personal lives through righteous conduct or by following the precepts laid down in the scriptures as God's eternal commands. They viewed life as an orderly progression of events from one stage to another, with God as its source.

When humans adhered to that orderly process and followed the way of life the scriptures recommended, it ensured peace, balance, stability, happiness, and prosperity. They believed that if they followed the righteous path upheld by him, it ensured them the fulfillment of their desires, the attainment of their goals, and the support of the gods. Otherwise, they thought people would succumb to evil desires, Dharma would decline, and their lives and the world would become chaotic and disorderly, filled with suffering.

Jayaram V

Probably, similar ideas prevailed elsewhere in the ancient cultures where people lived in close proximity to Nature and experienced awe and wonder at its marvels. The Sanskrit word 'ritu' (season) or rīti (tradition or the way of things) is derived from the root word 'rta.' We can find similar-sounding words in other Indo-European languages also, like 'rhythms' in Latin, 'rhythm' in French, 'rhythms' in Greek, and 'rhythm' in English. They convey the same meaning: order, beat, pulse, meter, pattern, flowing, and harmony, which convey that the ancient cultures probably discerned the order and regularity hidden in creation and attributed it to God, Nature, or some supernatural power.

Establish harmony and order within yourself

The idea of Rta, or the universal order, as God's personification is the cornerstone of Indian spirituality. The practices aim to re-establish the same order and regularity within the practitioners by helping them control their chaotic minds and bodies and their nature-driven actions through self-control, discipline, and devotion. These practices inspire and motivate the aspirants to establish peace, harmony, stability, and equanimity within themselves, thereby allowing them to escape from the disorderly, chaotic, and impermanent world. One can see the idea of Rta as the basis of the Yoga philosophy and practice also. The mystic diagrams (yantras) used in Tantric rituals also personify it. Creation, preservation, and destruction are orderly processes, and we, too, can harness their power by invoking the deities who are responsible for them to purify ourselves and escape from this world.

The purpose of yoga is also the same. When practiced correctly and systematically, it removes the impurities of the mind and body, suppresses the modifications (vrittis) of the chaotic mind, and establishes peace and stability so that the yogi's mind becomes one-pointed and centered in itself and enters the perfect and blissful state of equilibrium, sameness, and oneness. Each living being is a combination of order and chaos, the same principles that govern the whole existence. The eternal Self (Purusha) in the body represents order, peace, stability, harmony, regularity, universality, and infinite power. The body, the mind, and the senses represent afflictions, ignorance, duality, disorder, chaos, suffering, instability, and lack of control. They prevent us from knowing who we are and our true nature. It is by removing the chaos of the mind and body with the help of yoga and returning to that pure Self and merging with its pure consciousness one can re-establish order and discipline and experience peace and happiness.

Our suffering increases in proportion to the extent we distance ourselves from the order and regularity within ourselves, and our minds become chaotic. We will not be effective or find peace and happiness unless we are in tune or harmony with ourselves or our essential nature. Our suffering also increases if we live in a chaotic world that is filled with disorder, perversion, and evil influences. While we cannot control the world, we can surely control ourselves and our essential nature and establish peace, order, and harmony within ourselves.

We can do it in several ways: by restraining our minds and senses, practicing discipline, controlling our impulses, passions, and desires, keeping our surroundings clean, protecting our environment, spreading peace and happiness, organizing things, avoiding waste, exemplifying divine qualities, and so on. We can bring order to our lives by attaining perfection in our thinking, conduct, and actions through disciplined effort, discernment, and righteous living. By nourishing the gods in us through sacrifices and mystic chants (mantras) and purifying our minds and bodies through virtuous actions, we can reconnect to the inner rhythm (the Rta) or God's eternal vibration (nada) that reverberates silently within ourselves and connects us to the rest of creation.

The Absolute Truth, whom we venerate as God, is one seamless, absolute Truth that the moon and sun do not shine and the mind cannot reach. His creation is a holistic and seamless union or synthesis of multiple realities and diverse truths in which order and chaos coexist as the opposites of the same force. Our world and minds and bodies, which are an integral part of it, are also a mixture of both chaos and orderliness and subject us to both, depending upon how we organize our lives and bring order and discipline into our lives.

If peace and happiness are the goals, we must establish harmony, peace, and perfection within ourselves through discipline, restraints, austerities, and devotion. We must live dutifully and virtuously, align our chaotic lower nature with the stable higher nature with God as the role model, and remain in control of our desires, thoughts, and actions to connect to the indestructible silence and harmony hidden deep beneath our surface consciousness.

Jayaram V

The Four Faces of Suffering

Suffering is universal and is the common factor of all life on earth. Whoever is subject to impermanence cannot escape from suffering. As humans, we suffer continuously, whether we are aware of it or not, when we have or do not have problems. Any discomfort, unease, or inconvenience is suffering only. As long as the mind is subject to afflictions, disturbances, and modifications (vrittis), and as long as it is unstable or restless, it is not free from it. In the Yogasutras, Patanjali says, "For the one who has discrimination, everything is suffering." Philosophically speaking, living on earth is in itself a great suffering. The very process of living and even mundane tasks we perform for our survival, such as eating, breathing, walking, or working, also produce suffering, although we may not consciously experience it. We may take pride in what we have or envy what others may have.

Indeed, all living beings deserve compassion because we are put into a situation by forces that are beyond our control without asking where we are bound to the actions of Nature and are forced to live inside our bodies as prisoners. From the time we are born, we suffer constantly for one reason or another. We suffer for having or not having something, doing or not doing something, or choosing or not choosing something. We suffer when we are busy or when we are idle. We suffer for having too much wealth or not having enough. Practically every thought, desire, emotion, action, and feeling we experience contains in it a seed of our suffering. Birth is suffering. So is death. Eating is suffering. So is digestion. Breathing is suffering. So is walking or speaking. Every transformation or change we experience in our lives is a potential source of suffering. Impermanence, which is the essential nature of our existence on earth, is the main cause of our suffering. Our ignorance, desires, egoism, and our attachments aggravate it.

Religions do not offer much solace because they remind us how imperfect and sinful we are and what fate awaits us in the end if we do not mend our ways and follow their methods. Some religions regard us as born sinners. Some portray us as ignorant and deluded, caught in the web of life and bound by our own failures and actions. Because of the continuous outpouring of such teachings, most people rarely feel comfortable practicing their faith or finding solutions from them. Theologically, we have no clear explanation of why the world exists, why we are here, and what purpose we serve here. Some people do find a lot of comfort and solace from their faith. However, it requires a lot of effort, sacrifice, and discipline on their part, which only a few can achieve.

By reading our scriptures, we find some answers but not all. The Buddha said that we suffer because of desires. But this does not explain why we were created imperfectly to experience desires and suffer from them. Life would have been better if we were perfect or flawless, but it did not happen. A life in heaven is often offered as a solution to this problem, but it does not explain why we are allowed to go there straight without spending our whole lives here and suffering in the process. The scriptures do not offer convincing answers to resolve such contradictions and moral dilemmas. Instead, we have to rely upon faith as a test of our devotion, with no guarantees or certainties.

The world is a vast cauldron of seemingly meaningless activity, where people search for happiness in the fleeting bubbles of impermanence. Those who have experienced the rigors of life understand how suffering permeates our lives and influences our thinking. We suffer when we are in conflict with reality, with truth, with the way things are, and with ourselves. We suffer when we are not what we should be, when we desire what should not be desired, or when we perform actions that should not be performed. We suffer when we do not follow the ordained laws, follow them wrongly, or follow the laws that should not be followed. We also suffer when we fail to discern right from wrong, become deluded about ourselves and our identities, pursue wrong goals, or uphold falsehood, as much as when we perform righteous actions and uphold Dharma with evil or selfish intentions. Suffering, it seems, is an unavoidable burden we all must carry until we are liberated. Part of it is inherent in our lives, and part of it arises from our actions and inactions. Our scriptures suggest that suffering comes to us as a guide and teacher to teach us valuable lessons about ourselves.

In worldly matters, it is difficult to accept the notion that suffering is a corrective process and a spiritual expediency. However, from the words of enlightened masters, it is what we learn. Suffering is a corrective process or a perfecting mechanism. It is built into our existence as an answer to Nature's imperfect and clumsy mechanism. Nature brings the perfect Self and puts it in the most imperfect and gross form we call the body. Our suffering is proof of Nature's failure to create perfect forms and living conditions on Earth. From our observation, knowledge, and understanding of the mortal life in this world, the following truths about suffering emerge. When we examine them, we will understand a great deal about suffering and how we may resolve it.

1. Suffering is a state of mind
2. Suffering is self-created
3. Suffering is here to teach us lessons
4. Suffering can be overcome

Suffering is a state of mind.

Although we tend to equate pain with suffering, they are not the same. Pain is mostly physical, and suffering is mostly mental. Most of the time, pain is the cause, and suffering is the result. When we are in bodily pain, what ensues from it is mental suffering. Others may not agree with this subtle difference, but it is how I see them both. When the body becomes numb, one does not feel pain at all, even if it is grievously hurt. From hypnosis, we learn that both pain and suffering can be induced in normal people through simple suggestions. In a hypnotic state, it is possible to make people cry in pain or feel sad and depressed, even if there is no real cause. Such incidents amply prove that suffering is a state of mind and a conditioned response to certain events and situations. We suffer for a multitude of reasons, some of which are real and some imaginary. Our thoughts and beliefs play an important role in creating and perpetuating our suffering. Many times, we aggravate our suffering by overreacting, exaggerating, awfulizing, and focusing on the negative.

Because suffering is a subjective state of mind, people differ in their tolerance and responses to suffering, depending upon how they perceive troubling situations and interpret them. Some remain hopeful even when the world is crashing around them, while some lose hope and feel depressed even for minor setbacks. Some cope with suffering in unhealthy ways, such as avoiding, escaping, withdrawing, submitting, drinking, taking drugs, or even committing suicide. With such self-defeating methods, one may buy peace temporarily, but they create more problems in the end, calling for even greater involvement. There is a saying that you attract what you resist. If you resist suffering, you attract it more. Suffering is a condition, like a disease, which should be dealt with in the right way, at the right time, and with the right attitude.

We think mostly about our problems and difficulties. However, it is wise to think about the suffering of others along with ours and pray for their welfare. When we look at others' suffering, our suffering becomes lighter and tolerable. We owe our gratitude to countless people who participate in our lives and help us greatly with their toil and support. Expressing our gratitude may not be enough to discharge the debt we owe to them. We should try to help others in whatever way we can. In the process of helping others and sharing their suffering, very likely we forget our own and experience peace and contentment. We should not only think about the suffering of human beings but the suffering of every living creature on earth. We must have compassion for everyone, including plants and animals, because everyone who lives here suffers, without exception, and is connected in some way with everyone else.

The world is a harsh place. Therefore, everyone who lives here deserves respect and compassion. That includes plants and animals. We owe them a debt of gratitude because they help us in many ways, often at a great cost to themselves. By becoming offerings in the sacrifice of life or creation and serving others in different ways through that sacrifice, they earn meritorious karma and evolve from one birth to another. They do not have as much ability and knowledge as we do to survive or protect themselves from danger. They are totally at our mercy. Therefore, it becomes our sacred and obligatory duty to protect them from mindless destruction and unnecessary suffering and help them evolve so that someday they will also attain human birth and strive for liberation.

Spiritually speaking, suffering arises from our delusional thinking, which in turn is caused by our limited knowledge, attachments, desires, wrong values, mistaken identities, and egoistic thinking. We suffer quintessentially when we do not perceive the world clearly, make wrong decisions, indulge in irrational behavior, or respond to situations inappropriately. We suffer when we make mistakes, judge ourselves harshly, think irrationally, harbor ill feelings towards others, indulge in vice, or develop attachments to things that are difficult to attain or sustain. We suffer when we pursue the wrong values and goals or engage in actions with evil intentions. Much of our suffering happens internally, under the surface, without us becoming even aware of it because we assimilate much of it unconsciously and accept it as a natural condition. We suffer from mundane situations also, such as standing in long queues, becoming stuck in traffic jams, or feeling ignored or neglected in social gatherings. However, we do not give them much attention. We take them in our stride and move on to deal with other and more serious problems. We become so accustomed to dealing with them that we do not even consider them problems but matters that need to be endured as a part of our daily lives.

Suffering is self-created

Our suffering comes from our thoughts, actions, inactions, reactions, desires, conditioning, beliefs, attachments, attitudes, relationships, and associations. It is mostly self-created and self-inflicted. We may blame others for our suffering, and sometimes rightly so. However, it does not help us much to feel better. Others may play a role in aggravating our suffering, but always in a script written and approved by us. Our suffering may arise from extraneous factors beyond our control, but we have the freedom and the ability to deal with them appropriately according to our knowledge and intelligence.

It is perfectly natural to feel wronged and vindictive when others interfere with our lives and interests. However, how will that feeling help us? We should rather focus on how to resolve our suffering and how we may benefit from the experience of suffering and the resolution of suffering. Classical yoga identifies five causes of suffering: ignorance, egoism, desires, aversion, and clinging to life. We suffer in situations such as the following, which keep recurring in our lives like waves in an ocean.

- When we do not get what we want.
- When we get what we do not want.
- When things do not happen as we expected.
- When things happen differently from what we expected.
- When we have what we dislike.
- When we do not have what we like.
- When we are united with what we detest.
- When we are separated from what we love.
- When we lose our dearest friends and relations.
- When we empathize with others' suffering.
- When we compare ourselves with others or envy them.
- When we lack discretion and make mistakes.

Our suffering may arise from unintended actions, unexpected events, and situations over which we may have no control. However, they may be manifestations of your previous karma. You may not be able to control what happens to you, but in the aftermath of a tragedy, you always have a choice to deal with it. Ultimately, your suffering is your creation and how you may deal with it rests with you.

Suffering is here to teach us lessons

Suffering comes to us because of our inner imperfections, inappropriate actions, and reactions. It is a gift of God, delivered in a thorny package, with a cryptic message, very much like a practical cruel joke played upon us, to let us know our failings and shortcomings. In essence, it is a note of caution or admonition. Our suffering is mitigated to the extent we learn from it and correct ourselves. If you are a spiritual person, you will accept suffering willingly and embrace it because it is a sign of God's love for you and His willingness to help you on the path. If you have serious problems in your spiritual practice, it is an indication that you have awakened all the demons of your consciousness, who now want you either to surrender to them and admit your failure or transform them and move on. The very presence of suffering in your consciousness is an indication of egoism and attachment. Any egoistic attempt on your part to resolve your suffering will only increase it further. From a spiritual perspective, if you suffer for any reason, it is an indication that you are egoistic. It is as simple as that.

You may overcome suffering by inflicting more suffering upon yourself through rigorous austerities. However, it may not be the right choice unless you come from a tradition that regards suffering as a virtue. Some religious traditions do recommend painful methods of self-denial for liberation. They may be helpful in some cases because all paths eventually lead to God only. However, they may not work for everyone equally. Some may even feel discouraged and stay away.

Extreme methods of spiritual practice are considered regressive by many traditions since they hurt the body and endanger one's mental and physical well-being. They may even strengthen the lower nature and demonic qualities since the deities in the organs of the body, who are by nature pleasure-loving, do not participate in it. Therefore, these traditions recommend benign and agreeable methods to discipline the mind and body and practice self-control. In other words, using extreme suffering to resolve suffering is not a good idea. One may use it to overcome desires and attachments, cultivate virtues such as patience and tolerance, strengthen resolve, or correct one's methods and practices. Suffering arises from our imperfections and failures. It contains within itself a hidden message, revelation, or teaching.

Therefore, when it arises, we can take the message it intends to deliver and act accordingly. When you go through an unpleasant experience, ask yourself why it happened and what you may learn from it. Identify the causes and your role in creating your suffering. It may be some desire, attitude, belief, need, fear, quality, or deficiency that might have attracted it and which you must resolve for your own good. See what you can learn from it or how you may benefit from it. We can also learn from the suffering of others or the suffering that is endemic to our existence. Every day, we are presented with many opportunities to learn from our imperfections and mistakes and the suffering, restlessness, or anxiety they produce.

Suffering can be overcome

You can either deal with your suffering in empowering ways or learn to live with it with forbearance. Like any other manifestation in our objective reality, suffering manifests in our lives due to our desires and attachments or due to the thoughts and actions they induce. At some point, it will disappear if we change our ways and learn from it. In the end, depending upon how you respond, you are either cleansed by it or crushed by it. You always have choices to deal with it or respond to it. Those choices depend upon you and your knowledge and awareness. When you have a problem, you must give it proper attention. You must find the root cause or causes, which may take time if it is not apparent, and take appropriate actions. Thus, the resolution of suffering is very much a problem-solving or decision-making process, which depends upon your knowledge, intelligence, discernment, determination, focus, and initiative.

Suffering can be resolved passively or aggressively by changing one's methods and responses or by changing oneself. One can escape from it or become indifferent to it. They are all useful strategies used by both worldly people and spiritual practitioners. On the spiritual path, the emphasis is more on finding the ultimate and everlasting solution through purification and transformation to cultivate or strengthen the virtues of tolerance, resilience, resolve, endurance, detachment, indifference, etc. In worldly life, it is more on resolving or removing the causes or adapting to them. One can temporarily reduce or remove suffering by addressing its causes, or one can cultivate strength and fortitude to remain undisturbed by it. Both approaches are effective in their respective ways. Here are a few important and well-known methods pursued in various cultures and traditions to overcome suffering.

Self-effort: While theistic traditions believe in God's intervention in human and worldly affairs, non-theistic traditions emphasize self-cleansing through self-effort for spiritual liberation or liberation from suffering. Buddhism and Jainism recommend this approach. Although they differ in their approaches to the problem of suffering, they believe that the onus of overcoming suffering by themselves or with the help of others rests solely upon each person.

Surrender: Any response or reaction to suffering arises from the ego. Therefore, while worldly people resist suffering or act upon it to control it or resolve it, spiritual people are advised to give up their egos and endure their suffering as an austerity to cleanse themselves. Some recommend surrendering to God and letting him address the problem. In either case, you surrender your egoistic desire to address your suffering and leave the problem passively to fate, God, or circumstances. Surrender implies faith, trust, and giving up personal opinions, doubts, and reservations one may have about the teachings and methods one practices.

Self-transformation: We are conditioned to live and thrive according to circumstances, pursuing our egoistic desires and attachments in an ignorant and deluded state, oblivious of our spiritual nature. Due to impurities such as ignorance, egoism, delusion, cravings, and attachments, our outgoing minds and senses extend into objective reality and become bound to the world, whereby we create suffering for ourselves and maybe for others. When the impurities are removed through spiritual practice, we develop the moral and spiritual strength to cultivate sameness and remain indifferent to suffering.

Right living: Much of human suffering arises from sinful karma, which results from indiscretion and desire-ridden actions when people sacrifice their virtues and pursue wrong livelihoods or paths to make a living or achieve their goals. Hence, one needs to live righteously, cultivate virtues, and pursue the right aims through righteous actions to end suffering. Each tradition has its version of what right living and right actions mean. You must be familiar with whatever teaching or faith you follow to know that you are progressing in the right direction and not producing further suffering for yourself.

Knowledge: Ignorance is inherent to our very nature and existence. Ignorance is why we are bound to samsara and why we suffer birth after birth. Ignorance may mean different things to different people. According to Buddhism, it means ignorance of Dharma or the four causes of suffering and the Eightfold Path. According to Hinduism, it means not knowing that you are an immortal and indestructible Self, not your mind and body, and you can escape from suffering by becoming established in it and attaining oneness with it. In Islam and Christianity, it means disobeying God's laws and commands and succumbing to evil desires and temptations. Whatever the method or teaching, all traditions assure that with the right knowledge and discernment, you can escape from suffering and attain eternal life.

Self-control: Most traditions identify the activity of the mind and senses as the root causes of desires and attachments, which lead to suffering. Therefore, they recommend restraint of the mind and senses to practice self-control, subdue desires, stabilize the mind, and establish it in peace and equanimity. The Bhagavadgita prescribes self-control (atma-samyama) and exclusive devotion as foundational to the practice of all yogas to overcome suffering on a lasting basis. It is also foundational to the practice of Right Living in Buddhism.

Service: According to Hinduism, devotion to God can be expressed in several ways. One of the best ways to practice it is by performing sacrificial duties and serving God's creation selflessly. By engaging in charitable actions, nourishing the hungry or the needy, or helping others, one can transcend selfishness and forget one's suffering in alleviating the suffering of others. When you serve others and make yourself a sacrifice or offering in your devotion to God, you will connect to the rest of his creation through empathy and compassion and open your heart to his eternal love.

Purity: The mind is fickle and unstable, and we are driven by desires and evil tendencies because of the presence of three chief impurities: egoism, desires, and delusion. These impurities promote and perpetuate desire-ridden actions and deluded behavior, which leads to sinful karma, suffering, and bondage. The impurities are why our suffering persists and keeps intensifying until we resolve them and cultivate purity through virtuous living. We should, therefore, focus on cultivating purity and divine nature to resolve suffering.

The Awakened Life

Acceptance: We suffer because we react and respond differently to different situations due to likes and dislikes or attraction and aversion. We suffer when we have to deal with things, people, and situations we dislike or are separated from those we like. The dualities of life, craving and clinging, are why our suffering never ends. Knowing that all things and phenomena are empty in themselves but produce suffering due to desires and attachments and practicing self-control, we can learn to accept things as they are without judgment, desires, likes, and dislikes and experience peace and equanimity even when we are exposed to the dualities of life or the causes of suffering.

Emptiness: According to Daoism, form is an illusion. Reality is the space invisible and hidden in the form. That space is actually responsible for the form. Therefore, we should become empty, formless, unassuming, humble, invisible, silent, and yet poignantly universal, like space rather than form. Buddhism and Hinduism suggest a similar approach but with different theological explanations. When we are empty or when our minds our empty, all the causes that produce suffering also disappear. Hence, through emptiness or by becoming a nobody, we can resolve suffering.

Detachment: We cannot be free if we are bound to the world through desires and attachments or if we cling to worldly things and pleasures and become involved with them. Our attachments are like the roots that penetrate deep into the soil of life and do not let us be free. They become obstacles to our independence, happiness, and freedom from suffering. Therefore, if we want to overcome suffering, we must become detached from the things that bind us to this world. It can be done only by practicing detachment and renunciation and letting go of all desires and attachments.

Conclusion

From a spiritual perspective, suffering is an inescapable fact of life, and surrendering to God and cultivating virtues is one effective means of overcoming it. Those who do not believe in God may follow their respective methods according to their best discretion, remembering that suffering can be mitigated only through corrective actions without causing suffering to others or subjecting oneself to undue suffering. Despite their fundamental differences, most traditions agree that suffering can be overcome through righteous paths, with the help of God, with individual effort, or by both. Up to some point, we may consider suffering as an obstacle to our happiness and enjoyment. However, when we expand our awareness and see that it is also an effective means for our growth and transformation, we will accept suffering and learn from it. Even if you are not a spiritual person, you can learn from your suffering and transform yourself.

Follow the simple rule: if you know how to resolve suffering without hurting yourself or others, do it. If you cannot, accept it, endure it, learn from it, and cultivate better awareness about it. When you make mistakes, at some point, you may have to deal with their consequences. It is the truth of life. Those who follow wrong paths, pursue inappropriate goals, engage in perverse actions or perform them with wrong intentions, make wrong choices, or let their imperfections prevail despite clear warnings will eventually be forced by circumstances or their karma to realize their mistakes and mend their ways. The law of karma, which is interwoven in our world of cause and effect, is inviolable and inexorable. If you are wise enough, you will learn from your mistakes and imperfections and avoid repeating them. When suffering comes, the wise ones look for the message it intends to deliver and act accordingly. If they are unable to find it, they take refuge in God or their higher nature and seek help and guidance. Most importantly, they acknowledge that suffering is the fire in which they can pour their sinful karma and attain perfection, illumination, enlightenment, and liberation. If you accept suffering as a corrective process with which you can overcome your imperfections and weaknesses, you will learn to accept it with tolerance and understanding and let yourself be transformed by it.

Manifesting With the Right Intentions

May Indra give thee ability. May he give brilliance and wealth to his votary. Rigveda.

Thou art the fiery brilliance; give me that brilliance. Thou art valor. Give me that valor. Thou art strength; give me that strength. Thou art power, give me power. Thou art wrath, give me wrath. Thou art conquering might, give me might. Yajurveda 19.9

May we be free from debt in this world and free from debt in the world to come. Atharvaveda

The human mind can manifest reality, although it may take a while for people to work on it and develop the ability. By channeling your thoughts and desires in the right direction, you can create the life you want to lead. However, only a few succeed in using that potential. One can attribute the failure to a lack of knowledge, effort, faith, and conviction. We are not speaking here about magical thinking or the deluded that one can influence the events in the world or materialize reality without corresponding effort. We must know that we are subject to many natural limitations. Therefore, we cannot accomplish everything through the mind's manifesting power. We still need to work hard, overcome obstacles, and keep persevering to execute our thoughts, plans, decisions, and dreams and translate them into reality. Within our natural limitations, sustaining our motivation and beliefs, we can still harness the powers and potential of our minds and accomplish a lot. If we know clearly what we need to accomplish, we can work on it. We can strengthen our faith and resolve and persevere in our actions to realize it. Those who aspire to harness it should not fall into the trap of deluded expectations and magical thinking we mentioned before. However, they should know that even actions can be sustained, influenced, or reinforced by thoughts and beliefs.

Thoughts and intentions are equally important

Never underestimate the power of your thoughts and intentions. They are not just fleeting ideas but the driving force behind your actions and the blueprint of your life. Understanding and harnessing this power can empower you to take control of your destiny. It has been repeatedly stressed by many that our intentions influence our thoughts and actions and, thereby, our lives and destinies. With strong determination and faith in ourselves or God and with persistent and goal-oriented effort, we can achieve whatever goal we intend to achieve. By planting a thought or an idea firmly in our minds and constantly thinking about it, we can vastly improve the odds of it being executed in real-time and set in motion its actualization.

This is not mumbo-jumbo or an irrational thought. We are not saying that you can sit in a cave and transform the whole world with your thoughts. We are saying that we can use our minds to establish precise and realizable goals or form a clear picture of the end we intend to achieve and harness its power further to keep it alive while we work at it. It proved true in the case of many who shared their experiences through writings, films, and books. They have proven that the human mind is a powerful actualizing machine and that our thoughts and intentions have the power to motivate us and drive us toward our intended goals. They have shown through their examples that we can create the desired reality or vastly improve the chances of its happening by imagining it or by building a clear image or picture of it, sustaining it with beliefs, thoughts, affirmations, or visualization, and persevering until the end.

Whether we are aware of it or not, our conscious and subconscious minds influence our thoughts and desires and, thereby, our actions. Within the limitations to which we are naturally subject, we can accomplish a lot by harnessing the hidden potentials of our minds. We can accomplish much of what we desire or intend to happen by reinforcing our thoughts, beliefs, faith, resolve, motivation, and determination. Through them, we can attract what we deserve or desire. We can manifest our most dominant and persistent dreams and desires with corresponding effort.

Our thoughts gain strength to the extent we pay them attention, visualize them happening, reinforce them with conviction and affirmations, and work on them. True, one cannot just imagine it and forget it. The mind must be consumed with it and become fully established or absorbed in the belief that it will happen, given the right circumstances and with the right effort. The same holds for everything we seek. It holds even for our relationships. They strengthen to the extent we pay attention to them, think of them, care for them, nurture them, and respect them. They wither if we neglect them, ignore them, disrespect them, or fail to take care of them. If you always think of yourself as if others do not matter, in the end, you will be left alone. Therefore, set your mind with firm thoughts on the goals you want to accomplish. Reinforce them with repetition or affirmations, and actualize them through planned and sustained effort.

You are not separate from the World

Every thought that we send out into the universe returns to us with renewed vigor, gathering strength from thoughts of the same kind that exist in the universal consciousness. The world seems to exist on the sound principle of giving and taking and responds to both good and bad actions, although, at times, it may not happen for reasons we cannot fathom. However, in most cases, it works like a wall and bounces back whatever we throw at it as if it does not want to be in our debt. If you send out love, it returns love. If you send out negativity, it returns negativity; if you criticize someone, most likely you will receive criticism in response; if you help someone, the person who receives your help will reciprocate in some way, if not immediately, later when he finds an opportunity.

Our actions also leave ripples on the surface of life. Positive actions attract positive rewards, and negative ones lead to negative consequences. Through our actions and thoughts, we constantly create waves in the ocean of samsara, which precipitate our realities, teach valuable lessons, and shape our destinies and personalities. Whatever we give comes back to us either as a reward or punishment. Every question is answered, although we may not always discern the answer or learn from it. Every aspiration is challenged or fostered according to our faith and resolve. An invisible thread runs through us all, connecting us to the universe or the Supreme Being who controls all this or created all this. The web of life in which we live ensures that we are impacted not only by our thoughts and actions but also by our collective thoughts and actions.

The word is not separate from you. It is an extension of your mind. You are connected to it through your mind. A part of it lives in you as your inner world, filled with its images, impressions, and memories of your interactions with it and its objects. Therefore, if you think that what happens in the world outside is of no concern to you, you are mistaken. What happens to the world also leaves its ripples in you, although you may not be aware of it or immediately understand how it may affect you. Your mind is the bridge between

Manifesting With the Right Intentions

you and the world. Your senses are the limbs or organs of your mind, which interact with it and fill you with knowledge about it. Hence, you must know that you are connected to the world, even if you renounce it and live in a cave.

Just as the collective consciousness arises from our collective thoughts, collective karma arises from our collective actions. When a majority of humanity engages in hostile and destructive thoughts and actions, they awaken chaos and destabilize the world through their collective failure to uphold the right values, protect the world, or ensure peace and unity. If we live selfishly and ignore what goes on around us, as if it is not our concern, at some point, we will be swamped by the same forces that disturb the world. Therefore, you must not ignore your social responsibility in performing your duties or pursuing your goals. You must know that what you think about yourself, the world, and others is important since you do not live in isolation, and a part of the world lives in you as your very consciousness and your essential nature.

You attract what you resist and fear

Fear is a mental affliction that interferes with our ability to see things clearly and objectively. Fear restricts our vision and our ability to deal with our problems effectively and decisively. Therefore, whether it is in worldly life or spiritual life, it is a major stumbling factor. Fear denotes egoism, lack of trust, and lack of confidence in oneself and God. Fear can seriously compromise and impede your mind's power to manifest. It not only influences our thoughts but also our actions and conduct. When it dominates our thoughts, what we fear consciously or subconsciously or what we do not want to happen may happen. It can disturb or frighten even the bravest souls because no one is truly free from it. In the Bhagavadgita, Arjuna felt anxious and fearful at the thought of fighting against his kin and losing his name, family honor, and respect if he killed them. Such fears are common, and they arise, especially when we are attached to things. Because of attachments, people may be afraid to express themselves, be themselves, or freely execute their thoughts. If our fears are persistent, we may fail to perform our duties or reach our goals.

One way to deal with them is by acquiring the right knowledge and developing a proper understanding and perspective about them. If you are well informed, you will be in a position to assess the situation correctly, know what you are dealing with, and overcome the uncertainty. In the Bhagavadgita, Arjuna's mind rested in peace when he came to know that he was an eternal Self and he was supposed to enact his dutiful role as a warrior in a divine drama enacted by God. He realized that he was about to take part in a war that was destined to happen and in which the fate of all the participants was already predetermined.

Faith is another important antidote to fear: faith in oneself, God, or both. Faith arises from beliefs and convictions and usually precedes or follows knowledge and experience. If you sustain your faith and keep working at your goals, at some point, fate or circumstances will test you to see how far you can go despite obstacles and difficulties.

Moral purity is another sustaining factor that helps us in actualizing our thoughts. It gives us extraordinary confidence, courage, and fortitude to deal with our problems and difficulties. The evil ones live in constant fear of the consequences arising from their sinful actions. The pious ones live with the certainty that they will be taken care of by the divine laws and God himself. It is said that of a non-violent person, enmity and hostility disappear, and even cruel animals shed violence and act peacefully. It is because the purity of pious souls touches everyone and everything and temporarily transforms them into their likeness. Therefore, in their presence, even the evil ones act piously against their wish.

Being True to Yourself

People often blame others for their problems because they do not want to assume responsibility or feel guilty. They live in denial, refusing to acknowledge their shortcomings or accept responsibility for their failures and shortcomings. The truth is that we are responsible for our actions. Even if others are involved, the fact that we undertook and performed those actions makes us primarily responsible for them and their consequences. This realization is not a burden but a source of empowerment. It is the law of karma, and the understanding of it gives us the power to shape our lives, not escape from it.

The truth is that whatever happens to you or in your life does not happen by itself without your involvement. Even external causes, the intervention of luck, or acts of God may arise because of something you did or did not do. A combination of factors precipitates your reality. Some of them may have been active for a long time in your consciousness or as a residue of your past without your knowledge and working silently to precipitate your current reality. Therefore, when events happen or when situations develop in your life, whether to your liking or not, you must take responsibility for them and introspect to know why or how you let them happen. If you analyze them with an open mind, you will learn from your experiences and improve yourself. Every mistake is a lesson, and every lesson is a step towards growth. Our imperfections show up frequently in our actions and achievements, but they also show us the path to becoming better.

It holds well in almost all other aspects of our lives, too. We should take responsibility for all the events and happenings in our lives, whether we can trace their causes to ourselves or not. Our positive and negative thoughts, feelings, and emotions influence our lives. For example, our suffering is mostly self-created. So are our joys. We let things happen or not happen because of what we think or believe. Subconsciously, we sabotage our joys, success, and happiness with negative and self-destructive thoughts and create obstacles for ourselves. We fail to reach goals due to fear, guilt, or the belief that we do not deserve what we seek. If we are in conflict with ourselves or if we suffer from doubt and fear, we become the problem, not the solution. We may blame others for our failures and suffering, but probably those "others" come into the picture because of your thoughts or your actions in the past.

Self-introspection, therefore, is not just necessary but urgent to ensure that we do not stand in our way to success or fulfillment. Sometimes, we may not be aware of how we end up becoming a problem to ourselves. The thoughts or emotions that precipitate our reality may remain hidden from us, buried deeply in our subconscious minds. They may precipitate situations or reality against our surface thoughts and expectations. If you want to attain prosperity or invite abundance, but somewhere in your subconscious mind harbors a powerful thought or fear that it is a lot of work, you may not deserve it, or it is beyond your level or capacity, you may find yourself short of that goal and not realize why it happens to you. Any negativity you may have towards any goal you want to attain can prevent you from reaching it. If you entertain negative thoughts about wealth or wealthy people, you may overlook many opportunities in your life that would have otherwise helped you attract wealth and make yourself happy. If you think that you are not born to enjoy a good life or experience happiness or fulfillment or if you believe that they are reserved for only a few lucky individuals, very likely you will deny yourself many opportunities and feel miserable.

Therefore, if you want to take control of your life and realize your goals, you must spend considerable time in introspection. You must examine your whole life, including your thoughts, motives, fears, beliefs, and memories, and cleanse yourself of all the negativity that you harbor with or without your knowledge. You must become a mindful witness to yourself, your thoughts, intentions, and actions to know your conflicts and self-sabotaging thoughts. If your spiritual goals are not properly aligned with your worldly goals you may remain conflicted in pursuing them. In other words, you must expand your knowledge and awareness and strengthen positivity to welcome all thoughts and possibilities without judgment or prejudice. With an open mind thus established, you can develop an inclusive and holistic philosophy of life in which you can accommodate a wide range of thoughts, feel comfortable with yourself, and establish a central or the ultimate purpose of your life around which you can organize your goals and actions and build your life or reality.

Jayaram V

Understanding Desires and Intentions

In spiritual life, we are constantly advised to overcome desires and attachments to cultivate equanimity. However, in worldly life, we know that we cannot live without pursuing desires. Indeed, they are the basis of all life-related activity on this planet and the continuity of all life. Without desires, life cannot continue and many people will not find any purpose or reason to engage in actions or ensure the order and regularity of life. In the Bhagavadgita, God says that He engaged in actions for the welfare of the world, even though he has no desires and is indifferent. He exhorts humans also to follow his example and perform actions without desires. We know that everyone cannot practice it. Hence, in Hinduism, the pursuit of wealth (Artha) and desire (kama) are included, along with obligatory duties (Dharma) and liberation (Moksha) in the four chief aims of human life. Up to a certain stage in our lives, desires are necessary to fulfill our obligations and participate in God's creation to support it and ensure its continuity and orderly progress.

In other words, we should not dismiss all desires as evil or harbor any negativity toward them. Certain desires are necessary for our well-being, and certain desires must be avoided by all means. We learn about them from our scriptures, from our experience, or by cultivating discerning wisdom. However, in any case, whether they are good or bad, we should not entertain any negativity about them but know them as the signs of Nature working in us and through us. From mindful observation, we can discern that all actions and movements in our minds and bodies begin with a desire to overcome something, achieve something, adapt to something, oppose something, or repel something. The same holds true for all organisms. It is the main motivating power and the source and the beginning of all that manifests in their lives or their consciousness if they possess it. In its purest and pristine state, each desire is an expression of one's active will. In its weakest state, it bubbles up as a mere wish, hope, or aspiration and in its primal state as an impulse or instinct. Whatever they may be, we cannot deny that desires are life's sustaining force. They are why we are here, why the world continues, why we continue, why life goes on, and why we pursue various goals and seek fulfillment through desire-ridden actions.

The problem is not desires but intentions

The problem with actions and their consequences, at least in worldly life, is not desires but intentions. It lies in ignorance, wrong thinking, or more specifically, the lack of discretion or discernment in pursuing our desires or engaging in actions because of them. The issue is not whether actions or desires are inherently good or bad, but whether we exercise discretion in choosing, deciding, or performing actions. Actions and desires are deemed worthy or unworthy, wholesome or unwholesome, and conducive to life and happiness or to destruction and misery, based on the intention or purpose hidden within them. One may engage in actions driven by desires with either evil or righteous intentions. Outwardly, they may appear similar, but they yield different consequences or karma. For instance, righteous anger aimed at improving or transforming someone is certainly superior to destructive anger intended to dominate, destroy, avenge, or suppress others. Charity given selflessly to help the poor and the needy is certainly superior to charity given for egoistic reasons or to expiate for past sins. Thus, actions are judged as good or bad based on the intentions hidden within them. This is well illustrated in many scriptures. The Buddha also recognized this distinction. Hence, although he identified desire as the root cause of human suffering, he included the Right Intention as one of the eight precepts in the Middle Path, calling it samyak samkalpa (right decision, resolve, or intention).

The key to understanding the moral quality of our actions lies in our intentions. Having the right desires without attachment and performing the right actions without selfish expectations is neither sinful nor afflictive. For instance, if you desire the welfare of others without any selfish motive, no negative karma will attach to you. However, if you desire their welfare for your own profit, it may. The law of karma does not punish you for seeking wealth or material things in life if your intentions are good and if you want to help others selflessly. Suffering only arises when desires are pursued using the wrong means and with negative or selfish intentions. In such cases, our desires become dark, divisive, and self-destructive, creating suffering, conflicts, and divisions in the process. It is why, in Hinduism, selfishness is equated with evil, and followers are advised not to engage the organs in their minds and bodies for selfish purposes.

Jayaram V

Understanding Desires and Intentions

In the ancient world, ascetic traditions, such as Buddhism and Jainism, admitted rich people as lay followers and accepted their wealth for charitable activities, knowing that it would help the donors cleanse their sins and grow spiritually. The revelation that desire in itself is neither evil nor immoral is crucial in both worldly and spiritual pursuits. On the path of renunciation, it is obligatory for the ascetics to renounce all desires. However, even they distinguish between righteous and unrighteous desires. In worldly life, desires are still important and central to one's existence, peace, and happiness. Worldly people must pursue them with the right intentions, avoiding those that are explicitly prohibited, such as desires that involve unethical practices or immoral conduct. Our scriptures make it clear that in its highest and purest state, desire is a divine quality. It is the power that, when used correctly and with the right intention, propels us in the right direction and prepares us for a better life, progress, and happiness. Until we reach a certain state of perfection on the spiritual path, we must pursue desires to attain our desired ends for our good or the good of others. Eventually, spiritual people must renounce them. However, in the initial stages, they even come to the path because of desires only: the desire to attain liberation, know or purify themselves, explore the unknown or the mystic knowledge, or experience higher consciousness, peace, or equanimity.

Hinduism recognizes the fulfillment of desires (kama) as one of the chief aims (purusharthas) of human life. However, it puts Dharma (obligatory moral and religious duties) in front of it. Vedic people worshipped various divinities and offered them sacrificial oblations, seeking peace and prosperity for themselves and their kings. Hindus worship several gods, making them offerings and seeking their favors. In the Bible, we find the assurance that if you sincerely and persistently ask God for help, He will respond to you. Whether it is in Hinduism or any other religion, our prayers are but petitions and supplications in which we express our deepest desires and purest thoughts, asking God or a higher being for help and intervention. The Vedic mantras explicitly seek the assistance of various divinities for peace and happiness on earth. The Vedas do not deprecate desires but warn people against harmful thoughts and evil intentions.

All religions recognize the importance of virtuous living and right thinking. They are far more important than controlling desires. If we live ethically, we cease to pursue wrong desires. With the right intention, we can safely pursue both our worldly and spiritual goals. The Middle Path of Buddhism is all about thinking and living correctly, overcoming imperfections, and developing the right awareness of the Buddha's mind. In classical yoga also, one arrives at the state of detachment and renunciation through a long road of self-restraint and virtuous living. Desires exist in our consciousness as the propelling forces of our actions and lives. In Hinduism, we believe they are also responsible for our karma and bondage to the cycle of births and deaths. Collectively, they are responsible for our suffering as well as enjoyment and much of what happens to us in our daily lives. What this means is that we must have balance in pursuing our desires on the path of righteousness. If we pursue them with pure thoughts, we will have an opportunity to be part of this world and yet prepare ourselves for our spiritual liberation.

Intentions imply the use of willful and conscious decisions in the pursuit of goals. They gain strength and momentum from purpose and resolve and are reinforced by success and positive outcomes. Intentions also denote the involvement of attitude and determination in the pursuit of goals. Our intentions not only reveal our intelligence and attitude but also our true character. People are good or bad, moral or immoral, and honest or dishonest depending upon with what intention they pursue their aims and perform their tasks. If you pursue right aims with wrong intentions or wrong aims with right intentions, the consequences will be negative. If you want to understand people and their actions, try to know their intentions. It is, however, not easy because people can hide them or rationalize them.

One should always pursue material or spiritual goals with the right intentions and for the right causes or purposes, with a positive attitude and righteous conduct. Pragmatism and circumstances may often tempt us to ignore this fundamental principle. While one may temporarily escape from it, it is difficult to escape from the negative thoughts they produce, such as fear, guilt, etc. Whatever the difficulty or temptation, one should not entertain any intention to take from others what does not rightfully belong without paying the price. In manifesting thoughts or attracting abundance, one should not think of harming others, exploiting them, or gaining at their expense intentionally. If the intentions are good, decisions will be good, and the actions that follow them will be free from negative consequences.

Jayaram V

Manifesting Abundance for the Common Good

Abundance implies completeness, wholeness, and an inexhaustible supply of everything. Abundance can be experienced in worldly life as well as in spiritual life. The earth has limited abundance, but the material universe is filled with the abundance of everything. Even the Earth is filled with an abundance of things and great diversity. The Vedas affirm that everything comes to us from the Creator, the Lord of the Universe. He is infinite, eternal, indestructible, and the source of unlimited abundance. Even that which we think belongs to us or is created by us belongs to Him only because we exist in Him and are a part of Him. We are made up of the same particles, atoms, and elements that exist in the planets, stars, and galaxies. The same energy that flows in the universe flows in our bodies. We share the same gravitational force that keeps the planets, suns, and stars in their respective orbits.

The universe is a living and breathing embodiment of God. Indeed, it is a spectacle that never fails to inspire awe. Filled with billions of galaxies and other celestial bodies, some stretching across gazillions of miles, it reflects His infinity, vastness, power, and richness. Its sheer magnitude, beyond our wildest imagination, is a testament to the boundless abundance of God's creation. Just imagine how many planets may exist in it, filled with or made up of precious metals, hydrocarbons, rich minerals, and unknown compounds.

We represent a dynamic and intelligent aspect of the universe. Perhaps we share the consciousness of the Universe in all its glory. We are the living and breathing faces of God, the Creator or all, through whom He enjoys all this and marvels at Himself and His own vast creation. If you firmly believe that you are an inseparable part of him, you will not feel the need to assert yourself or define your territory. You will not compete with others to prove your superiority or suffer from negative passions such as anger, envy, or pride. When you live with the conviction that you are an eternal and individual entity with infinite capacities, you will regard your life in this world as an opportunity to transcend your limitations and experience infinite peace through oneness with the rest of creation. This state of oneness, often referred to as 'liberation ', is a state of unlimited abundance, where one is free from the constraints of the material world and experiences the fullness of spiritual abundance. You must remember these aspects of our existence if you want to attract abundance into your life and enjoy it.

To experience the richness of life, you must have faith in the inexhaustible abundance of the universe and your inseparable connection with God. If you draw a circle around yourself and think that you are separate from everything else, you will feel the weight of the universe pressing upon you. When you focus your attention on the dualities and the limited life you experience in your frail body and unstable mind, in difficult situations, even small problems may assume infinite proportions and disturb you. When you consider yourself small, weak, vulnerable, or alone, you will worry about your survival and continuity and build walls of defense around yourself. When you extend that thought process to the whole world and develop an attachment to it, you will project similar fears and concerns onto it and worry about our collective survival. You will see it as a small world in a hostile universe with a precarious climate and limited resources.

Abundance is not just a concept but a reality that permeates every aspect of God's creation, including us. It manifests in each of us as our abilities, energies, and faculties or as a potential waiting to be unleashed. We have an abundance of potential to set our goals and accomplish them with intelligent effort. We can store an inexhaustible amount of information in our brains, most of which remains unused even after we spend a lifetime on earth accumulating knowledge and memories. With our knowledge and intelligence, we can fathom the depths of the universe and understand the most complex ideas and subjects. Although we have many limitations, we have more skills, knowledge, and potential than are necessary for one lifetime. This abundance of potential should inspire us to strive for continuous growth and development.

The universe mirrors and manifests your thoughts and intentions. It responds to you according to your fears, desires, and expectations. If you think you are limited, you will be limited. If you think negatively, you will experience negativity wherever you look. If you are resentful, you will be met with resentment. If you suffer from the thoughts of scarcity, you will experience scarcity in your life. If you think you do not deserve a good life or the riches of the world, you will stand in the way of your success and happiness. Therefore, you

Manifesting Abundance for the Common Good

must not let your mind succumb to fear or self-doubt or entertain any negativity or thoughts of scarcity or failure in your mind. Instead, fill your mind with thoughts of gratitude, love, and abundance. Every time you succumb to negative thoughts of fear or despair, replace them with uplifting thoughts such as 'I am worthy of abundance, "I am capable of achieving my goals, 'and 'I am surrounded by love and support. ' With faith and devotion, you can seek God's help to overcome obstacles and open yourself to his abundant love.

At the same time, it is crucial to remember that God's abundance is not for us alone to keep or enjoy. We must share it with others and become a source of happiness and abundance to others. Whether it is knowledge, resources, talents, abilities, experience, wisdom, insight, or some superior skill, we have a responsibility to share His eternal riches and unlimited wealth with others because they also represent Him, possess His divinity, and are part of His manifestation. As the Vedas indicate, human beings should not think about themselves or their welfare only but also about the welfare of others, including animals and other creatures. They must serve gods, ancestors, pious and needy people, animals and other creatures through daily sacrifices by sharing with them offerings of food. They have an obligatory duty to preserve the earth and the world as much as they have to preserve themselves.

By sharing God's unlimited abundance with others, you can experience fulfillment, wholesomeness, and completeness in your life and foster a sense of connection and responsibility towards others. You must follow the same principle when you desire to attract God's universal abundance. Whatever you receive from God or the universe in any form, you must channel it for a greater or higher cause. You can serve Him by letting His abundance flow freely through you to others and helping them, knowing that all that exists here belongs truly to Him, and the best you can do is to facilitate its free flow and fulfill your obligation. You have the right to attract God's abundant treasures into your life and enjoy them. At the same time, you must be willing to share them with others, knowing that they do not belong to you but to Him only. You can attract God's unlimited abundance in one or more of the following ways.

- By praying with faith, devotion, humility, and gratitude so that you can earn God's grace and secure His abundant love.

The Awakened Life

- By cultivating knowledge and discernment so that you can pursue wealth with the right methods and for the right causes without making mistakes or incurring sinful karma.
- By helping others selflessly, doing God's work on earth, and becoming a source of abundance, peace, and happiness to others so that through their blessings and gratitude, you can keep channeling His abundance through you and performing His eternal duties as your own.
- By overcoming and cultivating purity and divine nature so that you can outgrow your desires, attachments, ignorance, egoism, pride, selfishness, fear, anger, envy, greed, lust, etc., and truly serve God and His creation without any moral conflicts or confusion.
- From a spiritual perspective, you should not seek abundance for your selfish or egoistic enjoyment or to increase your influence, power, or prestige. You should not seek it to compete with others, harm them, exploit them, or dominate them, but help them, cooperate with them, protect them, or set a good example. Therefore, think of abundance as a means, not an end in itself. Make use of any wealth you possess or attract through your thoughts and actions, such as your knowledge, positivity, wisdom, or material things, to help others, serve God, and spread abundant peace and happiness.

Understanding the Real Person in You

Aham Brahmasmi, I am Brahman. Brihadaranyaka Upanishad.

Tatvamasi, You are That (Universal Self). Chandogya Upanishad.

To understand the concepts discussed here, we need some familiarity with Hinduism or concepts such as delusion, liberation, the Self, the not-self, tattvas, and yoga. We will describe them as we present our ideas. If you are not interested in Hinduism or these concepts, you may skip this chapter and go to the next.

The first one is the concept of moha, which means delusion, or false or mistaken notion. It arises in the beings, especially in humans, due to the play of Maya. Because of this, they experience two fundamental mistaken notions or false understandings. One is the mistaken notion that the mind and body represent one's true identity. The second is that the world or the material universe that we enjoy through our minds and senses is real and all that there can ever be. These mistaken notions result in many complications for humans. They keep them distracted and deluded and bound to samsara, the cycle of births and deaths, and prolong their suffering by preventing them from knowing themselves and their essential nature, which connects them to the Creator himself with whom they share it. The fundamental purpose of human life is to overcome this problem and return to one's original state of absolute freedom and knowledge.

To understand this further, we also need to understand the composition of human personality according to Hinduism. The scriptures identify two fundamental aspects of the human personality: the Self and the not-self. The Self is pure, eternal, indestructible, and unchanging. The not-self is the exact opposite: impermanent, perishable, and mutable. They are also described as the body and the soul, the Field (Kshetra) and the Knower of the Field (Kshetra), Purusha (the Person) and Prakriti (Nature), or God and His universe. The Field is the Person's playground, where Nature enacts her play for His enjoyment. He participates in that Play passively as the Witness Self, enjoying it and supporting it but remaining uninvolved, undisturbed, immutable, and untouched. Usually, the scriptures refer to the Self as he and Nature as she.

These two entities, the Self and the not-self or the Person and Nature, exist in each living being. The being (jiva), a temporary formation arising from their union, is drawn to material things through desires and attachments and becomes bound to the law of karma and samsara (the cycle of births and deaths). Thus, the being is but a deluded Person or God. In this cosmic drama, as stated before, the Person (the Self) does not participate and remains undisturbed and untouched by the modifications of the mind and the body or the Field. However, he remains bound until the Jiva attains liberation, the ultimate goal of all life on earth. The jivas have to evolve spiritually through numerous births until they attain human birth, the only birth in which they can attain liberation.

From this perspective, human birth is precious, difficult to attain, and a rare opportunity for beings to qualify for liberation. However, liberation is still not guaranteed since they have to attain the utmost purity. Liberation, or Moksha, is the ultimate state of freedom from suffering and rebirth. It is achieved when the Person in the body returns to his natural state of pure awareness or consciousness, without the impurities of egoism, delusion, and desires, and realizes his essential nature as the eternal Self. It is also the essential nature of the Cosmic Purusha, known as Isvara or the Lord of the Universe, who resides in the Cosmic Body, material universe, or the Energy Field of Prakriti as its Lord and Controller, unlike the passive Purusha in each being.

Thus, Purusha and Prakriti represent the fundamental duality of all existence, from the highest universal level to the lowest level of a small living being. In the beings, the Purusha is passive, but at the higher levels of Creation, he is active and performs many functions to support it and ensure its continuity. His highest manifestations are his different versions performing different roles to uphold the creation. At the highest level, as the Lord of the Universe, he performs five fundamental duties: creation, preservation, destruction, concealment, and revelation. In the beings, Prakriti remains in control and keeps the Person bound to her. She uses her deluding power (Maya) to veil his essential nature and create an alternate reality or the illusion that the mind and body or not-self constitute the real Self. Maya, often translated as illusion, is a complex concept in Hindu philosophy. It is the veiling power of Prakriti that masks the true nature of the Self, creating a distorted perception of self-reality or ego-identity and subjecting it to ignorance and delusion, attraction and aversion, desires and attachments, and births and rebirths. In the deluded state, the jiva engages in the same five functions of creation, preservation, destruction, etc., but in a limited and ignorant way.

The physical self or the not-self is a creation of Prakriti. The material universe is also her creation. At the cosmic level, it represents her universal body. In a jiva, it represents the jiva's body. It is made up of her primordial parts, organs, or evolutes known as tattvas. They do not manifest equally in all. The lower organisms contain a few tattvas, whereas humans contain all of them. Hence, each human being in whom Purusha and Prakriti manifest fully is considered a small universe. The Bhagavadgita and some Upanishads describe the body as a holy temple with nine gates, in which the Self remains seated in the sanctum, the heart. At the same time, they consider it impermanent and impure and a cause of suffering and bondage.

In human beings, duality and delusion reach optimum levels since they possess Nature's higher evolutes (tattvas), namely the senses, the mind, the ego, and intelligence. They constitute the internal organ (antahkarana), which is responsible for the sentience or the feeling of being alive, active, conscious, and distinct. It is also responsible for the delusion that the physical body is the real self, and one has to pursue desires and material things to ensure one's survival and enjoyment. They remain in this state until they overcome their impurities through self-transformation, realize their essential nature as the eternal Self, and attain liberation.

In that journey of self-purification, yoga plays an important role. Yoga means a state, union, a philosophical system having the same name, or a method, spiritual path, practice, or technique that is used to purify the mind and body and attain liberation. The Bhagavadgita defines it further as the ultimate state of sameness or the restraint of the mind and senses. All these meanings are interrelated. Historically, in spiritual practice, many types of yoga are used to attain perfection and purification. The Bhagavadgita lists several of them, each distinct but related to others. Patanjali's Yogasutras describe the beliefs and practices of Classical or Ashtanga Yoga, in which yogis use eight practices to purify themselves and suppress the modifications of their minds and bodies. Buddhism and Jainism also have their versions of Yogas. Some well-known yogas are Karma Yoga, Jnana Yoga, Sannyasa Yoga, Bhakti Yoga, Raja Yoga, Hatha Yoga, and Dhyana Yoga. In recent times, many new yogas have surfaced, but they are mostly physical yogas that in some way perpetuate the deluded notions of the physical self.

The Awakened Life

The purpose of traditional yogas is to overcome the distortions and imperfections of our minds and bodies or our physical nature to realize who we truly are. Using that discernment or knowledge, yogis must withdraw their minds and senses from the sense objects and worldly things into themselves, renounce desires and attachments, engage in selfless actions instead of desire-ridden actions, practice detachment and dispassion (vairagya), and establish their minds in the contemplation of the Person in them or the Cosmic Lord of the Universe with unwavering faith and devotion. By persevering in their effort, with their minds firmly stabilized and absorbed in His contemplation, they must permanently overcome delusion about their bodies, connect to that Person in them, and realize that they are indeed that Person, who is eternal, immutable, and indestructible and whose essence is transcendental, pure consciousness. In that pristine state, they are no longer deluded, disturbed, or distracted and remain absorbed in oneness with the Person or God-consciousness in them.

The Problem with Your Extended Identities

This chapter delves into the profound consequences of our ego-driven identities. These identities, born from egoism, delusion, desires, and attachments, lead us to entangle ourselves deeply in the world. This entanglement or involvement results in our bondage and suffering. In this discussion, we will examine why they are problematic and what we can do to transcend them and establish the true identity that remains hidden within ourselves.

As deluded beings caught in the whirl of samsara, we extend ourselves into the world through several identities induced by egoism, delusion, desires, and attachments and become deeply involved with it, leading to our bondage and suffering. These identities arise from our births, family and social backgrounds, essential nature, appearance, duties, relationships, associations, roles, pursuits, peculiarities, etc. They act like our alter egos and draw us deeper into the world, making our escape difficult and laborious. They stand between us and the truth of ourselves, distance us from our essential or divine nature, and subject us to suffering and bondage. The wise ones know that these identities are superficial and distracting, and one should not become involved with them if liberation is the aim. Hence, spiritual people begin their journey of liberation by renouncing them to establish their minds in the contemplation of the Self or God until they reach the tranquil state of oneness and see the same consciousness pervading the whole existence. It is why, in the practice of renunciation (sannyasa), the initiates are instructed to take vows and renounce all their identities and become recluses without roots, past relationships, affiliations, and attachments.

The world is impermanent and unstable. None of the identities we establish with it to spread our roots, pursue our desires, or ensure our survival or continuity are permanent or real. They arise from our births and the various factors associated with our lives and actions and have no independent existence of their own. They are like extensions that grow from our egos to strengthen our claim upon the things we desire and ensure our preservation and continuation. Through them, we create our self-images, define ourselves to the world, pursue our goals, and protect our interests. We cling to them and act as if they are permanent and will last forever. This clinging and the delusion they reinforce with the multiplier factor make it difficult for us to look beyond them and recognize our divine nature, which remains hidden, and identify with it.

The real Person (the Self) who lives in each of us as our soul and represents our essential nature and true consciousness has no definitive name and form, no physicality or materiality. He is essentially an invisible, immaterial, formless, and abstract notion or ethereal entity without boundaries, tangibility, and materiality. Neither the mind and the senses nor intelligence can reach him or comprehend him. Hence, we cannot objectify and create a clear identity out of him or form a relationship or association with Him. He is but the Supreme Being Himself. Hence, for most people who are conditioned by duality and delusion, it is as if the Person in them does not exist. They find it difficult to accept that pure identity of theirs and become established in it.

Your most basic identity arises from your name and your body. Your body is like your personal ID that you carry everywhere. It defines you and introduces you to the world, helps you create a space around you, and establishes various relationships with the world to pursue your desires and goals, own things, and ensure your continuity and self-preservation. After the personal identity associated with your name and form (namarupa), your family name is another extension that helps you draw yourself into it and establish a relationship with it to pursue your goals or form other relationships. Whether you use it or not, or like it or not, it is certainly a defining aspect of your public persona. Depending on your circumstances and comfort level, it may either work for you or against you. Some people take pride in their family names and use them profusely to their advantage. Some wish they could forget about it. If the family has a bad reputation, it becomes a problem for those who are born in it. However, for those who are born in reputed families, it is certainly an added advantage. It creates an aura around them and helps them ride on the success and reputation of their families. In the past, in Hinduism, family lineage was considered central to a person's life, reputation, profession, marriage, social standing, etc. It is still relevant to many families who can trace their lineage back to several generations.

Apart from these basic identities associated with their personal and family names, people also take pride in the group identities associated with their castes, races, tribes, cultures, religions, the languages they speak, the professions or occupations they practice, the regions and nations to which they belong, etc. They prevent people from seeing the world or themselves clearly and objectively, without filters, biases, likes, and dislikes. They also strengthen group identities and collective egos and often lead to major conflicts and suffering for large populations and groups. For thousands of years, they shaped people's behavior and determined the course of history. Even today, they are very powerful social factors. In the Hindu community worldwide, caste is a major dividing factor and a major source of friction. It is also a major obstacle to our spiritual growth. It is such a powerful deluding force that even spiritually enlightened teachers and renunciants often fall into its trap and take pride in their caste identities and use them to establish their authority, promote themselves, or attract followers.

However, our involvement with the world through ego-driven identities does not end here. In our outward search for happiness and security, we extend our minds and senses into the world and form numerous other identities. For example, some people develop almost a passionate admiration for a leader or a celebrity and become their ardent fans. They become obsessed with them, worship them like gods, and spend their lives in an imagined relationship with them. Then, some people develop identities from their political and ideological affiliations. They become conservatives, progressives, socialists, communists, radicals, etc. Some take up social or cultural causes and become activists. In recent times, several new identities have emerged due to the popularity of the Internet, discussion forums, and social networks. They keep people busy and distracted and prevent them from looking into themselves and knowing themselves without filters by having an honest dialogue with themselves.

These identities define us collectively to the world. In the course of our lives and interactions with the world, we become so wedded to them that we go to great lengths to protect them and preserve them. Each of them deludes and binds us to the world. Each of them complicates our relationship with the world, with others, and with ourselves, making our liberation difficult. They are also impermanent, just as our bodies are. Although we may not like to think about it, they do not last forever. Some last for the duration of our lives. Some may outlast us and remain in the memory of those who remember us, but in any case, most of them will be forgotten sooner or later. All the identities and memories associated with us will become buried in the sands of time at some point, leaving no trace of our existence for posterity.

Spiritual people should become aware of how we complicate our lives, our involvement with the world, and our liberation by establishing these numerous identities and reinforcing them through our actions, desires, and pursuits. From the spiritual perspective, they are, but the numerous ways in which Maya plays her game induce delusion in us to distance us from the reality of ourselves or from knowing the Person inside us. She keeps us apart from ourselves and God, draws us increasingly into her Field of activity, and keeps us under her control so that the world can continue and the cycle of creation progresses normally without major interruptions. Each of them adds to the restlessness of our minds and senses and keeps us distracted and preoccupied with the external and inconsequential aspects of our lives.

Identities associated with places, regions, religions, races, genders, languages, cultures, institutions, nations, ideologies, sports, professions, etc., also become an obstacle to overcoming ignorance and delusion and cultivating an all-inclusive awareness or establishing the mind in God or the Self. People use them as mental crutches or little props to fulfill their desires, gain support and influence, or establish control. In worldly life and material pursuits, they extend our reach, boost our egos, secure our interests, and strengthen our pride, self-importance, belongingness, and feelings of brotherhood.

While we are easily drawn to these limited identities for personal or emotional reasons, we do not think much about the universe in which we live. Although we are surrounded by it from all sides and know its existence, we do not feel any affinity with it. We identify ourselves with people we know and admire, the places, regions, or countries where we are born, the professions we practice, the groups we join, or the religions we practice, but we do not think that we belong to the universe where we live. Whether we acknowledge it or not, we are an integral part of it. It is the Ultimate Field, or the Field of all the fields, that stays with us always, wherever we go and whatever we do. Whether we are asleep or awake, we are never separate from it. We are born in it and die in it. We are also its numerous manifestations, whether we acknowledge it or not. We are its numerous faces, voices, forms, and manifestations. We are its intelligent, emotional, and self-aware formations through which it probably speaks to itself, observes itself, and tries to fathom its depths in a state of duality and awe. Steeped in our limited identities and attached to them, we do not realize this vast truth about ourselves, whereas it is the only identity that should matter to us and which will probably in future save this planet and humanity from self-destruction.

The Upanishads declare the material universe as the body (field) of God (Brahman). They exhort us to transcend the field of forms to experience the field of the formless. We can do so only when we go beyond the appearances of our limited identities and our attachments and identify ourselves with the universal Self or the Cosmic Person who also lives in us as our true identity. To experience oneness with Him or establish our identity in Him, we have to renounce all these superficial identities, withdraw into ourselves, and empty our consciousness, letting go of everything and every notion of duality and individuality. When you are empty, you are full. When you are asleep, the Person in your body rules. When you detach yourself from your limited identities, you become comfortable with the idea of being one with the Cosmic Being and improve your chances of experiencing transcendental unity with it. When you extend your identity to the universe and speak for it, you become its voice and its face. This is the truth. This is the absolute and the highest identity, to which the Upanishads point and towards which the yogis progress in their spiritual journey. The idea of universal belongingness, which is enshrined in our religion, becomes a reality only when we transcend the limited identities with which we become involved and develop an expansive and limitless vision.

Cultivating Sameness and Tolerance

Do you avoid people and situations because you dislike them or are uncomfortable with them? Do you prefer the company of only a few people you like? Do you have set opinions about how the life, the world, or people should be? Do you tend to criticize mentally or mutter to yourself when you watch television or read news or social media posts? If your answers to these questions are affirmative, do not feel upset. Consider yourself a perfectly normal human being who is subject to attraction and aversion, dualities, and polarities of life and cannot easily let go of your opinions, prejudices, beliefs, expectations, attachments, likes, and dislikes. You probably want to live in a certain way, stay within your comfort zone, and avoid taking risks or breaking your daily routine. In this, you are not alone.

We are conditioned by our experiences and perceptions to look at the world through a narrow prism of values and beliefs that are deeply ingrained in us, with which we agree or resonate and with which we accept them to be true. For example, due to many factors, people in almost all parts of the world face prejudice and discrimination in workplaces, schools, campuses, personal relationships, and elsewhere. Even the most educated people often indulge in them or suffer from them. Nowadays, indeed, it is more widespread in the most advanced nations in the world due to the increased migration of people and the pressures the changing demographics create. In many countries, if you belong to a minority community, you have to cope with discrimination. Even in countries that boast of individual liberties, you will not be treated according to your merits but your social or racial background. Religion is another divisive factor. It divides people, creating deep-rooted prejudices and difficult to overcome negative thoughts. People bring the same attitudes into their personal and social relationships, working environments, businesses, and neighborhoods.

Our expectations, preferences, and notions of right and wrong significantly influence our thoughts, behaviors, and relationships. They can either enrich our lives or limit our potential for growth. By cultivating an open mind and embracing life's opportunities, we can expand our worldview and experience the richness and diversity of life. This shift in perspective can also foster spiritual growth and a deeper understanding of human suffering and the need for compassion.

The universe is supported and protected by God's unconditional love. It is filled with his all-pervading presence just as he supports all of us and witnesses our actions and reactions as the Person (Self) in each of us. All this exists primarily because He is its indweller and source. The world exists despite all the shortcomings because He does not interfere with it and does not stop supporting it. He remains neutral and lets the world run its course. He may help his devotees and listen to their prayers but does not punish those who ignore him or deny His existence. It is because He is free from likes and dislikes, judgments, egoism, and the need to prove himself by showing his true powers. He is equal to both good and evil, although we tend to attribute motives and conditionality to Him. He is the power that facilitates and promotes everything in the universe secretly, silently, and unassumingly, ensuring things like water, air, fire, the earth, and space act according to their inherent nature. He does not micromanage our lives but ensures that the laws of the universe keep things under control and ensure order and regularity.

Despite our egoism, desires, attachments, and other impurities, we have the potential for growth. We can overcome these obstacles by transcending delusion and egoism, and through the practice of yoga, we can cultivate sameness. While this may be challenging for many, it is not impossible. We may not achieve perfection, but we can incorporate aspects of it into our daily lives, developing tolerance and understanding for situations we may not agree with.

We may not attain the perfection of the great souls, but we can try. We can learn to appreciate others, suspend our judgment, accept life's ups and downs rather philosophically, and express gratitude for all the blessings we enjoy. We can learn to agree rather than disagree, appreciate rather than criticize, and understand people and their motives without judgment. If we cannot do it in certain circumstances, we can learn to be silent and reflective. We may not be able to love everyone unconditionally, but every day, when we wake up, we can send a prayer of peace and love into the universe, wishing for the welfare and happiness of all. We can avoid hurting and harming others, pray for the welfare of plants, animals, and all sentient beings, feeling compassion for the suffering they go through and the sacrifices they make to facilitate our lives. We can express our gratitude to all those who are, at this very moment, striving hard to keep the world going and helping others.

All that we experience here is God's universal body. It is also your extended body. The same Person who lives in you also lives in the whole universe. He is in you and outside you. You are connected to it just as you are connected to your body. You are inseparable from it just as you are inseparable from your body while you live in it. You can connect to it through your thoughts and actions or in the four states of your consciousness, just as you can connect to your mind and send thoughts into it. By extending the same love, you can expand your vision and transcend your smallness or selfishness. Everything that happens within you or in the world outside is the work of God. All the divinities, angels, and celestial beings of the higher planes, as well as the demons and the destructive beings of the lower world, belong to the universal Self and represent His manifold aspects. They also exist in you as your potencies, thoughts, organs, and mental objects.

In other words, you can connect to the whole universe through your inner universe or microcosm. It is possible only when you do not block your vision with desires and attachments or likes and dislikes and become a universal witness without choices, preferences, likes, and dislikes. Even a little practice in this direction will broaden your consciousness and release you from the limitations and restraints to which you are bound. You may not reach the ecstatic heights to which the sages ascend during their meditation. However, by loosening your bonds and opening your heart unconditionally to the diversity and complexity of life, you can extend your love to others and feel an affinity with them. There is an underlying unity in the world. We feel it when we see ourselves in others and extend our love towards them. This is the essence of what the Upanishads teach us to cultivate: seeing oneself in others and others in oneself.

You may think that if you protect your respective interests and possessions, you will be safe. In your eagerness to be something and have something, you may build walls of separation around you and refuse to break them down. However, the safety that comes with such a strategy does not actually set you free. Having the things that you cherish and hold in esteem may satisfy your ego, but it does not guarantee you peace and happiness. Freedom comes when you do not feel the compulsion to defend and protect anything and when you develop an unconditional trust in the bounteous nature of God. It happens only when you overcome all the dualities and distinctions.

God exists in each of us as our very essence. He is the Person in each of us who supports, enjoys, and witnesses all the drama that takes place in our lives, minds, and bodies. By His presence, He connects us to the rest of the creation and gives us an opportunity to see the truth of ourselves and our essential nature from the great heights to which we can elevate our consciousness. If there is one virtue that leads us to experience the presence of God amidst us, it is the wonderful virtue of looking upon the whole universe or creation as an extension of our personality or consciousness with sameness or without desires, conditions, expectations, and judgment. It will open to you the wonderful, expansive vision of the seers and the liberated souls who remain established in it without duality. What is the use of being a vegetarian, virtuous, religious, or moral if you lack compassion or cannot see others without bias, judgment, or negativity? Of what purpose are knowledge, devotion, and intelligence if you cannot treat others with respect, even if you disagree with them and their ways of life?

Surrendering to God means abiding in oneness with him and forgoing everything that you hold in your mind as yours. It includes your desires, likes and dislikes, and everything that defines you and separates you from Him and the rest of His creation. If you are God's exclusive devotee and if you truly believe in Him as the all-pervading supreme reality, you will not be bothered by the inconsistencies, imperfections, and impurities you see in the world. You will accept them as His numerous manifestations. You may be tempted to judge others based on your moral and religious values. However, if you do not accept others, you will remain limited, deluded, constricted, and separated from Him and his creation. Your knowledge and spirituality will be of no use if you see the world with prejudice or judgment. Spiritual practice and all the knowledge we gain from the study of scriptures should open our minds and hearts to the possibilities of experiencing the presence of God in diverse forms and conditions. If that does not happen, we should look for other avenues rather than continuing them. Accepting people without conditions comes from selflessness, which can be cultivated by tempering one's ego and controlling its habitual movements. It is difficult to practice compassion and tolerance if one is deeply involved with material pursuits. However, if one persistently controls one's cravings and clinging, one will rest one's mind in peace and equanimity.

If you want to bring God into your life, try to root out your prejudices as a part of your spiritual growth, even if it is difficult to practice. For that, you do not have to socialize with everyone or submit to evil people. You can practice morality and resist immorality, but not judgmentally or egoistically. Neither God nor Nature takes sides. Transformation and renewal in our universe do not happen due to likes and dislikes but as a natural process (dharma). Nature does not favor the weak or the strong but creates circumstances that may work well for some and not so well for others. If you cultivate friendliness (mitrata) and harmlessness (ahimsa) towards the whole creation, you, too, will not take sides. What is important is the attitude with which you view others and view the dualities dispassionately without disturbing yourself. For that, you have to broaden your vision and embrace everything within the field of your perception without preference and prejudice. Accepting people without conditions comes from selflessness, which can be cultivated by tempering your ego and controlling its habitual movements. It is difficult to practice compassion and tolerance if you are deeply involved with material pursuits. However, if you control your cravings and clinging with persistence, you will rest your mind in peace and equanimity.

From the discussion so far, the following conclusions emerge.

1. You may not attain utmost perfection in sameness. However, you can control your impulse to react, resist, judge, and criticize, and you can treat others and situations that disturb you with tolerance and understanding.

2. You can outgrow your egoism and selfishness and cultivate an all-inclusive awareness, treating others and the whole existence as an extension of your consciousness. If you see the world and others with that understanding and awareness, you will treat them equally with tolerance and sameness.

3. All beings who are caught in the whirls of samsara are subject to suffering and bondage. They deserve your compassion and understanding. If you cultivate a healthy, spiritual relationship with yourself and feel connected to God's creation, most likely, you will feel compassion for others. You will see your suffering in their suffering or relate to them through your suffering.

Jayaram V

Cultivating Sameness and Tolerance

4. You can develop a reflective and philosophical attitude toward life, reduce your involvement with the world, cultivate detachment from your physical self, and establish your mind in the Person (Self) in you. By meditating on the impermanence of things, you can become indifferent to gain and loss or the dualities of life.

5. It is the nature of the mind to judge people and situations, express opinions, and criticize others even when it is unnecessary or no one asks for it. We often turn this judgmental nature against ourselves through negative self-talk and keep oppressing ourselves. Through practice, thoughtful reactions and responses, practicing silence, understanding, and tolerance, overcoming likes and dislikes, and controlling our desires and expectations, we can overcome this nature.

6. Reduce your expectations and prepare for surprises. Life throws many surprises and does not always happen according to our likes and dislikes. If you are prepared, keep an open mind, and stay calm, you will be in a position to deal with the problems and difficulties in your life.

7. As the Bhagavadgita says, focus on performing your actions sincerely and leave the results to God. Accept whatever results or consequences that arise from them.

The Importance of Faith

To deny knowledge, experience, and the known is to invite the unknown. Jiddu Krishnamurthy

We are afraid of this total destruction of the known, the ground of the Self, the me and the mine; the known is better than the unknown, the known with its confusion, conflict and misery; freedom from this known may destroy what we call love, relationship, joy and so on. Jiddu Krishnamurthy

The faith in spiritual things that is asked of the sadhak is not an ignorant but luminous faith, a faith in light not in darkness. Sri Aurobindo.

So, at first, to begin with, one must be able to get out of the ego. Afterwards, it has to be, you understand, in a certain state of inexistence. Then you begin to perceive things as they are, form a little higher up. But if you want to know things as they really are, you must be absolutely like a mirror: silent, peaceful, immobile, and impartial, without preferences and in a state of total receptivity. The Mother

Faith, a deeply held belief in something that transcends the material world, precedes knowledge and experience. We rely upon it to make sense of the world when we lack adequate information or when our knowledge and understanding are gaps. Having faith or beliefs is not a delusion. Treating beliefs as facts is delusion, but treating them as beliefs that require validation is a balanced view of what faith truly represents. We do not have to necessarily depend upon our senses or direct experience to validate them. We can rely upon other means, such as circumstantial evidence or the knowledge found in the scriptures or confirmed by the experts. It is especially true in the case of transcendental truths that are beyond our senses and cognitive abilities.

We do not know whether these 'other methods' lead us to the truths we want to verify. However, considering the limitations of our mental faculties, there seems to be no better alternative. You do not have to believe in them because tradition says so, but because it is how the doors of knowledge open to you. Tradition, the accumulated wisdom and experience of countless people who lived in the past, represents a valuable source of knowledge and understanding. It is through tradition that certain values, beliefs, and practices have been held to be true, and we can benefit from them instead of brushing them aside as a vestige of the past.

Jayaram V

We can neither solely depend upon facts to perform actions or make decisions nor discard all beliefs because we do not have proof. In fact, in most cases, we rely upon beliefs rather than bare facts to make important decisions. We trust intuition, common sense, or gut feelings on many occasions when we do not have sufficient information. Indeed, it is wise to rely upon faith or beliefs when we engage in uncertain and unpredictable actions and cannot properly assess their outcomes or consequences. Even if we have facts and our actions are based upon them, we still have to rely upon faith and wait patiently until they yield expected results and validate our initial assumptions and expectations. Even in science, we depend upon faith. We formulate new hypotheses and test them to validate our assumptions, discover new facts, gather new evidence, or gain new insights. Indeed, living in an uncertain world like ours, we cannot continue for long without the faith that life will go on and we will reach our goals and find fulfillment.

However, it is also true that we cannot solely depend upon faith only. Even if we start with faith or certain beliefs, at some stage, we need to find the truth about them and decide whether we should still rely upon them or discard them and move on. All beliefs, and even faith itself, are perhaps irrational unless they are grounded in reality or reason. Belief in God, a transcendent and omnipotent being, is not irrational because we have many reasons to believe in Him. For those who do not believe, those reasons may look unfounded, but for those who believe, they are valid and reliable. The heart is more reliable than the mind in matters of faith. The heart relies upon the distilled experience of one's whole life in responding to situations, threats, and opportunities, whereas the mind relies upon pure facts.

This discussion is not to convince anyone who does not believe in God. Belief in God is a matter of one's personal choice based on one's life, upbringing, and circumstances. If you do not believe in Him, perhaps it would not make any difference to you. At the most, your liberation will be delayed or you will have to depend upon yourself to resolve your problems or improve your life. However, you will not be punished for your lack of faith. The Supreme Lord is not vindictive, although some traditions may believe so. History proves that belief in God is not essential to be spiritual or attain liberation. Many philosophical systems of Hinduism and at least two major religions, Buddhism and Jainism, do not believe in a Creator God. Yet they prescribe rigorous practices and a strict code of conduct for their followers for self-purification and liberation. Their belief in the non-existence of God does not make them any more or less evil, immoral, or irreligious than those who believe in Him and worship Him with unwavering faith and exclusive devotion.

However, tradition says that if you believe in God, your faith should be consistent and strong. You should wholeheartedly and unconditionally surrender to God and work for your salvation. In matters of faith, ambivalence is worse than disbelief. A weak faith is as good as not having faith. As the Bhagavadgita declares, God rewards His devotees according to their faith and devotion. In whatever way they approach Him, He reciprocates in the same manner. However, those who worship Him with exclusive devotions, with their minds and hearts fully established in Him, consider them the dearest and take care of their welfare. Therefore, in the theistic traditions, which consider God as the upholder of all, faith carries a lot of importance.

God speaks to us every day, yet we are unsure

The house in which you live needs no proof that it exists. However, if you live in a dwelling that is as vast as the universe, perhaps even larger, what proof can convince you that the One who built it and upholds it as its Supreme Self is also the same Person who lives in you as your individual Self and upholds you? You may see but a tiny fraction of the universe, which may not convince you that it is the work of a Cosmic Being. How can you know a person if you do not see him fully or see only a fraction of him? Those who lack vision may not see others but know definitely that they exist because they can still ascertain their existence by other means. Their knowledge depends mostly upon their remaining senses, common sense, and personal experience. Their knowledge of others may be incomplete, and their reality may be different, but no one can dispute the fact they know. In other words, certain truths cannot be established fully or conclusively. Still, they can be accepted and used for our knowledge and understanding.

Our knowledge of existential truths can arise from many sources, and they need not be perfect or conclusive. Even the knowledge arising from reason and perception need not be accurate since one may still make mistakes in drawing conclusions or inferences due to the distortions to which our minds are vulnerable. Hence, in most cases, the idea of a person we hold in our minds and the truth of that person in reality will be vastly different because we do not see them or think about them clearly. In most cases, we rely upon beliefs and assumptions rather than perceptions to make judgments, draw conclusions, or perform actions without even realizing it. Many do not realize that beliefs, assumptions, preconceived notions, biases, and feelings drive our actions and decisions as much as facts and reality. Although we are rational, we cannot say that we are always rational or act rationally.

If beliefs and assumptions influence our thinking, actions, and relationships, why are we so particular about relying upon facts or direct evidence in matters of God or faith? Why should we exclusively depend upon facts to know Him or His whereabouts when we are not that particular about facts in many critical aspects of our lives, including the relationships we form with the people we meet based on our surface impressions and a few interactions? We cannot be an invisible presence. We can only discern it through other means. The same holds true for God, the invisible Being. We can infer His presence only through His footprints and numerous manifestations. Even that knowledge arising from inference is inadequate. We can also rely upon the testimony of scriptures and the accounts of spiritually enlightened people. Even with all that, we still need faith to sustain our belief in Him and establish our minds in His contemplation. Even with all the knowledge we gather from different sources, we still need faith to continue on the path of liberation. The Vedas clearly state that one can truly know the Brahman, the absolute, supreme Reality. This predicament is expressed in the Kena Upanishad, which declares that even gods do not know much about Brahman, the Supreme Reality.

Indeed, we cannot know the Supreme Reality of God, ascertain the truths of him, or clear our doubts about him conclusively by any means. We cannot also depend upon reason, empirical evidence, or direct observation. We may draw knowledge from other sources, such as intuition, scriptures, or the knowledge and experience of those who attained Him through oneness. Still, we need to faith to use that knowledge and sustain our practice. We need unwavering faith and devotion to take refuge in Him and establish our minds in Him. Faith is the only bridge or the raft that we have to reach the other shore. In other pursuits, we may require faith that much, but in spiritual and devotional practices, we cannot do without it.

The Awakened Life

Rationalists may scoff at the idea, but the fact is that even they rely on faith to arrive at their conclusions.

The dualistic schools of Hinduism maintain that the material universe, made up of both animate and inanimate objects, is God's universal body. If you believe in that, you know that you are always in direct contact with him and never separate. Just as you are present in your whole body, He is present in every aspect of His creation, including you. Since He is present everywhere, you do not have to travel to some destination to find Him or meet Him. You just need to realize Him, wherever you are, including your mind or consciousness. You can find Him through worship, devotion, sacrificial actions, renunciation, or contemplation. If you have the faith that he exists in you, you can in the silence of your heart and mind. This may appear like an absurd idea to some, but it has been proven by countless yogis, seers, and saints who found Him within themselves and left behind accounts of their deeply spiritual experiences.

Those who insist on the proof of God's existence assume many notions about Him. They also rely upon their beliefs and even irrational arguments to refute him. If you think God is a being with a definitive form or physical body, you are bound to mistake him for a human-like entity rather than an invisible, formless, and absolute Supreme Reality. You will demand proof of his existence and confuse yourself. It is what most rationalists do. However, our scriptures affirm that God pervades His creation and is not distant from it. He is all-pervading, which means He does not exist only in specific places such as heaven but everywhere. The scriptures also affirm that He has numerous forms, some visible, some invisible, some with form, and some without form. Therefore, we may be asking too much when we want to see Him in specific ways, ignoring His omnipresence right before us and inside us. The Person who experiences all this through our minds and bodies is Him only.

When you stand in front of an ant, it cannot see you as you are and does not know whether you exist as an entity. It may sense a part of you, but you cannot see your form or personality. It does not know who you are, even if you stare into its eyes or touch it. It may see some moment and perceive a threat, but it does not know what it is dealing with. The ant's inability to comprehend your presence or existence does not mean that you do not exist at all. You do not exist for it. You do not need or depend upon the ant's validation or approval for your existence or continuity. You will not try to declare your presence to the ant to feel assured. Unless you are irrational, you will leave the ant unharmed and move on. We are more like ants when we search for a truth like God, who is vast and complex and greater than the universe.

At the outset, we said that mistaking beliefs as facts is delusional. There is no one way to know any truth conclusively. Even ordinary truths can be seen from different perspectives. However, many times, we think egoistically and refuse to see or acknowledge different points of view or different narratives and interpretations about the same subject. When we are attached to our beliefs and opinions, we cling to them even if they are defective, illogical, incomplete, and incorrect to others. When you become attached to a particular belief in God, when it becomes a part of your identity, and you cling to it, refusing to let it go, know that you are subject to delusion and denying the expansive and all-inclusion vision of God. The One you worship will be a limited reality, a point of view that can very likely create friction and clash with other theories and points of view with which it does not agree. Once you develop an egoistic pride in your beliefs and relationship with God, you develop a whole mythology and assumptive knowledge around it to sustain your myths, faith, and fervor and delude yourself. This is what happens to those who cling to their beliefs, mistaking them for facts. A more balanced approach would be to acknowledge beliefs as beliefs and facts as facts and not confuse one for the other. It is even better if you put your beliefs into practice and see how far you can go and whether they stand the test of truth.

Beliefs are difficult to sustain without corresponding devotion or commitment. When people go to a place of worship, they usually put on their best behavior, act piously, and think religiously, feeling virtuous and proud of their faith or allegiance. In contrast, when they step out of them and return to their daily routines, they become their normal and practical selves and forget much of what they learn from the faiths and scriptures they follow. Those who worship God and act piously in public but engage in unethical business practices, how good are they? How do they reconcile their beliefs with the guilt that arises from their actions? If people believe that they can compartmentalize their religious beliefs, values, and practices and practice them selectively on certain occasions and forget them conveniently at other times, they are sadly mistaken. Faith in the eternal God must be inseparable from the reality of oneself and one's life. They must be integrated into one's consciousness and a way of life so that whatever one thinks or does becomes an offering and an opportunity to worship Him and earn his love.

None can find God or attain salvation with deluded beliefs and inconsistent and superficial actions. They may put those who indulge in them on the path to transformation but do not lead them to God. He is found in the depths of your mind when it is engaged in exclusive devotion. When your senses are quiet, your mind is at peace, your ego is resting and relaxing, your thoughts are asleep in the lap of silence, and your emotions have retreated into a quiet corner, then only you will find Him in the silence of your heart and in the purity and tranquility of your consciousness. You will find Him when you put your desires to sleep and when you let go of your egoism, delusion, and worldly attachments. When you empty your mind, give up your possessions, and live and act as if you do not exist at all, except as a shadow, then only you will find Him in every aspect of your life. When you transcend your selfishness and egoism, you expand your consciousness to comprehend his universality and transcendence.

Therefore, to know God, you must develop the right vision and see Him everywhere and in everything. You can have faith and a set of beliefs, but they must be free from delusion and desires. Your actions must agree with them and reinforce them. You must cultivate knowledge and develop a pure heart and a reverential and devotional attitude that leads you on the path and connects you to your source. If you persevere on the path, practicing practice self-control, selfless actions, detachment, concentration, meditation, and devotion, you will attain sameness and oneness and see the whole existence as an extension of the Person in you, your innermost Self. With your mind becoming empty like an empty shell, devoid of all movements and modifications, you will awaken Him and fill it with the light of His pure consciousness.

Overcoming the impurities of egoism, desires, and delusion is the biggest challenge in this effort. However, if you keep faith in God and persevere, you will succeed. In short, do not demand proof of God to engage in spiritual or devotional practices. If you do believe in God, it is a different matter. You can pursue whatever doctrine you hold to be true. However, if you believe in Him and pursue Him, you should rely upon your faith and worship Him unconditionally for your good, peace, and happiness, or liberation. God does not make Himself known to His devotees unless they worship Him with unwavering faith and devotion and remove the walls that separate Him from them.

Spirituality For Worldly People

Few people turn to spiritualism, and still fewer actually practice it because spiritual life does not fit into our notion of success and happiness. The ego takes little pride in being spiritual because, in spiritual life, you have to make many sacrifices and forego your pride and comfort. In worldly life, success means having lots of money, power, and status. Spiritual life does not offer any of these. In fact, it demands their opposites characterized by a life of renunciation, austerity, and self-effacement. Because of that, many people prefer to stick with their worldliness and pursue their simple pleasures. The urge for self-realization is felt by a few in whom the latent impressions (samskaras) are fully burnt. The ancient ascetic traditions of India were aware of this human predicament. Therefore, they offered a compromise to ordinary people to practice spiritual materialism or worldly spiritualism by admitting them as lay followers and giving them an opportunity to follow a few simple rules and restraints to calm their minds and prepare themselves for their next births.

If you come to spiritual life out of frustration, anger, dejection, and disappointment, think again. Spiritual life is going to throw more and more of it until you either learn to live with your suffering or run away from it. If you turn to a life of renunciation or asceticism, you are likely to lose many friends and comforts and you are going to be criticized or misunderstood by society. You may also suffer from doubts and despair as you encounter difficulties on the path. If you believe that you have genuine spiritual aspirations, please examine your motives and whether you are really ready to take a plunge because if you change your mind in the middle, you may find it difficult to readjust to worldly life once again.

For an ordinary person, spiritual life is dull and unappealing. There are hardly any incentives on the path for the worldly-minded. During your practice, you have to spend a lot of time practicing virtues and removing your negativity and weaknesses. On the path, there are no immediate rewards. Until you reach perfection, you may not experience anything. Most likely, you will experience many emotional disturbances recurrently as you deal with your habits and your persistent thoughts. Out of millions of people who become interested in spiritual subjects, hardly a few really turn to asceticism or monastic life.

In the material world, you have the freedom to pursue your dreams and desires unabashedly and rejoice in your success. But on the spiritual path you have to exercise restraint and stop seeking looking for rewards and fulfillment of desires. To expect results and rewards is against the principles of spiritual life. Spiritual people have to relinquish egoistic seeking and their attachments, including their attachment to the fruit of their actions. They have to renounce what defines them and sets them apart as individuals, including their opinions and their particular likes and dislikes. They have to abandon their notions of success, failure, right, and wrong in order to be non-judgmental and equal in their attitude and behavior. They may also have to change their opinion and attitude towards the meaning and significance of success because what is deemed as success in real life may actually be a failure in the spiritual world and vice versa.

Because of such difficulties, we find few serious adherents to spiritual life. Most people remain on the fringes of spirituality without actually leaving their worldly ways, participating in a few spiritual practices now and then so that in case afterlife or eternal life really exists, they are not left behind. In life, we do not find many spiritual aspirants, but many spiritually curious people who dabble with spirituality, reading spiritual books, participating in spiritual events, performing rites and rituals, following a guru, visiting temples and other places of worship, promoting their faith and so on. Some may go to the extremes of joining a secret cult or promoting a spiritual tradition or a particular ideology. While the world appreciates superficial spiritual engagement, genuine spiritual effort mostly goes unnoticed. A majority of people are just this-worldly, and the idea of spiritual life does not really appeal to them. You will hardly receive any encouragement from society if you renounce the world and lead a dedicated spiritual life. Instead, your motives and your sanity will be questioned.

A dedicated spiritual life is not suitable for many, especially in the present-day world. Our world is not conducive to spiritual life. If people perceive you as a spiritual person, they will either draw a circle around you and treat you as a venerable saint or doubt your motives and integrity and move on. In the absence of any support or encouragement, you need a lot of courage and conviction to stick to your beliefs and follow the spiritual path chosen by you. Practically, with no support from your friends and family and with no certainty about your future or your survival, you have to live by the thread of your faith and deal with the problems and difficulties you face on the path with grace and humility. You also have to deal with a lot of resistance from your mind and body as you struggle with your instincts and dominant emotions. When you are engaged in spiritual activity, you come into conflict with Nature since you have to transcend your natural qualities and impulses. From Nature's perspective, every spiritual aspirant is an aberration who needs to be discouraged and taught a lesson if necessary. Renunciation and liberation do not fit in the natural scheme of things. Nature prefers people to remain engaged with their lives naturally, according to the laws that are set in motion. If you want to go against it, you have to pay the price and accept the suffering that comes with it.

Spiritual life is not necessary for living on earth. Nevertheless, you are never complete without it. The worldly life does promise a lot but delivers little. If you pursue worldly life with single-minded devotion, you will get to see only one side of life. You may see what is around you but not what is inside you. You will see what you can gain or lose in the material world, but not that which has always been there inside you as your essential Self. If you pursue material life solely and wholly with full passion, you will be like the one-eyed bandit who sees the world just like everyone else but misses on the perspective. In a limited way, worldly life is necessary for our happiness and the continuity of the creative process set in motion by God. Through our worldly activities, we need to fulfill our individual and family responsibilities and keep the wheels of life and society running. We have an issue with it because we become too deeply involved with it, forgetting the true purpose of our lives and our essential nature.

The phrase "spiritual life" is used here to denote a way of life in which you do not live for yourself but for the sake of the spirit or the Self that is hidden in you, identifying yourself completely with it. Your definition of spiritualism may not be the same as the one mentioned here. For some people, spiritualism means dealing with ghosts, paranormal powers, medium-ships, séances, and witchcraft. In some traditions, it means leading a contemplative, serene, and virtuous life with or without worshiping God or contemplating upon Him. Whatever your approach may be, it is used here in the most traditional sense of living for the sake of the Self (atma), with the Self as the center of our being and awareness. The yogis refer to the Self as God (Iswara) or cosmic being (purusha). Some religions call it soul instead of Self. You may give it any name you want, but if you live for the sake of the eternal principle that exists in all and if you are serious about knowing it, you are a spiritual person.

In some faiths, there is a clear distinction between spiritual life and worldly life. There is no concept of spiritual liberation in them in the same sense as in Hinduism, Buddhism, or Jainism. They hold that eternal life is granted to everyone who follows God's laws, follows His way, and adheres to religious duties. In these traditions, you may renounce the world and shun worldly pleasures, but the purpose for which you do it is different. According to Hinduism and Buddhism, whether you lead a worldly life or a spiritual life, your primary purpose is to work for your salvation, making use of every opportunity that comes your way for your self-transformation.

Hinduism is considered a way of life because it encourages a divine-centered life, in which you make an offering of your life and your actions to God to free yourself from the burden of karma. It does not matter which path you choose, as long as you make decisions and perform your actions without any desire for the fruit of your actions and offer them to God as a sacrificial offering. Although Buddhism does not believe in the existence of God, it projects a way of life in which the practice of the Eightfold Path is an important and essential component. Both religions uphold a holistic way of life, in which you move slowly and gradually into spiritual life while performing your obligatory duties and your day-to-day responsibilities. Both religions agree that until you are ready for the life of renunciation, you should live responsibly and virtuously, working on your qualities and impurities and preparing for your liberation.

The holistic way of life suggested by these traditions provides an opportunity for their adherents to fulfill their material and spiritual aspirations without disrupting their lives. According to these traditions, it is not necessary that to lead a spiritual life you have to become a monk or an ascetic. You may remain engaged with the duties of the world and yet consider yourself as a spiritual person because it is your essential nature. You may think that you are a physical entity. However, a deeper reality is hidden in you, which becomes evident only when you disengage yourself from the objective world and look into yourself with dispassion and equanimity.

The Awakened Life

It is also not necessary that you have to go to a remote forest or a glacial cave to practice meditation or seek salvation, but right here and right now, wherever you are, through the things that you seek and the actions that you perform. According to them, to lead a holistic life, you need awareness, sincerity, commitment, and interest in the deeper and not-so-apparent aspects of life. You need to train your mind and the senses to change your mindset to be mindful of what is going on in you and around you and discern the reality that is hidden in you. The following suggestions are meant to help you lead a holistic life in which you involve your whole personality and your life's many opportunities to lead a consecrated, divine-centered life and experience peace and happiness.

Contemplate upon death

In worldly life, we rarely think of death. The very thought of death makes us feel uncomfortable. Although death is inevitable, we would rather do anything to divert our attention from it. We want people to be life-oriented and think of life and achievement, even if life is full of problems and challenges. We appreciate people who defy death in their heroic ways and survive against the odds. Although the fear of death lurks in our minds, we deal with it effectively and live as if death is a remote possibility.

However, on the spiritual path, you have to come to terms with death and learn to accept it as a natural and normal process. You have to contemplate upon it till you exhaust all your thoughts and emotions associated with it and overcome any fears and reservations you may have about it. You have to spend hours contemplating upon it to become aware of the true nature of life and the futility of the worldly activities in which people waste their time. When you focus on death and think about it deeply, you realize the impermanence of your existence and perceive how you are caught between the pairs of opposites in an ever-changing, phenomenal world. You also realize how your fear of death limits you and compels you to search for security and certainty and how it makes you act in predictable and defensive ways. When you consider both life and death as the two faces of your suffering and bondage, you cultivate sameness towards them and accept death as a renewal and regenerating process. In Buddhism, as well as in Hinduism, images of death are used in visualization techniques to contemplate life and death and cultivate detachment and dispassion.

Identify yourself with your innermost Self

In normal life, we identify ourselves with our names and forms. We deal with people according to their appearance and their outward behavior. If we have an appealing personality, we are happy and proud. If not, we suffer from low self-esteem. We have this fixation with our looks even though we know that eventually, we become old and wither away. The body is just a sheath, an outer covering, like the clothes we wear. It is vulnerable to death and disease and subject to constant change. Someday, it will become old and fall away. If you identify yourself with your physical self only, someday you are bound to feel disappointed about yourself and the way you look. Our scriptures vouch that we are not mere physical beings but individual souls caught in the acts of Nature and imprisoned inside our bodies. Therefore, they suggest that we should consider ourselves as immortal and effulgent beings rather than mere physical entities and live accordingly. The world may deal with you according to your looks, the color of your skin, or your gender, but you do not have to treat yourself in the same manner.

You should identify yourself with your innermost Self and live accordingly, focusing your attention on it constantly, even when you are engaged in your daily tasks. If you persist, you will become fixed in that thought and accept yourself as an eternal, formless, invisible, and radiant entity. You develop detachment and witness consciousness. The Upanishads describe that the Self is smaller than the smallest atom and larger than the material universe. Some speak of it as a radiant blue dot, and some as a small mysterious particle hidden somewhere in the body. You will not be able to perceive it physically. However, you become aware of it as you withdraw into yourself and contemplate upon it without distractions and disturbances.

Extend your vision

Usually, we do not think far or look beyond our immediate concerns, as we habitually focus on the immediate, the pressing, and the urgent. While such expediency may help us to cope with our daily pressures, it also limits our ability to focus on the larger and more important aspects of life. When we focus on small issues and the immediate problems and ignore the larger picture, such a restricted vision of life makes us rather narrow-minded, frivolous, and fickle. In contrast, if you treat yourself as an eternal being and view your life on the scale of eternity, your thoughts and your approach to life will change completely. Our scriptures affirm that you are not a mere physical being who lives here for a lifetime but an eternal Self who is caught in the grip of life and struggling through the web of phenomenal happenings. You have to believe in that and extend your vision so that you will not waste your time on frivolous activities but live in the larger interests of your eternal Self, working for your salvation and making use of the opportunities to overcome your suffering and experience peace and happiness.

If you have a spiritual bent of mind, you know that you are here for a reason. You know that your liberation and your happiness are in your hands. If you do not work for it now, your next life will be much harder to live as your actions and imperfections begin to bear fruit. It is, therefore, necessary that you look at yourself as an eternal soul whose existence stretches beyond the current life and who needs to be eternally free. When you stretch your thinking from the immediate to the infinite and from the physical to the spiritual, your priorities will change, and your attention will shift from the finite to the infinite. You will also develop compassion towards other beings as you realize their essential spiritual nature and identify yourself with them. Most importantly, you will consider your life as a unique opportunity to work for your liberation and become free.

Accept the impermanence of the world

We know how impermanent and inconsistent things are in our world. Yet we spend a great deal of time trying to deal with it and protect our lives from it. To allay our fears and feel safe and secure, we accumulate things that are impermanent by nature. We hold on to them to promote our interests and secure our lives. Sadly, material wealth does not adequately address the problem of impermanence that is inherent in our lives. With material possessions, you may experience pride but not freedom from anxiety and fear of loss. Whether you are rich or poor, you cannot escape from aging, death, and sickness. They are the irrefutable facts of earthly life. Whether you accept it or not, at every turn and twist of your life, impermanence keeps rearing its head.

You cannot escape from impermanence, and you cannot avoid the death and decay of things. However, you can learn to accept it and live with it without feeling disturbed by the suffering it creates. We suffer from the transience of life because of our cravings and attachments. If we practice detachment, we do not suffer from loss or gain. If you aim to experience peace and stability, it makes sense not to become entangled in the attractions of life and live with the awareness that, eventually, you will be separated from everything that you dearly love. When you are free from the world and its influence upon you, you become equal to the dualities and uncertainties that appear in your life. The best solution to the problem of impermanence is detachment, from which comes the ability to accept the pairs of opposites with equanimity.

Surrender to God

It is difficult to think of God when you are very busy with the daily problems of your life. It is also difficult to understand Him conceptually or intellectually because our conscious minds cannot comprehend the reality of God. According to our knowledge, intelligence, beliefs, and prejudices, we may vaguely form an idea of Him and form a relationship with Him. However, it may not be the right one and it may not satisfy our curiosity or our doubts. In material life, we usually approach God to seek His help to fulfill certain desires. It is essentially a selfish approach, an extension of the selfsame worldly attitude and an attempt to make use of the power of God for our benefit. In spiritual life, we may still approach Him with certain desires and intentions. However, we must look to Him with a different mindset and an attitude of surrender and devotion, accepting Him as the source of everything and every manifestation and acknowledging Him as the real power behind our actions.

Our scriptures suggest that God is the real power behind our actions and manifests our reality according to our thoughts and desires. Every scripture that is based upon God's revelations declares that devotion to God leads to either liberation or eternal heavenly life. God is the real doer. He is our true manifesting power. We have the ability to perform our actions and fulfill our desires because of Him only. We are here because of Him. He is our protector and benefactor. If we do not give Him due credit for the help we receive and if we assume ownership and doership for our actions, we become responsible for them and the consequences arising from them.

Therefore, our scriptures suggest that to live freely and escape from the consequences of our actions, we need to relinquish the notion of doership and offer all our actions and their fruit to God with love and devotion. The Bhagavadgita declares that we are never separate from God because we exist in Him and we are an inseparable part of Him. This whole universe is inhabited by Him, and He is the true power behind all movements. We see Him all the time. But we do not recognize Him. He is with us all the time, but we do not acknowledge His presence. Our actions are part of His actions. However, we do not know it. We find it difficult to accept God in unconventional ways because we do not feel convinced about His omnipresence. It is a sign that our faith is incomplete.

Cultivate friendships with spiritual people

Spiritual people need protection from negativity and worldliness, especially in the early stages of their practice. They need motivation and encouragement from others to continue their practice. If you are a spiritual person and spend more time in the company of worldly people, their worldliness will demotivate you and make you feel discouraged and depressed. According to our scriptures, the best way to practice meditation is to remain isolated from worldly people and practice it in secluded places. In ancient days, spiritual people shunned society and went to forests to practice asceticism. They lived in groups, under the watchful guidance of their masters, and practiced various disciplines, maintaining minimal contact with worldly people. The same was true in respect of people who retired from their household duties and went to forests to practice renunciation (sanyasa ashrama). It is hard to shun society in today's world because civilization is everywhere, and the forests are now very sparse. They are hardly suitable to practice meditation without feeling disturbed. Besides, the state regulations may not allow anyone to live there. Therefore, we have to come out with our ingenious ways to live in seclusion and safeguard ourselves from unhealthy influences. Here are some ways to do it. Firstly, you can create a sanctuary in your own house, choosing a place to practice meditation without disturbance. Secondly, you may stay in a retreat or an ashram if you can afford the money and if you like the rigid routine. Thirdly, you may look for like-minded people in your community with whom you can participate in group meditations and devotional activities. Lastly, if you do not find right-minded people, you can still keep your mind busy by practicing meditation, reading spiritual books, participating in some religious activity, listening to devotional music, or helping others.

Jayaram V

Practice meditation

Meditation creates profound changes in the way we think, feel, and observe the world around us. Through meditation, we come to know about our minds and bodies. We become sensitive to the world within us and the world around us and develop control over our thoughts, desires, actions, and impulses. Meditation makes you thoughtful, receptive, open, and attentive towards everything, including your mind and body. Through contemplation, you will be able to probe the depths of your consciousness and become familiar with your life and your experiences. In fact, meditation is the best way to remain connected with both the spiritual and material aspects of your life and remain balanced.

There are also other physical and mental benefits associated with regular meditation. It reduces stress, dullness, and negativity and increases awareness and tolerance. If you practice meditation regularly, you will become emotionally stable. If you practice breathing exercises regularly, it will energize your body, reducing your dependence on caffeine and other stimulants. With visualization techniques, you can reach out to your subconscious mind and plant powerful ideas and suggestions for your inner transformation. Practice meditation to free your mind and body from afflictions and experience peace, stability, and balance. Meditate naturally any time of the day or hour, with your eyes open or closed. Develop a reflective and attentive attitude to observe life and experience peace through awareness and understanding.

Cultivate virtues

Spiritual life is built upon the foundation of good conduct (sila). Commitment to right living is essential for spiritual life. It is impossible to progress on the path without corresponding inner transformation. One should stay free from impure thoughts and attacks from evil forces by remaining clean. Self-transformation is a self-purification process. If you are not willing to cultivate virtues, you should remain practical and pursue your worldly goals rather than risk your health and your peace of mind. Certain qualities are indispensable to spiritual life and self-transformation, such as patience, truthfulness, non-stealing, harmlessness, compassion, charity, selflessness, right attitude, devotion, surrender, humility, tolerance, forgiveness, courage, detachment, and love. We need them to transform the ego and the lower nature. However, self-transformation is not easy because to accomplish it, one has to break many habits of the mind and body and subject them to rigorous discipline. What you want to remove or transform becomes active in your consciousness and offers stiff resistance. It is a process during which you have to pass through innumerable challenges and tests and survive the pressures and the pain. If you are not ready for it and if you do not have the required moral and spiritual strength, you may stir up latent negativity in your mind and find the whole experience rather disturbing.

Pay attention to the events in your life

Mindfulness is a simple but effective technique to know the underlying causes of your behavior and sharpen your senses and sensitivity. With mindfulness practice, you come to know a great deal about yourself and your motivation. You realize how your perceptions and desires influence your thoughts and how you act and react habitually to different events and circumstances. You may learn the techniques of mindfulness from books or experienced masters. Alternatively, you may cultivate witness consciousness to observe yourself passively and dispassionately. These techniques enable you to observe the objective reality closely and precisely, with dispassion and attentiveness, and become aware of your thoughts, feelings, emotions, desires, motives, actions, and reactions. When you are mindful, you see the world, the people, things, and yourself with profound awareness and without judgment. With mindfulness, you may not read other people's thoughts or develop supernatural abilities, but you learn a great deal about human behavior and motivation. Through uninterrupted awareness, you learn to see things as they are and perceive the truth hidden behind the masks people wear and the illusions they entertain.

Focus on the task rather than the result

In worldly life, people do not easily give up on their hopes and dreams. They strive hard to reach their goals and fulfill their desires, if necessary, at the expense of others and their peace and happiness. However, spiritual people cannot show the same behavior. They have to tone down their aggression and their selfishness and cultivate sameness towards both success and failure. According to our scriptures, spiritual people should be interested in performing their actions but without desire for the result of their actions. They should perform them without egoism, without taking credit for their success or failure, and without any anxiety or worry about the outcome. According to the Bhagavadgita, actions in themselves are not binding, but our desire for action and our attachment to the result are. The means are also important. One should employ the right means with the right intention according to the moral values that are upheld by the scriptures. Actions should be performed as a sacrificial offering to God, with dispassion, disinterestedness, and detachment.

The actions that you perform for yourself are not the same as the actions that you perform in the name of God, even if the nature of the actions is the same. One binds you and makes you responsible for your actions, and the other sets you free because you are not seeking personal gain while doing them. From a psychological perspective, if you focus on the results of your actions, you may suffer from fear and anxiety, and you may not perform them well. However, if you focus on your actions without worrying about the results, you have better chances of perfecting your techniques and improving your performance. Technically speaking, the results of our actions are not in our hands, however diligent we may be in executing them. You may improve your performance through the right effort, but there is no guarantee that it will lead to the right result. However, you can always be sure of performing your actions as sincerely as possible.

Stop defending yourself

Egoism is a major obstacle on the spiritual path. You have to deal with it constantly as you perfect your practice. If you have a strongly formed ego because of your education, upbringing, family background, or social status, you have to spend a lot of time dealing with it. The ego manifests itself in many ways in our thoughts and actions. Responding to criticism, trying to defend oneself, or clarifying one's actions to win the approval of others are signs of egoism. In worldly life, you need a strong individuality to protect yourself from others and to stand for your beliefs and values. Nevertheless, in spiritual life you are not expected to protect your ego or strengthen it. Actually, you have to weaken it by cultivating humility and practicing virtue. When others criticize you, blame you, or question your motives and honesty, you have to use the opportunity to cultivate equanimity and control your egoistic urge to defend yourself or blame them in return.

There are some ascetic traditions with a long history that actually encourage their followers to indulge in offensive behavior and reprehensible public acts to invite public criticism and discourage people from worshipping them. They do it purposefully to clear any egoistic desire they may have to attract public appreciation and veneration. When you are on a spiritual path, people may assume that you are a holy person and approach you with respect and reverence, which may inflame feelings of egoism and self-importance and distract you from your path. These traditions make sure that the practitioners remain levelheaded and stay clear of worldly people and public adulation. While such harsh methods may not be necessary, it is still important for spiritual people to keep their egos under check by not defending it, by not promoting it and by not giving it importance.

Unity and Diversity of the Human Body

From a universal perspective, there is nothing else but the Self. It is the "I am of I am" that certain Prophets encountered in the past in the most unusual circumstances. It is the realization of the chant "Aham Brahmasmi" (I am Brahman) or "tatvamasi" (this is That). It is the highest state of self-absorption (samadhi), where the world comes to a standstill, and everything is in perfect equilibrium. People do not understand this concept until they see the world through an expanded awareness, lit by the presence of God or the liberated Self from the inside. It is difficult to explain this unitary aspect of our consciousness because we do not experience it until we remove all the impurities and imperfections and let the brilliance of the inner Self emerge through our consciousness. When we indulge in the activities of the senses and pursue sense gratification with egoism and selfishness, we fail to grasp the underlying reality of our consciousness and our inseparable connection with it. When we are drawn into the outer and apparent objective reality, we remain isolated and bound to the world and its myriad distractions. It is only when we withdraw our senses from the objective world and look into our inner realms, cultivating virtues, stabilizing our minds and bodies, and surrendering to God, that we become aware of the reality that is hidden from our surface consciousness.

The five bodies around the Self

According to Hinduism, the human body is made up of five sheaths (kosas) or bodies. The outermost one is the physical body, made up of flesh and bones. It is called the food body (annamaya kosa) because it is formed from the food we eat. It is also the grossest and densest of all the remaining sheaths. The next one is known as the pranic body (pranamaya kosa). It is made up of the energy created from our breathing activity. Hence, you may also call it the pranic or the subtle energy body. The third one is called the mental body (manomaya kosa). It is made up of all the elements of the mind and consciousness. The fourth one is the intelligence (vijnanamaya kosa) body. It is the higher mind that is responsible for our analytical, conceptual, rational, and intellectual skills. It enables us to discern things and make intelligent and rational decisions. Finally, we have the innermost sheath known as the bliss body (anandamaya kosa). It is in direct contact with the inner Self and reflects its blissful state and happiness.

Although, for description purposes, we refer to these bodies as layers or sheaths, they are not actually arranged in successive concentric circles. Functionally or conceptually, they are different, but structurally and spatially, they are indistinguishable in our personality. We refer to the physical body as the outermost and the bliss body as the innermost based on our ability to access them either through our senses or through meditative self-absorption in transcendental states. The physical body is the first one to be experienced with the help of the senses and the bliss body is the last one to be experienced in our deepest state of inner tranquility through the practice of yoga and after going through extensive purification. Once we pierce through the bliss body, we come face to face with the effulgent Self, referred to in yogic tradition as Iswara (the Lord) or Purusha (Cosmic Being).

The five bodies are not present in all living beings. They develop according to one's level of evolution in the spiritual hierarchy and the number of senses present in the body. In plants and animals, only the physical, pranic, and mental bodies develop. In our case, all five bodies are present but not necessarily in the same proportion. Just as there is diversity in their appearance and behavior, people differ in the composition of their gross and subtle bodies, depending upon how they use them. In some people, the outer bodies develop more as they focus on their physical and mental growth. In some, the subtle bodies develop more as they purify and stabilize their minds and develop a keen sense of observation and discernment. To develop the five sheaths fully, one needs to focus on one's physical and spiritual development and integrate the different components of the personality into a composite whole, with the Self as the center. The integral yoga of Sri Aurobindo aims to integrate the diverse aspects of the human personality, in a similar manner, around the psychic center and prepare it for the descent of higher planes of consciousness through surrender, devotion, and intense aspiration.

There is also another interesting aspect about the five bodies. As we move from the outermost to the inner, individual distinctions and variations among the bodies begin to disappear so that our innermost bodies are hardly distinguishable from one another except perhaps in their densities. This is true in the case of not only our personalities but also the entire creation. Outwardly, the material things are different and distinct. However, as we go deeper into their essential nature, the distinctions begin to disappear. Even from a scientific perspective, we know that, outwardly, the properties and physical characteristics of material objects may vary. However, at the atomic and subatomic levels, they contain the same particles and energy. In the innermost aspects of creation, all dualities and distinctions disappear, and everything eventually resolves itself into pure energy and consciousness. In their deepest states of meditations, the seers and sages of ancient India saw this fundamental unity hidden in the entire manifest universe and identified them as male (Purusha) and female (Prakriti) aspects of creation. In the following discussion, we explore this subject in further detail.

The physical plane

Every animate and inanimate object in the material universe is a distinct and unique entity that you can recognize and categorize based on certain qualities and distinguishing features. These distinctions are essential for our survival and sanity. Our physical appearances declare to the world who we are and, to some extent, what we are. Even if you undergo plastic surgery, you can still be identified based on your DNA, fingerprints, or the iris of your eyes. We use these distinctions to navigate our way through the world and manage its complexity and diversity without feeling overwhelmed. We use them to establish our relationships with others for our collective and personal good. Physically, at the most basic level, Nature has made sure that individually we stand out as separate individuals, without any confusion, so that we have no problem knowing whom and what we are dealing with. Imagine how life would have been if all people and beings looked alike, like the clones or the robots in some science fiction movie. Life would be chaotic, if we cannot hold people accountable and responsible for their actions and if we cannot prove our existence based upon our appearance.

The energy plane

Diversity exists at the level of the pranic body also, but not as much as in the case of the physical body. If the earth element characterizes the physical body, the fire element characterizes the pranic body. We call it the pranic body because, physically, breath, energy, or prana sustains it, and prana is its physical and outward aspect. Actually, it is the energy (pranic) body. Enveloping each individual is an energy field, which is known as the aura and which can be perceived with subtle senses. Inside the body, energy flows through several invisible channels. Problems may arise if these channels are blocked for some reason.

Behind the physical forms and appearances, what sustains life is energy in its various forms. Some energy is gross, and some is subtle. Some are free-flowing, and some are locked up inside the body and the cells. In yoga, we identify it as life energy (prana). Energy is hidden in all animate and inanimate objects, both in gross and subtle forms. It is also present in all living beings as both static and dynamic energies, which manifest as inertia (jada) and activity (chaitanya), respectively. Besides these, several subtle energies also exist in us in latent form, which wake up during spiritual practice and manifest as supernatural powers (Siddhis).

Depending upon the presence of the three primordial modes (gunas) of Nature (sattva, rajas, and tamas), energy may be either vital (rajas), pure (sattva), or gross (tamas). The first one is responsible for worldly desires and passions, the second for intelligence and reason, and the third for extreme passions, indiscretion, and antisocial or sociopathic behavior. Dynamic energy may move through the various nerve centers in the body and the chakras in the region of the spine along the path the kundalini energy is believed to flow. The movement of energy in the human body is responsible for the vitality, energy, and health of each individual. The static energy of the body is locked up inside our cells and atoms, while dynamic energy circulates through various life-supporting systems and invisible channels.

We derive our energy mostly from the earth through the food we eat. Some come from the air we breathe, some through the thought forms we exchange, and some directly from the vibrations of the universe and higher divinities. Truly, every object grasped by our senses is a potential source of subtle or gross energy. According to our scriptures, it is possible to derive energy not only from the food we eat but also from various other sources. It is also possible to increase certain types of subtle energy in the body by practicing austerities and self-control. Some people develop the ability to channel the energies of the mind and the body from one part to another or from one person to another, usually for healing. We also accomplish a similar objective through prayers and chants. In some traditions, spiritual gurus

Unity and Diversity of the Human Body

transfer part of their spiritual energy to qualified disciples to awaken their awareness or remove their obstacles. Spiritual practice is mostly about the transformation of various types of physical and subtle energies so that the body becomes fit for radiating the brilliance of the soul.

We learn from our scriptures that when an advanced yogi performs austerities for a specific period with great determination (sankalpa), a subtle heat (tapas) is generated in his body because of the transformation of sexual energy (retas), which gradually moves up through the spinal column and enters the head region as pure brilliance (tejas). In certain spiritual practices, the practitioners seek the help of the Mother Goddess and request Her to enter them and purify them completely so that they become fit for the descent of the divine consciousness.

The energy body is a very powerful component of the human personality. We can influence and transform it through austerities and specific breathing techniques (pranayama). Thoughts and emotions, food, karmic actions, religious and spiritual practices, purity and morality, the grace of Shakti (Mother Goddess), and a host of other factors play an important role in creating each being's energy field.

The energy body is within the grasp of the senses, but only in a limited manner. They cannot grasp the diversity of the energy body as clearly as they can perceive the physical objects. We may feel the energy present in the human body and recognize people based on their energy levels as weak or strong. However, it is difficult to identify individuals solely based on their energy levels or energy patterns. Maybe in the future, we may do it if someone invents a machine or an apparatus to draw the energy maps of each individual and if we find peculiarities in them. Until then, we have to be content with our broad classification.

However, in the spiritual realm, it is said to be possible to perceive the energy bodies with the help of our subtle senses. According to the personal accounts of several adept yogis, we understand that those in whom the inner eye has awakened can see the auras that surround people and objects and know about them. By looking at the auras, they can dwell upon the past and future of people, their problems, and their most personal secrets. There are also certain systems like Reiki, which teach us how to study the energy fields of people and purify them. Although not everyone may be able to distinguish individual variations in our energy fields, from these accounts we know that it is possible to do so.

In the epics, the Ramayana and the Mahabharata, and the Hindu Puranas, which deal with the ancient lore, we read about the use of energy shields and destructive weapons, which could be activated with concentrated mind power. While we are not certain whether they happened here on earth or elsewhere, they allude to the possibility of using our energies for creative and destructive purposes. Because the pranic body is between the physical body and the mental body, it influences both of them. It influences our mental stamina and our overall capacity to bear the pressures of life. It also determines the quality of our thinking, our enthusiasm, and our emotional energy.

The mental body

Some diversity is discernible in the mental body, although not to the extent that we can identify people solely based on their mental traits. The water element dominates the mental body and makes it plastic. It is an aggregation of our thoughts, emotions, feelings, memories, perceptions, desires, attitudes, instincts, and impulses. It is nourished by the senses and sustained by the ego, or the ordinary self, which has a hold on all the five sheaths. Although it is inside the physical body, it has no definite form, and according to occult descriptions, it may extend well beyond the body into the aura or the energy field. The mental body has a deep connection with the physical body and it is attached to it firmly. It also has some control over the physical and pranic bodies, which also exert their influence upon it. Unlike the physical and pranic bodies, the mental body is beyond the senses and cannot be perceived physically. However, it can be reached through the inner senses. The mental body is the bridge between the two outer and two inner bodies and also, being pervasive, and influences each of them definitively.

It is difficult to distinguish individuals purely based on their mental qualities. However, based on mental traits, we can categorize them into distinct personality types, such as emotional, stable, aggressive, submissive, friendly, unfriendly, extroverted, introverted, normal, abnormal, positive, negative, and so on. But the distinction ends here. We cannot identify individual solely based on their mental makeup. The mental body is not subject to the same limitations as the physical and pranic bodies are. It is formless and almost limitless. In the

Unity and Diversity of the Human Body

mental plane, we transcend many limitations of the physical body and lose much of our individuality as we share the same mental qualities and abilities with others. The mental body has a direct connection with the pranic and the physical bodies. For example, from the pranayama exercises, we know that with breathing practice, we can calm the mind and soothe the nerves. When the physical, mental, and pranic bodies are in harmony, we experience good health and pleasant feelings. The mental body is vulnerable to external influences and disturbances because of its dependence upon the senses. If the mind is not stable, it is difficult to gain knowledge, suppress the desires and the latent impressions, or go deeper into the subtle planes. Since its transformation is vital to experience higher states of self-absorption, the various techniques of yoga primarily aim to control and stabilize it.

The intelligence body

Actually, it is the higher mind, also known as the intelligence body (buddhi), which separates humans from animals. We share the lower mind, which is primitive and impulsive, with the animal world. The higher mind gives us the ability to think rationally and know the difference between right and wrong and good and bad. It is one of the highest aspects of Nature present in us, which reflects the brilliance of the Self and which is responsible for our logical, creative, analytical, and intuitive abilities, common sense, and discrimination. The intelligence body is the source of all our wisdom, having the ability to discern truth, solve our problems and steer us through the challenges of life. It maintains direct contact with the mental body but remains somewhat detached from the physical and the energy bodies, because of which we do not see its presence much physically, except in the brightness of the face, the intensity of the gaze, and the vibrations of the spoken words.

We cannot distinguish people exclusively based on their intelligence, except in the case of exceptionally brilliant people who stand out for their knowledge and intellect. As in the case of pranic and energy bodies, we can make some distinctions among people based on certain criteria such as the level of intelligence (IQ) and problem-solving skills. In ancient India, people were grouped into categories based on their ability to remember. We do the same now, although in different ways. The intelligence body does not develop equally among all people. It develops well in those who are well-educated, knowledgeable, wise, philosophical, and introspective, such as artists, scholars, scientists, writers, philosophers, spiritual masters, leaders, and men of great knowledge.

The intelligence body represents the swiftness and agility of the air element. Since it is very abstract and intangible, it leaves few impressions on the physical body. It receives light from the Self and, in turn, shines in the mental sphere as brilliance. From there it reaches the physical body in the form of wisdom and erudition. Intelligence is a very important aspect of human consciousness. It is a quality which puts men on par with the gods. Without it we will be equal to animals. In animals, the intelligence body is almost absent. Hence, those in whom the intelligence body awakens or in whom it develops fully are called the twice-born. They are well qualified for spiritual life. However, they also need to remove the influence of their egos from their intelligence.

Diversity in the bliss body

The fifth and the most mysterious component of our personality is that which is awake when we are physically asleep. It is the bliss body, which represents the ether, the fifth element, which is invisible and mostly unknown. We may also call it the divine body or heavenly realm because it encases the soul directly. Since it is in direct contact with the Self, it reflects its essential nature, which is bliss and illumination. The bliss body is too remote to be experienced physically, except during sexual union and in deeper states of tranquility. It develops fully only in exceptional individuals who have transcended their physical nature and who have purified their minds and bodies well enough to experience transcendental states of self-absorption (samadhi). The yogis who taste the sweetness of their bliss bodies would never return to worldly life and seek the small pleasures of physical life. Self-aware and self-absorbed, they attain eternal freedom when they depart from the world.

It is difficult to categorize people according to their bliss bodies because the bliss body is universal, indistinguishable, and devoid of any qualities, modes, or distinctions. Everyone possesses the same type of bliss body without any variations. It is also too remote from the physical and mental bodies to come into direct contact with them. It is beyond the senses, the ego, and the mind. We cannot control it because we have no direct contact with it through our minds or our senses. We may probably experience it in our deep sleep state, but no one knows or remembers. It is free from entanglements and detached from the objective world. We may develop some intuitive idea about its nature, but we cannot define it or distinguish it. It is the last layer to drop off when the Self is fully liberated.

The human and superhuman

We have seen that the diversity and individuality of the human personality are most visible and striking in the physical body and become less evident and less distinct in the subtle bodies. Our identities are very discernible in our physical and mental bodies. In the subtle planes, we come closer to God and the human archetypes. In the deepest core of our personalities, there is more generality than specificity and more unity than diversity. In the depths of our consciousness, we transcend our distinctions and become abstract, sharing the essential nature of creation with the rest of the things. There, we become uniform and almost indistinguishable. As we move from the outer to the inner, the veils that separate us from others begin to fade. We experience the expansiveness of our consciousness and our essential divine nature. While our individuality remains well preserved in our outermost gross body, it disappears completely in our innermost subtle body.

Our physical and energy bodies have a lot in common with those of plants and animals, while our mental, intelligence, and bliss bodies have a lot more in common with those of gods and celestial beings. In the bliss body, we come closest to God, which we experience only when our senses are asleep and our minds and bodies are at rest. For these very reasons, our scriptures suggest that if we want to move closer to God, we have to withdraw from the outer gross bodies and turn inwards to reach out to the deepest layers of our consciousness through contemplative and meditative means. If you develop attachments with your outer bodies, you will be restless because they are usually unstable and subject to the influence of the senses and the ego. However, if you go deeper into your subtle bodies, you will experience greater calm and stability because the subtle bodies are more stable and do not come under the influence of the senses as easily.

The human personality is a temporary formation that exists for the duration of a lifetime and then drops off. It needs to be transformed and enlightened in all the five planes to facilitate the liberation of the Self. It is equally important how you develop them. If you focus solely on the physical body, you will strengthen the animal nature and aggravate your baser instincts and animal nature. However, if you focus on developing your subtle bodies, you will strengthen the divine nature in you and use your intelligence and discretion to cultivate wisdom and equanimity.

The five-body meditation

Here is a simple meditation technique with which you can discern your five bodies, connect to them, and strengthen them.

Sit in a lotus position with your legs crossed. Close your eyes and gently relax your whole mind and body, starting with your toes and gradually moving up. Focus on each body part as you relax gradually, letting go of all your worries and tensions. Once you are in a state of deep relaxation, keep mindful of your physical body, from the tip of your feet to the top of your head. Pay attention to the physical sensations, the sounds and smells coming from outside, and any tension and discomfort you may experience in your body. Think about your self-image and how you feel about it. Think about how you are different from others and what distinguishes you. Think of all the different identities you assume and the roles you play frequently. Think of your health, your food choices, and how the food you eat may have influenced you and your behavior. Think of how your appearance changed over time and how you may look in the future. This is the meditation on your gross physical body or the food body.

Next, think of your pranic body. Pay attention to your inbreathing and outbreathing. Think of all the ways in which you receive energy. Feel the energy in you. Feel it flowing through every limb in your body, feel it flowing out and into you and connecting you to the whole akasic energy flowing around you from all sides. Imagine how you may be receiving energy from the space around you through your breath and how your energy levels are sustained by it. Think of the energy you release during emotional outbursts and the energy you receive from other people through their thoughts, words, actions, and emotions. Feel the energy present in your body and the energy field around you. Think whether it has any connection with your consciousness and whether your consciousness is also a form of subtle energy only. Feel the physical, mental, sexual, and subtle energies present in various parts of your body and how they are helping you. Feel your connection with the universal energy of the

Unity and Diversity of the Human Body

Mother Goddess and envision your luminous energy body as her projection. Visualize yourself as a mass of pure energy shining brightly like a glowing sun and connected to the universal energy from all sides. This is the meditation on the energy body.

Now, turn your attention to your mental body and visualize it as an aqueous mass filled with luminous thoughts, emotions, feelings, and memories. Visualize various mental objects leaving it or dropping into. Expand that mass of free-flowing consciousness mentally as far as you can and fill the whole space with its luminosity and vibrations. Imagine thought-forms of different colors, shapes, and hues coming in and going out of your mind like little whirls of radiant light. Imagine a golden lotus gradually opening its bright petals in your mind and radiating luminous light. Visualize as if you are a pure mind with no body, weight, or sensations. Cleanse your consciousness, visualizing a bright white light pervading you from all sides, flowing into the top of your head from the sky above, and cleansing your consciousness until you feel a vast, expansive peace pervade your whole being. This is the meditation on the mental body.

Next, turn your attention to your intelligence body. Become aware of reasoning and analytical skills, when you might have used them, and when you were satisfied or wanted to improve. Examine your thoughts and see whether you can discern things correctly, know right from wrong, how you are different from others, and how you can improve further. Think of what decisions you made and how they influenced your life and actions. Visualize yourself as a radiant being full of wisdom and intelligence. Think of how intelligence is different from the memorial mind and how you can use it to practice self-control or make the right decisions. This is the meditation on the intelligence body.

Finally, think of your bliss body. Reflect on the happiness and what it means to be happy, joyous, and fulfilled. Recollect moments of happiness and pure joy you experienced in the past. Visualize yourself as a radiant being filled with pure happiness, joy, and unending bliss, floating freely in the universe, self-absorbed and completely free, holding on to a beam of light, your inner Self, and feeling an exhilarated feeling arising from it and filling you from head to toe. Feel your oneness with the blissful Self and think how its brilliance is reflected in your being and removing all traces of darkness, sadness, and negativity in you.

Spend at least five minutes contemplating each body. To make the practice even more effective, add your own imagination. Once you are done, slowly become aware of your surroundings and open your eyes.

Seeing Things as They Are

Dōgen Zenji lived in Japan in the thirteenth century AD. He was the founder of the founder of the Sōtō school of Zen Buddhism, who started the practice of Zazen, sitting meditation. After his initiation as a monk in Kyoto, he went to China and practiced Zen for several years in a monastery and returned to his native village in Japan. According to one story, after he returned from China, one day, he met a villager in a street who asked him what he had learned in China from his teacher. Dōgen said to have replied that he learned that his eyebrows were horizontal and his nose vertical. Upon hearing it, the villager could not understand what he meant and wondered why the teacher spent so much time learning such a trivial thing. He missed the point that Dōgen learned to see things as they were without distortions, expectations, and delusion.

It is indeed true that the more we study and learn, the less we see because our seeing becomes clouded by the knowledge that we accumulate. With that, seeing becomes a repetitive recollection and superimposition of what we already know upon what we see. That severely impacts any further learning from new experiences, study, or observation. Education adds layers of complexity to our thinking and perceptions, which is why the more educated we are, the greater the difficulty we face in overcoming our distorted views and cultivating the right awareness. After years of study, many forget to remember the simple joys of life or look at the world without any pretensions. We are inundated with so much information every day from various sources that simple matters do not attract our attention at all unless they are unusual in some way. In our preoccupation with complex issues and daily problems, we do not have time to pay attention to simple and mundane matters. We take them for granted. We use generalizations and stereotyping to process the overwhelming amounts of information that keep coming every day.

To see things clearly, objectively, and mindfully, we must be free from mental blocks and filters, possess clarity and discernment, and be free from cravings, passions, delusion, and egoism so that nothing stands between the seer and the seen. We must be equal to all things without judgment, likes and dislikes. Unless our minds are free from modifications and distortions, we cannot discern truths as they are or comprehend the true nature of things.

Seeing Things as They Are

In today's world, people are too busy to slow down, reflect upon themselves or their experiences, or observe mindfully what happens around them. They spend their time on matters that require their urgent and immediate attention or give them a break from their stressful life, ignoring the deeper aspects of life that would help them grow mentally, spiritually, or intellectually or help them expand their knowledge and awareness. Therefore, it is not surprising that in this information age, we have many people whose general knowledge about the world or the country in which they live does not compare well with those who lived a thousand years ago without any current amenities. For most, the world ends at the periphery of their interests, desires, and pursuits. They see a very constricted and fragmented world and reality through a narrow window of their limited interests and knowledge, according to their likes and dislikes or beliefs and biases, and ignore whatever does not catch their attention or goes beyond their comprehension.

If we want to see reality, we must be free from the mental pegs that bind the mind to a certain way of functioning and limit its ability to absorb information without distortions. We must free our minds from impurities, modifications, and limitations that interfere with our knowing and understanding and develop an inquisitive mind that can see and comprehend clearly without filters. Dogen alluded to this profound truth. He spoke about the unlearning process, the casting of the conditioned mind and arresting all its movements to relearn the pure and most basic skills of seeing and knowing things clearly and precisely as they are. It is when the mind is asleep it really sees. When it is not engaged in its usual business of thinking and building aggregates of structures and forms with the mind-stuff, it perceives the "pure presence of things as they are."

Much of the spiritual practice in any tradition consists of developing this basic skill through unlearning, emptying, unwinding, discarding, and casting off the unwanted and conditioned formations of the mind to learn to see things anew with curiosity, awe, and wonder like a newly born and to settle mindfully in the now and hear. When we work on ourselves in this fashion, we will learn how to cut through the maze of complexity we build in our lives and return to our pristine and natural state of simplicity, see objectively, and regain our natural skills of seeking, knowing, and learning, which we forget as we become involved with the world and clutter our minds.

Jayaram V

Seeing Things as They Are

You cannot see the world clearly when desires and attachments obscure your mind. To be attentive, you must be wide awake without desires, disturbing emotions, anxieties, and expectations. You must have the patience and tolerance to accept things as they are without judgment. Life becomes a blur when you are busy and rush through it to meet your goals and expectations. To see things clearly, you must be willing to wait, pause, and savor the moment. You must control your desires and see things without your mind standing in between.

The human capacity to observe and comprehend varies. These are not static skills and cannot be taken for granted. They can be improved or perfected through practice and training. They largely depend upon the mind itself, how chaotic or disciplined it is. At the most superficial level, it registers only a few surface impressions according to the desires, interests, and prejudices it harbors. The scope and depth of its observation and comprehension widen or deepen with practice as its outgoing nature is restrained and controlled. At this stage, it sees but does not fully grasp the truth of things without confusion and delusion. As the practice continues, it becomes even more restrained and rests in its natural, tranquil state, like a sea after an intense storm. It develops one-pointedness and intuitive awareness. In that advanced state of restfulness, free from feelings, emotions, memories, and other disturbances, the seer sees the world and the objective reality without judgment, interruptions, and discoloration. Beyond these, one enters the transcendental level, where pure awareness arises and persists, and the distinction between the observer and the observed disappears. This is the state of thoughtless, objectless, mental absorption (nirvikalpa samadhi), which is mentioned in several Buddhist and yoga texts.

Your mind is a facilitator as well as an interrupter. Left to itself, it stands between you and the world to conserve your energy and reserve it for more serious work and tasks meant for your survival. It does its best to keep you in a state of preparedness and readiness so that you will remain watchful and respond to any situation that may seem disturbing or troublesome for your peace and happiness or your survival and well-being. In the process, it filters a lot of useful information it deems unnecessary for the purpose and does not let you register or retain many memories that may prove burdensome for its normal functioning. In other words, Nature does not consider mindfulness practice to be required at all except in rare circumstances when your survival or well-being is at stake.

The Awakened Life

However, in spiritual practice, we arrest these natural functions of the mind and silence them to the extent possible so that we can become aware of the 'pure presence' of things as they are without their interference. You relearn to observe the world and grasp the true nature of things, or their impermanence and instability, without any framework of desires, expectations, preconceived notions, assumptions, like, and dislikes. If you are observant and mindful without becoming involved with your perceptions or the objects you perceive, be they your feelings and emotions or objects of the world, you will reach a point where all awareness rests on itself without your thoughts, movements, feelings, or emotions and the distinction between the knower and the known. In that pure seeing, the act of knowing dissolves into the act of seeing, leaving the seer with his seeing. In that unified state of focused awareness, observation becomes an inseparable part of effortless knowing. This is the goal spiritual aspirants cherish to free themselves from their minds' impurities.

The path to that cherished objective is not through mechanical or intellectual learning but through unlearning and emptying all that interferes with your seeing and knowing. In worldly life, we spend quite a lot of time educating ourselves to be competitive and successful. Modern education prepares us for the challenges we face in the world and helps us overcome the obstacles to secure a comfortable or even successful living. It teaches us how to be intelligent and successful in a complex, ambiguous, and competitive world. However, it does not teach us how to train our minds and senses and gain the right knowledge, the right view, and the right understanding. It does not teach us how to develop one-pointedness and see the world with clarity and discernment. You will learn that in the journey of your life if you are intent on cultivating it.

The world's profound wisdom is hidden in the simple truths of life. We ignore them because we may take them for granted or do not let our minds think about them. We may also let ourselves be distracted by numerous frivolous matters and waste our energies. The human mind is Nature's great marvel. We have to know its potential and faculties fully. All our knowledge, perceptions, memories, feelings, emotions, understanding, discernment, self-awareness, speech, etc., arise from it. Practically, it represents our identity and defines our lives and actions. At the same time, it is also inherently flawed since its essential purpose is not to enlighten us but to protect us. Therefore, if we want to bring it from survival mode to pure awareness mode, we need to purify it and prepare it for higher knowing and learning. In this regard, the following suggestions are useful.

1. **Practice mindfulness and become more observant.** Mindfulness practice is a very benign way to train the mind, remain in the present, and become more attentive and perceptive. It can be practiced everywhere. Even while performing routine tasks, such as breathing, walking, eating, sleeping, resting, reading, speaking, etc. You can practice it on yourself to learn more about your thoughts, motives, emotions, feelings, attachments, and states of mind.

2. **Slow down, pause in between, and live in the present.** We live in an age of rush. We hurry through our daily routines and have little time to relax or pay attention. By slowing down and pausing between your actions, you can reset your mind and return to the present. You can see the world around you in more detail. Life is impermanent. It is always in perpetual motion and is never the same. So is everything that surrounds you and exists inside you. What has perished or gone into the depths of time will not return. You may only see its variations and altered versions, which you may not even recognize. Therefore, it makes sense to use every possible opportunity to savor the precious moments of life and learn from your experiences and perceptions. We habitually ignore them in our anxiety to meet our obligations or reach deadlines. When you pause in between your work and look around, you give yourself an opportunity to regain your composure and your inner balance.

3. **Develop emotional intelligence.** There is a definite advantage in keeping your mind quiet by learning to observe your emotions and reactions, understand their underlying causes, and control your responses. You can stabilize your mind by observing and understanding your feelings and emotions and remaining detached or indifferent. If you persist, over time, your mind will be free from worries, anxieties, reactivity, and the usual mental chatter. With increased awareness, you will see the world with greater clarity, calmness, concentration, curiosity, and openness.

4. **Stay in the present.** If we are lost in thoughts of the past or future, we have little time to observe life or live in the present. We live for a limited time on earth. In that short span of life, we hardly stay in the present. This means we waste much of our lives not

truly living and experiencing life but reminiscing and worrying. If you stay in the present, you will experience life more profoundly and spontaneously without putting your mind on autopilot and having no true friends or genuine relationships. You will not respond to others with mechanical, superficial, and habitual reactions, responses, games, and rituals in which most people indulge due to their preoccupation with themselves. The mind and senses are, by nature, restless and outgoing due to desires, worries, and anxieties. You can bring it back by shifting your attention from the world outside to the world within you or to your immediate surroundings where also much drama happens.

5. **Suspend your judgment and critical nature**. In moments of profound silence, when we are alone or in the company of others, we observe the world more profoundly and minutely, setting aside our judgments and critical attitudes. Many times, we do not observe life at all or see others as they are because either they do not interest us or we judge them prematurely using our preconceived notions, surface impressions, or deep-rooted biases. Life becomes more interesting if you free your mind from likes and dislikes, preferences and prejudices, and observe life more profoundly and objectively. Our spiritual traditions greatly emphasize the need to cultivate detachment, renunciation, sameness, and indifference for this reason only. These virtues help us cultivate undistilled observation, free from the usual barriers that prevent us from seeing and knowing. If you suspend your judgment and remain detached and observant, you see things with greater awareness and discernment and without filters, distractions, and the usual disturbances that plague our minds.

6. **Become more reflective and thoughtful**. Most of the time, we are so busy with immediate and pressing problems that we do not find time to be alone or pay attention to our thoughts and feelings. Introspection is helpful in cultivating mindfulness as it makes us sensitive to our own thoughts and feelings and what happens outside. Therefore, spare some time, at least occasionally, to reflect on your thoughts and actions without judgment or critical attitude and without negative self-talk disturbing you, and become self-aware.

7. **Train your senses**. Your senses are extremely useful for developing awareness and becoming more perceptive about yourself and your world. Engage your senses mindfully to become more perceptual. Pay particular attention to forms, sounds, tastes, smells, touch, thoughts, and experiences to cultivate pure awareness. If you train your senses and see the world closely and minutely without becoming involved, you will experience life more profoundly and develop a unique perspective on the reality around you and inside you.

8. **Rest your mind and relax**. Rest is an important part of a disciplined and healthy lifestyle. Whatever the daily pressures, we need to take adequate rest and conserve our physical and mental energies. When we are tired, we tend to be careless. If we rest and recuperate, we will have more energy and stamina to spend our days and active time with enthusiasm and focus.

9. **Let go of your ego and the urge to control**. When you surrender to God or let go of your urge to control and resolve whatever you dislike or resist, you will also let go of the weight of the ownership and doership of your actions and find opportunities to relax and live in the present, unburdened by worries and anxieties. It does not mean that you should neglect your obligatory duties and responsibilities or your mindfulness practice. You must continue to perform to them, but without worrying about the results and accepting whatever happens as God's will or a learning opportunity.

Self-awareness means being aware of what happens in your mind and body. For that, you must pay attention to your thoughts, actions, feelings, instincts, and sensations and how they create your present reality and awareness. You must also know why and how your suffering arises and how your mind distorts your reality and keeps you deluded from knowing the truths of yourself or the world you see and experience. The mind personifies and exemplifies impermanence more than any other organ in our bodies. Its movements are never the same. It is always in flux. Even the feelings and emotions we experience have several gradations and levels of intensity. We do not experience any of them, be it anger, fear, envy, or pride, with the same intensity. They rise and fall with varying levels of strength according to the situation. Sometimes, we fear more, and sometimes, we fear less. The same is true about all other emotions. We must learn to label them and assess their levels of intensity to know them and remain untouched by them. We should not suppress them but learn to remain indifferent to them. It is possible only through observation and mindfulness practice.

If we become indifferent to the world and still our minds, we can see things as they are. Seeing things as they are means having better awareness and discernment. With mindfulness practice, you may not reach complete perfection in cultivating direct, nonjudgmental, and dispassionate awareness. However, even a little practice will open you to experience life more consciously and actively and resolve your problems and suffering with greater awareness and understanding. Through mindfulness and seeing things as they are, you can cultivate the right view. Through the right view, you will arrive at the right knowledge and right understanding (prajna). When you have the right understanding and discernment (buddhi), you will know what to do in any given situation. You will be close to the Buddha's mind.

Jayaram V

The Spiritual Aspects of Food

It is very fine to escape into meditation and, from the height of one's so-called grandeur, look down on material things, but one who is not a master in his own home is a slave. The Mother of Aurobindo Ashram

There is no universal diet that fits every body type. You must choose the right food according to your specific body type, your occupation or lifestyle, and your environment. Jayaram V

In social conversations and spiritual discussions, we often hear about the importance of a vegetarian diet in one's spiritual or physical well-being. In recent times, it has gained widespread recognition due to the increasing awareness about its importance as a healthy lifestyle choice. Some even scoff at it as an elitist fad. The fact is vegetarian diet has been the focal point of India's spiritual traditions for millenniums. This topic usually surfaces in many writings and discussions about Hindu, Buddhist, and Jain beliefs and practices. These traditions also promote the virtue of nonviolence and proscribe meat eating as a part of one's spiritual purification. Hinduism and Buddhism permit nonvegetarian food for lay people with certain conditions. However, Jainism prohibits it completely, without exceptions.

The question that frequently arises and evokes varied responses in today's conflicted world is why people should not eat animal protein when, biologically and physiologically, it is rich in proteins that are so important for our health, strength, and well-being. In this regard, we mainly come across three divergent opinions, each with its own spiritual and ethical implications.

1. Eating meat is not sinful, unethical, or evil. It is not against Nature either. Meat is a perfect human diet. God created animals to serve humans, especially for their nourishment and support, and to help them survive. They also help us in numerous other ways, apart from serving as food. Therefore, it is perfectly acceptable to use them for food as long we treat them humanely and do not cause them suffering or kill them unnecessarily. By using them for food, we are not violating any natural or divine laws. We are just letting Nature work through us.

2. Animal food is certainly sinful and should be avoided by all means since it is sinful to hurt and harm animals, and it results in

sinful karma. All living beings possess souls. They go through the same cycle of births and rebirths as humans and evolve from birth to birth. Animals are meant to serve humans, just as humans are meant to serve gods and nourish them through sacrifices by offering sacrificial food. Human life is precious because a living being attains it after innumerable births and deaths. Further, it gives all humans a unique opportunity to escape from samsara and attain liberation. Therefore, even though humans have the option to eat animal food, they should avoid it to purify themselves and cultivate divine nature and virtues like compassion to escape from samsara. It is especially prohibited for spiritual people since animal food strengthens animal nature, and eating it violates the practice of nonviolence.

3. Your food choices should depend upon your spiritual and material goals. Whether you are religious or irreligious, worldly or materialistic, you should live responsibly and minimize the suffering you may cause to others, whether they are humans or nonhumans. Further, indiscriminate destruction of life on earth will destroy the balance of life on earth and endanger our very survival. Meat is also not necessary for our survival. We can also secure protein from different sources without having to kill animals. Since there are strong reasons on both sides, one may use discretion and eat meat if they find it acceptable or if their lifestyles demand it. Otherwise, they should avoid it and rely exclusively on vegetarian diets.

Hinduism permits meant for certain categories of people. The law books permit eating meat for all people subject to several conditions and exceptions. In Buddhism, it is allowed, subject to monastic rules. As some historical accounts suggest, the historical Buddha ate meat when it was offered to him without his asking. He might have done it to exemplify renunciation or desirelessness. When you renounce desires, you must also renounce likes and dislikes. The desire to avoid or not eat meat is also a desire and a form of attachment to aversion. Therefore, the Buddha probably never objected if someone offered him nonvegetarian food. Thereby, he exemplified true detachment or freedom from attraction and aversion. In several schools of Buddhism, the monastic code allows eating certain types of meat. The Hindu law books also follow a similar approach.

The pros and cons

The choice of the non-vegetarian diet evokes varied responses and many lingering questions. It is not considered a problem for those whose religious or spiritual beliefs explicitly permit them to indulge in it. However, it becomes a problem, and people would surely like to know the moral or spiritual implications if they are explicitly prohibited from eating it or even cautioned against it. In today's world, meat-eating is not just a moral or religious issue. Several health problems are associated with it, besides its implication for the preservation and continuation of life on Earth. We are now aware that the Planet has already gone through several cycles of mass extinction, and if we have to believe the latest data on it, we may be near another and maybe just a few decades away. We may, therefore, continue to indulge in our old ways of killing animals for food and enjoyment, presuming that God will take care of everything. Alternatively, we may act responsibly, establishing proper controls to ensure that the planet survives and that life continues.

Food is the main source of our energy. What you eat becomes a part of you. Our bodies are essentially made up of the food we eat. Animals may or may not have souls. However, they suffer from pain and experience a wide range of emotions, just like humans. They react emotionally and experience pain, just like us, when they are hurt. They do have a longing for life as we do, fight for their survival, and do their best to propagate themselves. They may not have our intelligence, but they do have many qualities similar to ours and are better than humans in many respects. Most importantly, they are living things, and their survival is vital to our survival. Therefore, anyone with some moral compunction and educated awareness would not appreciate the slaughtering of any animals, especially the wild ones, and more importantly, those on the verge of extinction, and deem that as an act of cruelty and selfishness.

To understand the implications of meat eating, it is crucial to comprehend the significance of food in human life and how it may affect our mental, spiritual, and physical well-being, in addition to its health implications. This understanding becomes even more important if you have spiritual aims and believe in karma and the afterlife. When we think of the spiritual significance of food, the following truths stand out. By analyzing them carefully, we can ascertain the moral and spiritual implications of our food choices and where we need to exercise discretion.

- Food is a source of energy
- Food helps us in our transformation and liberation
- You share your food with the gods in your body
- Treat food as a sacrificial offering to God
- Follow the scriptures to cultivate discernment

1. Food is a source of energy

The material universe is filled with abundant energy of various types. All existence is the play of energy only from the most apparent to the most invisible. The same energy exists in every object of the universe in different forms and conditions. Food is also a form of energy that sustains and nourishes life on Earth. It is the connecting link and the universal feature of all animate and inanimate forms. Our scriptures recognize food as the source of all life on earth and in heaven. Even gods require food, which they receive from humans through sacrificial offerings. Thus, food is life-sustaining and responsible for the progress of creation. We receive energy not only from food but in other ways. For example, our subtle bodies receive vital energy from prana, the subtle energy that pervades the whole world. Energy is also exchanged through speech, thoughts, actions, blessings, mantras, prayers, blessings, touch, desires, devotion, and divine grace. The physical body receives nourishment mainly from the elements (fire, water, etc.) present in the food. Hence, it is known as the food body (annamaya kosa). All spiritual practices also involve transfer, transformation, purification, and cleansing of the various forms of energy present in the mind and body. Through spiritual practices such as yoga, we purify and transform the energy present in the body and awaken the higher energies (Shaktis) that assist us in our liberation. They purify our animal nature, reinforce our divine nature, and help us stabilize our minds in divine thoughts.

2. Food helps us in our transformation and liberation

The food we eat determines our essential nature and our predominant modes (gunas), namely Sattva, Rajas, and Tamas. These modes are responsible for desires and attachments. They are also in perpetual conflict and try to suppress each other to establish their dominance. They are also responsible for our karma and the suffering that follows since they induce desire-ridden actions and bind us to samsara. All three modes are problematic. As long as they are active, one is never free from desires or the modifications they induce through desires and attachment. These modes persist in our bodies and gain strength due to the food we eat. If we eat sattvic food, we strengthen the mode of Sattva and weaken the other two. The same happens when we eat the other two types of food. Therefore, spiritual people should pay particular attention to the food they eat. As far as possible, they should eat sattvic food only and avoid eating rajasic and tamasic food. Meat is predominantly rajasic and tamasic and strengthens animal passions such as anger, pride, lust, envy, and fear. Hence, those on the path of liberation or practicing yoga should avoid meat by all means. Meat eating is prohibited for spiritual people for other reasons mentioned below.

1. Meat eating strengthens rajasic and tamasic modes, animal passions, animal nature, and the grossness of the body. It also leads to the accumulation of other impurities, such as egoism, desires, attachments, and delusion, which delay liberation and prolong suffering and bondage.

2. When animal food is consumed without due process and with desires and attachments, the animal's karma, along with the energy present in it, is also transferred to the person who consumes it. At the same time, the animal receives a part of the person's good karma, which facilitates its evolution and a better life in the next birth. Therefore, the person who eats meat suffers from two disadvantages.

3. Those who believe in the law of karma should know the implications of killing animals for food or subjecting them to undue suffering. While killing in itself is a mortal sin and bad karma, those who eat meat by killing animals are further exposed to the risk of being born as animals in their future lives.

4. Animal food is not good for health because it contains cholesterol and several harmful substances. Therefore, even purely from a worldly or health perspective, it is better to avoid eating meat.

These are long-held beliefs, and we are not discussing their merits or demerits. It is sufficient to know that many religious and spiritual traditions do not view meat-eating favorably and advise people to exclude all types of meat or meat products from their food.

3. You share your food with the gods in your body

The body is a small universe in itself. In each body is hidden a Person (the divine Self), just as the Cosmic Self is hidden in the material universe or the whole creation. Both these worlds, the microcosm and the macrocosm, are similar in many respects. In the microcosm of the body, divinities also exist, presiding over functions of the organs in the body. They reside in the higher nature and regulate the higher chakras, higher tattvas, mental faculties, subtle energies, and divine qualities. Just as the gods in creation, they face constant attacks from evil forces, the demons, who reside in the body in the lower nature and regulate baser instincts, animal nature, and demonic qualities. Both the gods and demons in our bodies gain strength from the food we eat, the thoughts we entertain, and the actions we perform. If we eat sattvic food, we will strengthen the gods and give them extra energy to fight the evil ones. If we eat impure food, such as meat, we will nourish the evil forces and energize them. That will make it difficult for gods to control our inner universe and establish order and regularity.

Thus, food plays an important role in deciding which nature prevails in us in the battle between the gods and demons of our inner universe. If we eat food that is rich in animal energy, the demons gain strength, while the gods suffer due to lack of nourishment. If we eat food that is pleasing to the gods, they gain strength, while the demons lose their strength and diminish. When gods are strong, pleasant thoughts, positive energies, and sacred feelings arise in our consciousness. When demons are strong, we experience the opposite and suffer from violent emotions and negative thoughts. For the people who believe in the inviolability of the Vedas, this is not just a theory. It was what the Vedic people believed as they internalized rituals. By performing elaborate rituals, both externally and internally, they kept the gods in them and the macrocosm happy and contended. They assisted gods by fighting on their behalf against the demons in them and diminishing their strength. Therefore, spiritual aspirants should be careful whom they nourish through their food, thoughts, actions, desires, intentions, etc. They have to decide whether they want to strengthen their animal nature or divine nature and whom they want to assist through their thoughts and actions.

In today's world, gods must be having a tough time. They must be having tough times in our inner world also since most people do not nourish them well through their thoughts and actions. One can imagine what will happen if this trend continues. The gods will gradually lose strength and fade into the background as evil nature gains the upper hand and the demons take control of our minds and bodies. With their increasing presence, their bodies will become virtual hells, filled with baser desires, animal passions, emotional turbulence, pain, and suffering. With more people falling under their influence and gods losing control, the world will fall into chaos. Dharma will decline, and evil will gain ascendence. The Puranas suggest that when this happens, and the situation goes out of control, the Supreme God will incarnate on Earth as Kalki and destroy evil to start another cycle of creation.

According to our scriptures, the gods and demons are not merely symbolic or imaginary figures. They are real beings ever engaged in a constant battle to take control of the worlds they inhabit. For them, the earth (and our bodies) is a major battlefield because it is the only world where spiritual transformation and liberation are possible. If the gods lose control, it would be a major setback for our world and our spiritual progress. We should, therefore, live righteously and keep the gods in us stronger and in control of our minds and bodies, simultaneously doing our best to suppress our lower nature and evil tendencies.

4. Treat food as a sacrificial offering to God

The best way to ensure that we nourish the gods in us is by offering our food to God before eating it. God purifies the food when it is offered to Him with faith and devotion. He also ensures that the divinities present in the body receive their share of the food. Even if you offer food that is not pleasing to them, He will neutralize any impurities present in it and make it fit for them. According to the Bhagavadgita, those who eat food without offering it to God verily eat sin. Everything in the universe belongs to God. Even we belong to Him. The Isa Upanishad suggests that since He inhabits everything and owns everything, we should not covet what does not belong to us and find enjoyment in renunciation and doing our works as ordained by him. When you hold God as the true owner of everything, it makes sense to offer Him before you eat any food because it rightfully belongs to Him. Many religions encourage remembering and thanking God or offering it to him in gratitude before eating it. By your offering, the food becomes a sacrificial offering. Hence, no sin will touch you if you eat it. With that offering, the impurities present in the food become neutralized, and you will be shielded from them. Logically, you may eat any food once you offer it to God. However, as you develop deep devotion and cultivate the divine nature, you may not like to indulge in cravings or eat prohibited food. Apart from eating pure food, equally important is who prepares it, how it is prepared, and with what attitude since it may imbibe both positive and negative energies of those who prepare and serve it.

5. Follow the scriptures to cultivate discernment

The early Vedic Indians most likely shared among themselves the sacrificial meat they offered to gods during sacrificial ceremonies as the remains of the sacrifice to nourish the gods in them. Subsequently, meat-eating became a taboo when ascetic movements and faiths such as Buddhism and Jainism, with their emphasis on nonviolence and the renunciation of desires, gained prominence. Meat is still used for worship and spiritual transformation in a few left-hand rituals of Hinduism and Buddhism. Although Buddhism upholds non-violence as the highest virtue, its monastic code (Vinaya) allows meat-eating with certain rules and restrictions. The Hindu law books follow a similar approach. They prohibit certain types of meat and specify a strict code of conduct for the rest.

According to the Upanishads, food is a manifestation of the Supreme Being or Brahman. They affirm that everything manifests from food: the entire material creation, all the divinities, and living beings. Hence, they instruct worshippers to treat food with respect as a life-giving and life-nourishing divinity and perform sacrifices with it to uphold creation. Since the gross physical body is made up of food only, human beings will be better off by not eating impure food that promotes animal nature and keeping their minds and bodies free from impurities arising from it. By making intelligent choices with discernment, they can strengthen their divine nature and keep their minds and bodies in good health.

The Bhagavadgita recognizes the importance of food in purifying and spiritually liberating bound souls. It recognizes food according to the triple gunas present in them. They determine a person's essential nature depending upon which of them he chooses. Ideally, on the path of liberation, one should eat sattvic food to strengthen divine qualities. In worldly life, it depends upon a person's way of life or occupation. The distinguishing features of these three types of food are stated below.

1. **Sattvic food** is juicy (rasya), oily (snigdhah), stable or wholesome (sthirah), and pleasing to the heart. It promotes longevity (āyu), purity (sattva), strength (balam), health (ārogyam), happiness (sukham), and satisfaction (priti). This is the food of gods.

2. **Rajasic food** is bitter (katu), sour (amla), salty (lavana), very hot (ati uśhna), pungent (tikśhana), dry (ruksa), and overcooked or deep fried (vidahina). It increases the grossness of the body, incites passions, and causes pain, discomfort, and diseases. It is the preferred choice of worldly people.

3. **Tamasic food** is not fresh (yata yamam), tepid (gata rasam), putrid (puti), leftover (ucchistam), intoxicating or sleep-inducing, and impure (amedhyam). It promotes lethargy, inertia, ignorance, delusion, grossness, animal nature, cruelty, and carelessness. It is the preferred choice of those who possess an evil nature and have the least respect for tradition and convention.

From these descriptions, we can infer that meat is not a sattvic food. Depending on how it is cooked and stored, it is either rajasic or tamasic. Maybe it attains purity if offered to gods and accepted as the remains of a sacrifice, as in the past. However, that practice is now discontinued and prohibited by the mainstream practice of Hinduism. Therefore, those who want to cultivate purity and pursue spiritual goals should avoid meat and meat-based products by all means.

Purification, Transformation, and Liberation

In spiritual life, concepts are not as important as practice. To achieve progress on the path, the mind ought to be silent and empty without being distracted and dragged into objectification. However, concepts are important and necessary to cultivate the right knowledge and arrive at the right understanding of the methods we want to practice, the goals we want to reach, and the right solutions to the problems we face. We usually learn them from our teachers and scriptures or through self-study. Concepts such as the Self, the Supreme Self, the ego-self, samsara, rebirth, suffering, liberation, etc., strengthen and stabilize our faith and serve as lampposts on the path. However, as long as we are caught in them intellectually and entertain desires and expectations about them, our spiritual goals remain unattainable ends or distant dreams.

Liberation is a long and uncertain journey. We have no definitive roadmaps about it. It is a fluid process because the methods and the whole journey are not set in stone and can vary according to the seekers and circumstances. As one teacher expressed it, it is a journey through a pathless land. Perhaps that path disappears as soon as one walks on it, leaving no trace of it for others to follow exactly step by step. In this long journey, our minds and intelligence are not very helpful, except in the initial stages. As we progress, we have to renounce and transcend them along with the body to attain the pure intelligence and consciousness that exist beyond them. We must invent solutions as we face the problems. In this discussion, we will focus on a few important concepts about the process of liberation.

The physical self

Each living being (jiva) is a combination of the pure Self or the Person and the physical self, also known as the body or the not-self. The pure Self represents pure consciousness that is self-existent, eternal, infinite, and indestructible. For our discussion and understanding we may refer to it as the Self or the Person or both alternatively. The not-self or the physical self represents the field of energy and objectified consciousness arising from the mind and body, along with all the impurities. By body, we mean all its parts (tattvas), including the ego, the mind, and intelligence. The ego is known as aham in Sanskrit. In a human being, it represents egoism (ahamkar) or the illusion of being an individual, separate and distinct from others. It produces the feeling of separation and atomicity (anavatvam) or the false sense of having an existence that is complete in itself and independent of the whole creation. Hindu scriptures describe it as one of the higher productions or evolutes (tattvas) of Nature. In humans, it joins with intelligence, the mind, and the senses to form what is known as the internal organ (antahkarana) or the inner sense, which is responsible for all cognitive functions of the mind. The ego takes control of the physical Self (whole mind and body) and assumes its lordship, which is chiefly responsible for our bondage and suffering. According to the yoga traditions, the yogis who are intent on liberation and self-purification must silence their egos, cultivate discernment, and withdraw their minds and senses from the world through detachment and renunciation to attain the deeper states of self-absorption or mental absorption (samadhi). In this discussion, I have given egoism a more general and broader interpretation, not in the limited sense of having pride or the sense of superiority about oneself or one's virtues and abilities, which is how it is generally interpreted in common usage. From a spiritual perspective, the ego is a problem and a major obstacle. It represents your identity or the false of being a distinct person whereby you will experience attachment to your name and form, desires and delusion.

The physical self is also a problem on the spiritual path because it is the seat of many impurities that keep you bound and ignorant. You cannot discard it because your existence in this world depends upon it. It is also essential to achieve liberation. Spiritually speaking, your physical self is a temporary construct that veils your true Self or essential nature and appears to you and others as your true Self. It usurps your identity and appears to you and the world as you.

Human egos are self-preserving constructs that tend to clash with others for survival and continuity. It is in their nature to be competitive, controlling, delusional, and judgmental. Hence, when novices begin their journey, the initial resistance and obstacles they face are from their egos only. Their egos control them as long as they remain stuck in duality and diversity and cannot discern their essential nature or the oneness of the whole existence. However, as they progress on the path and cultivate discernment, they realize the truth of themselves and stabilize their minds in the silence of their minds to attain their deeper and tranquil consciousness, the door to the nondual state of pure consciousness. When they reach it through self-absorption, they become seers (drashtas) or knowers of themselves (jnanis). Cultivating this distinction is important on the spiritual path to overcome delusion, desires, and attachments and stabilize the mind in sameness, which, according to the Bhagavadgita, is the highest state of yoga or samadhi itself.

There is a certain tragedy about our physical existence or ego existence because it is the real sufferer, the visually impaired king, who is bound to his duty, lives in fear, is subject to duality, and cannot enjoy life since he suffers from endless wants and desires to fill the void that he experiences within himself or protect his kingdom. He is also unsure whether he is the real king or usurper. He is never free from fear because of the fear of death and the uncertainty of life. The thoughts of impermanence and fear of losing what he has always haunt him and make him self-defensive and overly protective. From our mental perspective, the physical self is the apparent self, mistakenly accepted by our logical mind (buddhi) as the real Self. It is an impurity that clogs our consciousness and prevents us from seeing things as they are. It cannot be washed away until we bring the waters of liberation, River Ganga, from the highest heaven and dissolve it.

The true Self

We believe that behind this apparent physical self, which is ruled by the ego, is the hidden consciousness or the pure Self or the Person (Purusha). If the ego with its henchmen (the mind, the senses, and intelligence) represents the surface consciousness or what we generally understand as the mind, the true Self represents the pure consciousness that does not belong to the mind or arise from it but exists by itself in everyone as their substratum or support. This real Self or Person is not associated with Nature even when it is embodied by it. Being the same in all, it has the same essential nature and consciousness of the Universal Self and is not subject to the limitations of energy, time, knowledge, skills, and space. Self-contained and self-supporting, it acts as the support for the physical self, enabling the latter to experience liveliness (chaitanyam) and dynamism of the mind and intelligence. It is described in the scriptures as the indescribable, eternal, absolute, stable, indestructible, blissful, and transcendental Self. Its essential nature is pure consciousness, which is otherworldly, self-luminous (svyamprakasa), self-existent, and self-aware.

The Self or the Person has the attributive knowledge of the material universe (dharma bhuta jnana) as well as self-knowledge (atma svarupa jnana). He does not participate in creation on its own but is rather drawn into it by Nature. He is not subject to transformation or suffering since He is separate from the body. Even when He continues His existence as an embodied soul, He remains untouched by the activities of Nature. Since He is indestructible, he survives death, and even though He is held in captivity by Nature, He is not subject to suffering, duality, or delusion. This Self or the Person is not an abstract notion or some philosophical concept but can actually be experienced in transcendental as well as wakeful states by yogis who transcend their minds and bodies.

The true Self has no materiality and no association with names and forms. Hence, it cannot be visualized or described physically or conceptually. However, as novices eager to understand it, we can use our imagination and guess vaguely what it can be or how it may exist. Imagine an invisible entity, nameless, formless, self-luminous, self-existent, completely free, silent, passive, detached, dispassionate, and without any predicates, mind, body, desire, thought, memory, name, form, senses, impulse, feeling, or emotion, but just a glowing light of pure consciousness, on which depend all things and in which exists the selfsame awareness of, "I am" all the time without any distinction, desires, wants, associations or attachments. Conceptualize a self-illumined entity without a body that can exist in all and, at the same time, extends beyond everything and pervades the whole universe. Imagine that which is not the mind, the body, the organs, the senses, the objects, or anything that you can perceive or know with your mind and intelligence.

According to the Upanishads, the Self that inhabits living beings is the same as the Universal Self. It is smaller than the smallest and larger than the largest. However, the Upanishads are not very explicit about their respective statuses, whether they are the same or different, and if they are different, whether any connection exists between the two. They describe the individual Self as Atman and the Supreme Self as Brahman. In the body, Atman is passive, but in the universe, Brahman, who manifests as Isvara in association with Prakriti, his materiality, is described as its presiding lord, controller, creator, destroyer, concealer, and revealer. They also admit that both the Self and Brahman are great mysteries. Nothing definitively can be said about them, their reach, power, potencies and abilities. They even go to the extent of saying that they are indescribable, indefinable, unknown, unfathomable, mysterious, and those who think they know him do not know him, and those who admit they do not know perhaps know.

The two Selves that rest on the Tree of Life

Thus, from the above discussion, we can discern that at least three entities participate in the process of liberation: the not-self or the physical self, the Person in the body (the individual Self), and the Cosmic Person in creation (the Supreme Self). Of them, a seeker of liberation has to transcend or silence the first one to realize the second and or the third. For our discussion, we will not distinguish between the individual Self and the Supreme Self but regard them as the same since they represent the same absolute, incorporeal, and infinite reality. That leaves us with two facets of creation: the Self and the not-self, also known as Purusha (Person) and Prakriti (Nature). They are the two faces of creation. Purusha, Brahman, or the Self, represents the pure, infinite, eternal, indestructible, and absolute consciousness without any trace of duality, division, or impurity. Prakriti represents the materiality, or energy and matter. Again, the Upanishads are not clear whether she is an independent entity or an aspect of Brahman. For our discussion, we presume that she is an aspect of Brahman only and manifests in creation along with him to set in motion the whole creation.

Thus, Purusha and Prakriti exist in all of us and the whole creation as inseparable companions. They represent the fundamental duality of the whole existence, like light and darkness, the yin and yang, the archetypal male and the female, the pure and the impure, and matter and consciousness, who coexist without having to meet each other or know each other. Maybe at the highest level or in their absolute state, they are the same, appearing as dual and interdependent in creation for the sake of manifesting diversity and staging a universal play.

Regarding these Selves, namely the physical self (Prakriti), the individual Self (Atman), and the Universal Self (Brahman), the various schools of Hinduism differ in their views about their respective status and relationship. The following are the different views of their relationship found in the scriptures of the schools of Vedanta.

1. Atman and Brahman are the same.
2. Atman and Brahman are different.
3. Prakriti represents Brahman's dependent materiality.
4. Prakriti is independent of Brahman and acts on her own.
5. Atman is an illusion. Brahman alone exists and is the only absolute reality.
6. Atmans are numerous and of different types. There is no Supreme Self.

It is not possible to discuss each of them in detail. For this discussion, we assume that the same Person (Self) appears in the jivas as Atman and in creation as Brahman, and His essential nature is the nondual state of pure consciousness. In the embodied state, He illuminates the ego present in the jiva's physical body (the Field of Prakriti), which results in the formation of an independent and ego-driven entity and the illusion of its distinction and continuity. This false self or ego assumes a separate identity, ownership, and doership of all actions due to delusion and duality and moves around, seeking and striving for the things it desires. The Brihadaranyaka Upanishad describes how the sense of individuality manifested from the Self.

"In the beginning, the Self alone existed in the shape of a person (purusha). Looking around, He saw nothing but Himself. Then He said, 'I am He.' Therefore, It became He by name. Therefore, even now, if a man is asked, he first says, 'I am,' and then pronounces any other name he may have."

According to this verse, the one Self became two and subjected itself to duality. In the Jiva, the ego takes control, which results in the ego experiencing the duality between the knower and the known or the subject and the object and assuming itself as the true Self, Lord, and enjoyer. While the Self ("I am") remains hidden in the background, it develops associations, identities, and attachments and becomes a separate entity ("I am he") by itself. In reality, it is an effect, not the cause. It is also an illusion or temporary and unstable construct that manifests due to the aggregation of physical and mental objects or the union between Purusha and Prakriti. It disappears when the Self departs from the body. The real Self is different from this apparent self and remains hidden in the materiality beyond its reach. The awareness of pure "I am" is our indivisible experience in the absolute state of pure Self or pure consciousness. It is also the state of God, Isvara, or the Universal Self. The awareness of "I am he or she" is the false notion that arises due to delusion and association with Prakriti or the objective reality.

Whether the Self is one, two, or many does not matter to the seekers of liberation. They must realize that they are not of this world and that they are different from their physical personalities and ego identities and have no real relationship with them. Knowing that the body and the word are traps or the Fields of Maya that keep them bound to samsara through desires and attachments, they must detach themselves from their physical nature, cultivate discernment, surrender their egos and identities, and establish their minds in Brahman or the pure Self with exclusive devotion. The Bhagavadgita recommends this approach to escape from samsara.

The importance of withdrawing from the world

The experience of duality is responsible for our desires, our likes, dislikes, and our attachments, which in turn keep our minds and senses restless and outgoing. If we want to return to our original state of tranquil and expansive oneness, we must withdraw our minds and senses from the objective world and search for the center of calm within ourselves. In other words, we have to withdraw from the state of "I am he" to return to the pure state of "I am." First, we have to know how deeply we are involved with the world and how we delude and distract ourselves from knowing the truths of ourselves and our existence. With that discernment and awareness, we must then transform and purify all the false notions we entertain about ourselves, overcome the desires and attachments that perpetuate them, dissolve the boundaries we create to deal with fears and insecurities we experience, silence the chaos of the surface consciousness and find the pure state of tranquility that is free from all these and in which the Self alone exists all by itself.

Transforming the ego is not easy because, in the process of stretching out and becoming involved with the objective world, like a tree whose roots penetrate deep into the earth, the ego becomes deeply entangled and entrenched with the objective world. It expands its sway in the field of its play through its mind and senses, pursuing its cravings, attachments, attraction, and aversion. It results in the formation of the jiva, a very complex being with numerous qualities and a distinct personality. The jiva possesses a physical body, which is a production of Nature, and the Self, which is God's reflection or God himself. The Self remains hidden in the body behind the five sheaths (kosas), the outermost of which is the gross physical body, and the innermost is the subtle, bliss body. I have already described these five sheaths in a previous chapter. Therefore, I will not repeat them. The five bodies belong to the domain of Prakriti (nature). Together, they serve as her Field (kshetra) or the field of jiva's experience, existence, and enjoyment. The physical self is not the real Self. It is not the one that needs to be liberated from samsara. It perishes with death, unlike the real Self, which continues and transmigrates from one birth to another. The real Self is untouched by impermanence, change, or all the processes. At the time of death, it leaves the body with a residual karmic body consisting of latent impressions (samskaras) and dominant memories, which act as the seeds for its next birth.

The process of self-transformation

Self-transformation is the key to our liberation. If we want to continue the unwinding and emptying process to escape from the entanglements we create egoistically through desire-ridden actions and from the weight of karma, we must cleanse our whole bodies and their sheaths until no residues and impurities are left. In other words, liberation requires an intense self-purification process, without which one remains deluded and bound to samsara. We accomplish it through yoga. While there are several ways to achieve this, the most popular methods are found in the Yoga Sutras of Patanjali.

1. **Purification and transformation of the physical body.** This is done by observing the five abstentions (yamas): abstention from violence, lying, theft, sexual pleasure, and ownership, and the five observances (niyamas): purity, contentment, austerities, study, and devotion to the Self. The body is made supple, strong, and free from inertia (tamas) by practicing yogic postures (asanas) and following a sattvic (pure) diet.

2. **Purification and transformation of the mental body.** This is done by withdrawing the mind and senses (pratyahara) and by practicing concentration (dharana) and meditation (dhyana) while continuing the five abstentions and five observances.

3. **Purification and transformation of the energy body.** This must be done by regulating the five vital breaths through pranayama and purifying the energy field in the body with mantras, visualization, and meditation. One should purify the nadis (nerve channels) and meditate on the chakras to clear the obstruction in them and ensure the free flow of prana through them.

4. **Purification and transformation of the intelligence body.** This must be done by cultivating knowledge and discerning wisdom to overcome attraction and aversion, desires, delusion, and distortions in thinking. By studying the scriptures and serving the enlightened masters, the yogi illuminates his knowledge with the power of sattva. With detachment and renunciation, while continuing all the practices mentioned above, his intelligence becomes pure and one-pointed with penetrating insight, free from confusion and delusion. Endowed with it, he attains equanimity, freedom from desires, sameness, clarity, simplicity, and nonjudgmental awareness.

5. **Becoming aware of the bliss body.** This is the innermost body beneath all the above and is suffused with the bliss of the pure Self. It remains hidden beneath all the sheaths and requires no purification. It becomes self-evident when all other sheaths in the body are completely purified, and the yogis experience self-absorption and oneness with the pure consciousness of the Self without any trace of duality or otherness.

Guru and God in Liberation

The process of liberation is complicated by the accumulated (prarabdha) karma of the past, which operates inexorably and incessantly, making any possibility of release difficult to achieve. Even if a yogi attains liberation in his body, he still has to clear his prarabdha until he departs from here to attain final liberation. The scriptures provide some clues on how one can resolve. We have already discussed the importance of self-purification and how the mind and body can be purified from the outer to the inner. One can also resolve it by means of virtuous conduct, righteous living or right living, renunciation of desires and the desire for the fruit of actions, sacrificial and selfless actions, devotional service, ritual worship of gods and goddesses, charity, etc. The Bhagavadgita states that one can overcome bondage to samsara by securing God's grace through exclusive devotion. Some teacher traditions of Hinduism also cite the grace of a guru. According to them, a guru is essentially God in a human body. He is a pathfinder with the ability to transform individuals and liberate them from karma and samsara by blessing them or transferring his spiritual energy to them through touch and meditation. He can invoke shaktis and request them to purify his disciples and assist them in their journey toward liberation. Since he attains oneness with the Self and possesses such extraordinary abilities, his disciples can look upon him as God's true representative on earth and seek his help in their transformation and liberation.

The Spiritual Laws That Govern Our Lives

If we peer into the night sky, as far as our eyes and our thoughts go and as far as our scientific instruments go, we seem to be utterly alone on a small, fragile, and insignificant planet in an infinite universe, surrounded from all sides by vast spaces filled with countless celestial objects, mysterious forces, and rather frightening cosmic phenomena. If we look at the magnitude of the events that happen in the universe on a cosmic scale at any given moment and the degree of randomness at which they happen, we must consider ourselves fortunate to be alive and thriving as a species and part of a dynamic world brimming with life. With our limited knowledge and awareness, we may perhaps never obtain a full picture of the universe and its multiple dimensions or comprehend its diversity, immensity, and the secrets hidden in its vast depths. However intelligent and informed we may be, we are but a minuscule aspect of this gigantic universe, and we will never be able to measure its depths or stand apart from the outside and see it. If at all we come to know about alien life forms or extraterrestrial civilizations, it would be limited and most likely by chance.

We are not sure why we exist here or what purpose we really serve. There are many questions about our existence to which we do not have a clear answer. Are we all alone? Do we have a destiny to fulfill? Do the gods, or does the highest Supreme Being, in whom more than half of humanity believes, control this universe or determine our destinies? Do they exist at all? Do they listen to our requests, prayers, and aspirations? Do they really keep a watch on us and protect our planet, or leave it to be part of a grand design whose course and direction we do not know?

If God is one and indivisible and the source of all existence, on the surface, it does not make sense why we should have so many religions, prophets, scriptures, and paths to salvation, and why none of the religions and the teachings of the prophets and incarnations have guaranteed peace or happiness so far in our world on a universal and permanent basis. Most intriguingly, why are religions, meant to exalt and refine us, responsible for so much strife, division, bloodshed, and suffering among people? If God founded religions, would it be possible that they would cause delusion, suffering, conflicts, and violence for their followers? Despite all the learning, knowledge, and accumulated wisdom of thousands of years and despite the values they learn, it is not clear why humanity lets destruction, cruelty, and immorality prevail in their communities in the name of religion, caste, tribe, race, nation, or region. These and many more questions are difficult to answer. Our religions declare that God is the Creator and Controller of the world, and He delivers justice and sets everything right by punishing the wicked and rewarding the pious. However, when we delve into the details of how He does it, each religion comes out with its own set of theories, beliefs, and practices that have little in common with one another. We are not sure whether the fault lies with the teachings of our religions and beliefs or with ourselves.

Strange but true, the world offers many conflicting pictures of harmony, disharmony, chaos, and order. On the one hand, it presents a picture of confusion and uncertainty, where no one seems to be really in control, where events seem to happen by chance or accident, and where nothing seems to be permanent or dependable. It is as if we are caught in the labyrinth of a meaningless life and aimless activity, with no particular purpose or direction, and as if the world is a blind and mechanical automaton that would run its course for the duration of its existence, like any other celestial phenomena, in the chronicles of the universe and eventually disappear forever. From this perspective, we have no justification for why we need to live orderly lives or care for the higher aims in our lives. The approach of the atheistic materialists (lokayatas) of ancient India, who believed in the physical existence of life, like the existentialists of modern times, makes sense.

However, if we look at the world more reflectively and observantly, hidden beneath all the turmoil and confusion, we cannot fail to notice the intelligent blueprint of the universe, manifesting itself in various ways as intelligent forms, patterns, shapes, aspects, laws, energies, dimensions, objects and rhythmic movements of the universe. The Hindus call it Rta or, more generically, Dharma, which they consider to be an integral part of our existence, inseparable and inviolable. The rta, or the universal rhythm, is considered to be the functional aspect of God. It is the very law of God, inseparable from Him, which ensures the unity and integrity of the universe and imparts to it a certain degree of orderliness and predictability, thereby rendering the world into a meaningful, living, and holistic system that can respond intelligently and appropriately to the events and actions that impact it from within and without.

In a broader and secular sense, Dharma, or the divine law, represents a righteous force consisting of invisible forces, intelligent laws, and inviolable principles that hold the entire fabric of creation together as one unit, acting like invisible celestial glue and protecting it from the excesses of conflicting interests, disparate wills, and clashing egos. One need not have to be a believer in God to appreciate the orderliness of the universe, its intelligent patterns and rhythmic movements, and the precision and certainty with which the natural laws work.

The order and regularity of the universe that surrounds us from all sides is as astounding and miraculous as the birth of a newborn baby or the glitter of the night sky. We may not know whether it will rain or shine today, but we know when the next season will come or when and where the sun will set or dawn. Science admits to the existence of an invisible universe that is far more intriguing than the visible one and accepts the inviolability of certain physical and chemical laws that are universal, predictable, and provable. However, the invisible world that science speaks of is but an extension of the physical world or an aspect of it and its laws are very much within the realm of our sensory world.

The spiritual laws, on the other hand, belong to an ultra-invisible world. They are mostly beyond the grasp of our minds, senses, and intellect, and science, in its current form and with its methods, cannot validate them with the same certainty. With its precise methods of study and observation, science may explore the atoms and the subatomic particles of the material universe, but it cannot fathom the subtle elements hidden in it or our physical and mental bodies. Nor can it deal with the intangible truths, which our senses cannot validate. It may unravel the functioning of the brain or the human heart.

However, it cannot reach into the depths of the human consciousness to know how subtle emotions and aspirations arise and how they compel us to act in certain ways that defy human logic. It may prove the existence of physical laws with great precision and in detail, but it cannot comprehend and substantiate the spiritual laws that govern our lives in secretive and subtle ways.

Jayaram V

Spiritual laws

The spiritual laws found in our scriptures or seem to be operating in the world do not belong to the realm of the physical but the mental and the spiritual or to the super realm where the mind and the senses cannot go. They are not easily understandable with ordinary mental effort. They are even more difficult to prove or validate conclusively because, unlike the physical laws, they do not confirm a particular pattern, mechanism, or process. Their success or failure depends upon many factors, some of which are within our control, some beyond, some known, and the rest unknown. They do not always happen in a predictable manner or in a definite time frame since they are governed by several conditions and forces that we have yet to understand fully. Therefore, we have some difficulty in admitting their universality or inviolability, without the aid of faith and belief.

While the physical laws of science can be proved by experimentation, the spiritual laws that govern our lives can be validated only through personal experience or close observation. They may also vary according to the situation since the forces that govern them are also beyond our comprehension. In the spiritual world, the senses play a minimal role. Since a lot happens invisibly in the background, the senses are least reliable in discerning spiritual truths. Just as physical laws depend upon many factors, spiritual laws depend upon many factors to produce results. They are also subject to many constraints, such as the following.

1. They do not always yield the same results or work predictably as the physical laws.
2. They cannot be demonstrated objectively or universally in all conditions and situations.
3. Their success or failure depends upon many conditions. Some of them are known and within our control, but not all.
4. These laws are also subject to many mental and spiritual conditions that cannot be created predictably in a testing environment. They make each experience and outcome personal and subjective.
5. We understand a little about what hidden mechanisms, energies, and invisible laws are responsible for them.
6. Our subconscious minds, which are not entirely within our control, may also influence their workings, making them even more difficult to predict, manage, or control.

7. Sometimes, they work better if we express our wishes, remain passive, and let them do their work without exerting ourselves, interfering with them, or trying to control them.

Types of spiritual laws

The spiritual laws that govern our lives and all that exist here can be divided into the following categories.

1. Physical laws
2. Natural laws
3. Divine laws
4. Spiritual laws
5. Universal laws
6. Eternal laws
7. Manmade laws

By becoming aware of these laws, by realizing them and by knowing their true purpose, we can transform our consciousness and transcend our limitations. However, they do not work for everyone universally. Past karma, readiness, purity, faith, devotion to God, right knowledge, divine grace, clarity, mental stability, self-control, etc. influence their outcome. We are not listing these laws here because they can be found in the teachings of every major religion and spiritual tradition. You may already know them or how to use them. By becoming aware of them, understanding them, and practicing them with devotion, faith, and commitment, you can harness the powers of your mind and body, lay the foundation for an enlightened life, and fulfill your destiny.

In creation, everything is subject to certain laws. Even gods and celestial beings are subject to them. The higher worlds and planes have their respective laws. Some of them are inviolable and obligatory. Some are optional or situational. They ensure the order and regularity of the worlds and their continuity. In our world also, we are subject to numerous laws, some known, some unknown, some enforced by ourselves, and some by the gods of the higher planes. Nature (Prakriti) has its laws. She enforces them to ensure that beings remain bound to samsara, and if they want to escape from it, they must follow certain laws and overcome their impurities. We may not know them all, but they operate silently and shape our lives and destinies. They help us to know the right way to live, resolve, suffer, gain the right knowledge, overcome delusion and ignorance, practice virtues, and perform actions in certain ways to escape from samsara.

Jayaram V

By following them, we can improve our mental and spiritual well-being, cultivate discernment and purity, know our essential nature, and stay away from those who harm us or delay our progress. Just as we benefit from scientific discoveries and our understanding of the material universe, we can benefit from our spiritual discoveries and exploration of the spiritual world. The Vedas, Upanishads, the Bhagavadgita, Yoga Sutras, several other sacred texts, and the teachings of great masters contain numerous laws that govern our lives and help us improve our lives and overcome suffering. By studying them and knowing them, we can transform our lives and establish peace and happiness within ourselves.

The Bhagavadgita on Suffering and Its Causes

The Bhagavadgita is primarily a treatise on human suffering and its resolution through spiritual means, using the knowledge of various yogas to overcome the impurities of the mind and body, escape from karma through desireless actions and exclusive devotion, and attain liberation. It begins with sorrow as the central theme expressed by Arjuna which prompts Lord Krishna to teach him the secrets of overcoming it, and thus ends on a positive note. Lord Krishna teaches him the righteous way to escape from karma through karma-sannyasa without the need to avoid his duties and responsibilities by performing his actions without the desire for their results and offering them to God with exclusive devotion. The scripture assures that you can end your suffering through selfless effort, sacrifice, purity, self-control, yoga practice, and exclusive devotion. As the warrior prince who is bound to his duties, family, worldly values, and samsara, Arjuna represents the predicament of human beings who are confronted with moral dilemmas that cannot be resolved easily with action or inaction. Its knowledge can be applied to any situation since suffering is universal, and like Arjuna, we are stuck in samsara and subject to karma. We all are warriors in our lives in our ways. We fight many moral and spiritual battles within ourselves and outside. When we are pitted against powerful forces, we also suffer from moral dilemmas and experience fear, confusion, and despair.

When Arjuna surveyed the battlefield standing on his chariot and looking at all those who stood on both sides waiting for the war to begin, he realized the weight of the war, the death and destruction that would follow, how knowingly or unknowingly he might become responsible for the death of many, including his cousins, other relations, elders like Drona and Bhishma, friends and well-wishers. As he thought about it, he felt that by fighting, he might bring ruin upon his family, lose his reputation, and become a source of misery to countless people. Overwhelmed by fear and confusion, he told Sri Krishna that he would not fight, saying he would rather live seeking alms rather than fighting in the war and earning the riches of a kingdom.

Jayaram V

The Bhagavadgita on Suffering and Its Causes

Lord Krishna responded by teaching him the secrets of avoiding karma without renouncing actions and duties and enjoying both the riches of the world and liberation from samsara. He reminded him that he should never abandon actions because actions were not responsible for the karma or the consequences arising from them. Desires were the cause. Therefore, one should understand the causes of desires and attachments and deal with them without giving up actions. He told him that his duty was to fight since he was destined to slay the enemies as they were already fated to die by God's will as a part of his divine plan. Arjuna was merely an instrument in making that happen. Therefore, he should focus on his actions without assuming ownership or doership of his actions.

We should not take the story of the epic Mahabharata and the incidents surrounding the discourse of the Bhagavadgita at face value. We need to decipher the lessons hidden in them to understand their real value and relevance to our lives. One must also discern the symbolism hidden in them. The earth is a battlefield (Kurukshetra). So are our minds and bodies. We all are warriors destined to fight against many visible and invisible forces within ourselves and outside. We have to perform numerous actions to survive in this world and fulfill our obligations to all those to whom we owe a debt of gratitude. At the same time, we must find a way to escape from the karma that arises from our actions. We cannot avoid living, and at the same time, we cannot stop living, fearing the consequences. Therefore, we need a way to balance our lives, continue to live normally, and yet escape from this world and our suffering without damaging our souls. The Bhagavadgita offers a safe and practical way to resolve suffering and live normally.

If a warrior of the stature of Arjuna, with his training and awareness and with Lord Krishna himself standing by his side as his charioteer, was unable to deal with his sorrow and handle the situation well, imagine the plight of ordinary people like us who cannot take God's help and timely advice for granted. Imagine how difficult it would be for them to make critical decisions in their lives without any help or guidance, which may conflict with their personal beliefs and long-held moral values and against their relations and interests. According to the Bhagavadgita, human suffering is real, although not permanent. It is caused by many factors, some of which are external and some internal. Since we cannot deal with external circumstances entirely on our own, we need the help of God. Even to deal with the most ordinary problems and situations, we need the help of God because we do not know the consequences that may arise from our actions. Therefore, we need the guidance of God anyway. To believe that one can manage one's life entirely by one's efforts may fit in some people's worldview, especially when they do not believe in God and want to take full responsibility for their lives. God may not punish them for it, but it will be nonbelievers' burden to assume responsibility for their lives and actions and accept the consequences arising from them. The whole world belongs to God and everything in it. One may assume part ownership, but one has to pay a price for it, which is usually in the form of karma and the suffering that arises from it. If you believe that God inhabits and moves all that exists here, including you and your life, you better bring Him into your life and let Him take center stage.

We suffer for various reasons, but primarily because we exist in a state of duality, and we are attached to life and its attractions. Some people tolerate suffering well. Some have very little tolerance. But, knowingly or unknowingly, everyone suffers without exception. Suffering does not mean experiencing just pain or sorrow. They are the most common and visible symptoms of it. However, beneath the surface of our consciousness, we are subject to many disturbances, pressures, fears, inconveniences, emotions, and conflicts. We are in a perpetual state of conflict with diverse forces of nature to remain healthy and active. We fight against the forces of aging, climate and several diseases to protect our bodies from harm and injury. From the soul's perspective, we are in a state of imprisonment. We are prisoners of Nature not just for one lifetime but several. Therefore, it does not make anyone who understands it happier.

Suffering is inherent in our existence. It is rooted in the very principles which are responsible for our survival and propagation. It is the price that we pay to continue on earth and perpetuate our interests and identities. We are programmed to suffer because, without it, we will not look beyond our narrow concerns and see life as the soul's predicament. Other than this, there is no apparent reason why we have to suffer in a world that is not conducive to uninterrupted happiness. Suffering is a subjective experience, a state of mind which arises from the conditions to which we are exposed. We may learn to be different, respond differently, and not suffer. However, it is not easy. When we are attached to things and pulled in different directions by our senses and our desires, we experience

The Bhagavadgita on Suffering and Its Causes

conflicts and confusion. The Bhagavadgita is an ancient scripture. It examines the problem of suffering comprehensively and offers many solutions to deal with it. It views suffering as existential, arising out of ignorance, delusion, desires, and actions, and offers many avenues to deal with it according to our propensities and personal beliefs. It identifies several reasons for our suffering, of which I have selected the following for our discussion.

1. Mistaken identity
2. Attachment and Involvement
3. Lack of True Knowledge
4. Impermanence
5. Lack of faith

Mistaken Identity

The Bhagavadgita raises a fundamental question: who are we? Are we merely the minds and the bodies? Alternatively, is there something else about us that we ought to know? We come across such questions in almost every culture and religion, and the answers keep changing as our awareness deepens. Even after thousands of years of human progress, we are still not sure what the right answers are to these questions because we do not have the proper means to ascertain metaphysical truths except through individual experience. We may learn from the spiritual experiences of others, but it may not be enough to rest our doubts or complete our quest because we hardly accept people at their face value. To gain a firsthand experience of transcendental truths, we must be willing to tread the path till the end, making necessary sacrifices and undergoing necessary transformation. Even then, we may not know everything about them because they are multifaceted, and we may not realize them entirely, or our minds may not be able to grasp them correctly.

Our beliefs play an important role in our attitude towards suffering and the problems we face in our lives. If we think we are mere physical beings, alone, and have to take care of ourselves, we suffer from uncertainty, insecurity, fear, and anxiety. When we look at ourselves from a narrow perspective, identifying ourselves with our minds and bodies, we do not feel much affinity with the rest of the world. We consider the world as hostile and unfriendly and view it and the people with distrust. In that frame of mind, we may not even feel connected to God unless we envision Him in concrete terms.

However, the fact is we are not mere mortal beings and are not here because of some random event. We are an essential part of God's creation, and beneath our minds and bodies, we are eternal selves. We have an eternal identity that is not of this world and stretches far beyond into infinity. We have to find that truth and become stabilized in it to overcome our doubts, fears, and anxieties. Arjuna's suffering arose from his mistaken identity. He believed that he was a mere mortal, a physical self, who was subject to death and destruction. He believed that others were also like him and faced the prospect of losing their lives on the battlefield. Lord Krishna had to remind him that he was not a mortal being but an eternal Self who was immortal and indestructible. He had to convince him that he should not fear death because there was no death for the Self, and the body would anyway disintegrate someday like the clothes people wore.

In today's world, we are excessively preoccupied with our physical and mental identities. We live as if nothing exists beyond our minds and bodies. Everywhere, we see a great concern and fixation with looks, appearance, beauty, health, and the problem of aging. We indulge in these attitudes because we have limited knowledge of who we are and lack the conviction that we are spiritual beings and immortal. If we think we are merely physical beings, we do not find a strong reason to think beyond our current lives, act selflessly, or turn to God and seek his help to perform our actions or manage our lives. We hope for transformation and look toward liberation and eternal life only when we regard ourselves as spiritual beings who are caught in the cycle of birth and rebirth and need to escape to realize our true nature.

Attachment and Involvement

Most of our suffering arises from our attachments. Arjuna experienced sorrow before the commencement of the war because he was attached to his family, friends, and relations, whom he did not want to harm by his actions. He was also attached to certain beliefs, values, and habitual thoughts, which made him suffer even more. He believed that if he fought, his kith and kin would die, and his family would fall into confusion without the elders and male members to guide them. He was worried that he would incur sin and earn a bad name if he killed his family members and close relations. His fears and doubts were grounded in his beliefs and the value system to

The Bhagavadgita on Suffering and Its Causes

which he was attached. He thought egoistically that he was responsible for his actions and would suffer from the consequences.

When we are attached to certain things in life, our thinking and reasoning become clouded by egoism and self-interest and we lose the ability to resolve our problems with clarity and confidence. Our attachments are responsible for the problems we face in our lives and the helpless we experience. Many times, we feel helpless to resolve our problems or overcome obstacles, because we do not want to change our thinking or adapt ourselves to the changing circumstances. Our attachments take root in our consciousness and influence our thinking and attitude toward ourselves, the world, and our relationship with it. From the time we are born, we develop attachments to various things. By the time we reach old age, we form so many attachments that we lose a great deal of our flexibility and adaptability to live our lives normally. Our most compelling attachment is with our self-image, the qualities that define our individualities and set us apart. The likes and dislikes, opinions, decisions, actions, reactions, dreams, desires, fears, and concerns we experience or act upon arise from our attachments. When we are attached to things, we do not think clearly or see things as they are. Many vices like greed, anger, selfishness, pride, and envy spring from them, which in turn lead to many other problems.

Part of Arjuna's hesitation to wage the war was due to his aversion to death. Being a warrior, he was not worried about his own life as much as he was worried about the lives of others. He was sure of his powers and skills but was afraid that his actions would lead to the death of many. Some of them were his kin and some were those who respected and held in high esteem. Besides them, he was also attached to many other things, such as his pride, status, beliefs, knowledge of right and wrong, his skills as a warrior, and his reputation in society. It is natural for the mortal being to be averse to death. Aversion to death arises due to attachment to life. Our physical personalities are subject to death and decay. Death is inevitable for all mortal beings. In a way, it is good because death gives us a brief respite from our suffering and an opportunity to view our past in retrospect and begin a new journey in a new body. If there is no birth, imagine how unbearable life would be with all the suffering we must carry with no time to resolve it. Death gives us an opportunity to unburden ourselves mentally, discard our worn-out bodies, and start afresh with a new body, an almost empty mind, and a fresh agenda for the next life based on our experiences and the lessons we learned. It is almost like getting a new lease of life and a fresh opportunity to rectify our past mistakes and start afresh.

A case in point is Bhishma, one of the notable characters from the epic Mahabharata. He was a great warrior who was given the gift by his mother, Goddess Ganga, to choose the time of his death and remain alive as long as he wished. In his long life, he witnessed many events unfold before him. As time went by, he became increasingly disillusioned with the developments in the royal family and the behavior of his grandchildren. It is difficult to say whether he lived happily as he saw his grandchildren feuding between themselves for the throne and going their separate ways until the war became inevitable. His suffering, too, arose because of his attachments to his family, his values, and his inability to show tough love. In the end, he died unhappily, suffering for several weeks, lying on a bed of sharp arrows, waiting for an auspicious time to leave, and watching the destruction of his family members and close friends. Bhishma's life exemplifies how conquering death does not resolve suffering if we remain in mortal bodies and do not renounce desires and attachments.

Lack of True Knowledge

Having the right knowledge is crucial for our happiness and well-being. Without it, we cannot cultivate discernment, make the right decisions, know the right way to practice spirituality or attain liberation. It is difficult to say what constitutes the right knowledge and how we may arrive at it. According to the Hindu schools of philosophy, right knowledge is obtained through the standard means of knowing: through direct observation (pratyaksha), from the verbal testimony of scriptures or knowledge experts (shabda), by drawing inferences from circumstantial evidence (anumana) and by comparing the known with the unknown (upamana). Of these, ancient Indian scholars regarded the first two as the most reliable. Patanjali recommended self-study (svadhyaya) to gain the right knowledge. Jnana Yoga is the path by which the knowledge of the Self, the highest knowledge, is pursued. On this path, in the early stages, yogis focus on self-purification to cleanse themselves to cultivate discernment, detachment, peace, and mental stability. In the advanced stages, they renounce all knowledge to unite with the Self and gain direct insight. Shankaracharya recommended hearing

The Bhagavadgita on Suffering and Its Causes

(sravanam), remembrance (mananam) and contemplation (nidhidhyasana) to acquire self-knowledge. To cultivate the right knowledge, the initiates must also overcome ignorance (avidya). In spiritual terms, ignorance means not having the right knowledge or having the wrong knowledge or wrong notions about the Self and liberation. The Upanishads distinguish two types of knowledge: the higher knowledge of the Self (vidya) and the lower knowledge of the world, the body, rites, and rituals (avidya). The latter is necessary for the householders to perform obligatory duties and uphold Dharma, while the former is essential for knowing the Self. According to Isa Upanishad, both types of knowledge are necessary to cross the ocean of samsara and reach the other shore.

Ignorance or lack of knowledge is at the root of our suffering. Arjuna's suffering was due to his ignorance and lack of the right knowledge. He was ignorant about himself, his destiny and role as a warrior, and many spiritual truths about karma and liberation, etc. He had mistaken notions about life and death, action and inaction. He was unaware of his spiritual nature and his connection with God. He had no knowledge of his true Self and the fact he was not the real doer or agent of his actions. These and other mistaken notions aggravated his suffering. He had some knowledge of the scriptures and some sense of right and wrong. But he lacked the discernment to choose the right solutions under pressure.

When we lack the right knowledge and discernment, we experience confusion and delusion, make mistakes, hold wrong beliefs, pursue wrong goals, fail to find the right solutions and aggravate our suffering. We also rationalize our erroneous arguments and actions, as Arjuna did. If we want to overcome ignorance and delusion, we must rely upon the standard means of knowing mentioned above. We must develop discernment through self-purification and rely upon the knowledge of the scriptures and enlightened masters. Arjuna turned to Lord Krishna for knowledge and guidance. We can also turn to enlightened people to guide us and help us find the right solutions for our problems. We can also take refuge in God and cultivate nearness to him or seek his guidance and help through prayers and worship.

Arjuna's suffering also arose from his egoism. He believed himself to be a distinct individual who was solely responsible for his actions and their consequences. He feared that his actions would result in sinful consequences and suffering. He assumed ownership and doership, identifying himself with his mind and body, not knowing his mind and body were responsible for his actions and he was not their source or cause. Lord Krishna taught him his spiritual nature was distinct from his physical nature and he should renounce doership and ownership and perform his actions as a sacrifice to God, without desiring their fruit. By that sacrifice, karma would not accrue to him.

Impermanence

Life is a battlefield on which you constantly battle the forces of Nature and your own lower nature to ensure your survival and continuity. In this battle, the most formidable foe is impermanence. Bhagavadgita sheds light on how impermanence is at the center of our suffering. That which is born must die for life to continue. Nothing is permanent in the mortal world. All things that come into existence in this world have a beginning, a middle, and an end. Only the Self is eternal and indestructible. By taking refuge in it and detaching ourselves from all impermanent aspects of our existence, we can stabilize our minds and find freedom from instability and change. Lord Krishna emphasized these aspects to Arjuna. He wanted him to cultivate sameness, overcome desires and attachments, renounce desire-ridden actions and their fruit, and establish his mind in the imperishable Self. Through sameness, self-control, and exclusive devotion to God, he could become equal to all and remain undisturbed by the impermanence of life and the fear of loss and gain.

Lack of faith

Faith means having belief in something to be true or not true with conviction. You may believe in God, but if you do not have the conviction, your faith will be weak and vacillating. Faith is of several types: faith in one's abilities, faith in one's beliefs, faith in one's sense of right and wrong, faith in one's values, faith in God, faith in the afterlife, and faith in the possibility of success and happiness. It is also positive and negative. You may believe in your abilities or your weaknesses. You may believe in the possibilities or the threats associated with a problem or a situation. Faith arises from knowledge, experience, awareness, and discernment. Faith comes from your religious background. One may believe in God or demigods. One may not believe in either of them. If we do not have faith, we may not feel confident about resolving our problems. Arjuna had faith in his abilities and his sense of right and wrong, which made him feel unhappy about the consequences of waging war. He felt that many people would die because of him and his excellence in warfare. He also believed that he had enough justification to fight the war. But as he neared the battlefield, his confidence was shattered by his other beliefs about family values and social responsibility. Lord Krishna revived his faith in God by showing Him His universal form and explaining to him the need for faith and devotion to God.

Conclusion

Suffering is an integral part of human life. We suffer for various reasons: false identity, lack of knowledge, attachment, and lack of faith. Our limited capacity to explore truth and understand it and our dependence upon our perceptions to know about the truths of life aggravate the problem. The causes that we have identified for human suffering are not the only ones. There are many other causes which we have not explored fully. Arjuna symbolizes the best of human beings who are knowledgeable, balanced, successful, able, and well-prepared for the battles of life. In times of crisis, even the best of the best show signs of vulnerability and desperation.

Arjuna lost his balance at a very crucial moment in his life. He lost faith in the cause for which he and his brothers decided to go for the war. He lost his discernment in knowing the right from the wrong. Because of years of preparation and commitment to truth and morality, he saved himself from destruction and downfall. He qualified for divine grace through his good karma and received guidance from God in the form of Lord Krishna. The Bhagavadgita is a comprehensive manual on human suffering and the various ways in which it can be permanently resolved with personal effort and help from God. Its knowledge and practicality are relevant and effective even in modern life. By studying it and following the solutions suggested by it we can transform ourselves and experience stability and equanimity.

The Purpose and Value of Spiritual Practice

Spiritualism deals with knowledge, beliefs, and practices associated with the spirit, soul, or the Self and continuity hereafter. It includes the study of ghosts, spirits, mediums, paranormal powers, occultism, and so on. However, we limit our discussion in this chapter to the knowledge associated with the Self or the Soul. In Hindu scriptures such as the Upanishads, the Self (Atman) is described variously as the Person (Purusha), the innermost Self, the highest Self, the deepest Self, the real Self, and the immortal Self. Atheism does not recognize the existence of God, the soul, or the self. The Charvakas of ancient India, also known as Lokayatas, were atheists and materialists. They did not believe in the existence of God, soul, or afterlife and considered death as the final liberation. They encouraged their followers to enjoy their lives without impeding the enjoyment of others and liver responsibly as long as they lived.

Different Beliefs about the Self

Belief in the existence of an immortal Self and its affinity with God or the universal soul is a common thread in many spiritual traditions. It is a belief that holds immense significance and even becomes a reality for many. However, there are exceptions. Buddhism does not believe in a Supreme God or an eternal Self. It believes that each being possesses an ego-self, not-self, or no-self (anatma) that is subject to impermanence and change. It rejects the notion of a permanent, immortal, and indestructible soul or Self. The idea of permanence is deemed unacceptable in this tradition, as the Buddha held that all things, by nature, decay and are subject to impermanence. According to him, things come into existence due to the convergence of various phenomena, creating the illusion of names and forms.

Each jiva is a temporary construct or an aggregation of material things, subject to transformation and suffering in the whirlpool of samsara due to desires and attachments. They remain trapped in this cycle, experiencing numerous births and deaths according to their karma arising from their desire-ridden actions, until they attain Nirvana, a state of perfect peace and liberation from the cycle of birth and death. In contrast, others hold the belief that the Self is eternal, indestructible, without parts, and indivisible. It always remains the same in its bound state as well as the liberated state. These diverse beliefs and practices offer a wealth of inspiration and motivation for those on a spiritual journey.

Beliefs about the spiritual nature of humans and other living beings are diverse and fascinating. Some even go to the extent of claiming that the whole existence is a spiritual entity, one universal body with a universal mind of which everything in it is an integral and essential part. Hinduism, Buddhism, and Jainism share the belief that all living beings, without exception, and even objects like rivers, oceans, mountains, planets, stars, and other celestial objects, may have souls and should be treated as spiritual entities. Jainism takes this belief a step further, asserting that every object in the universe, whether animate or inanimate, contains one or more souls and that sometimes they exist in clusters. They also believe that all living beings have the potential to evolve spiritually through the cycle of births and deaths to take birth as humans. However, if humans indulge in evil actions due to their sinful karma, they may be born in the bodies of lower life forms such as animals, insects, worms, etc. This intricate web of beliefs adds depth and complexity to our understanding of spiritualism.

Exploring the Nature of the Self

What is the nature of the Self? Is it material or immaterial, graspable or ungraspable? Both views exist. According to one view, each jiva possesses a subtle body called soul, etheric, or aural body. It is made up of fine matter that is invisible and ungraspable to the senses. It has a distinct form according to the body in which it resides and survives death. People with psychic abilities may see them or sense them and may even communicate with them. Hence, a lot of folklore, myths, superstitions and fears developed around such entities. The other view is that the subtle body (soul) is also an aspect of Nature only. Higher than that and beyond the mind and the senses is the Self, which is immaterial, transcendental, ungraspable, and indestructible.

Those who practice occultism describe the Self as having made of the finest particles of energy, finer than the subatomic particles, which resonate at a higher frequency and radiate light and energy visible only to those who possess psychic powers or paranormal vision. Of the five elements, ether (akasa) is the closest to the essential nature of the soul and may be associated with it. Since it is similar to the same as space, which serves as the medium of sound, it can be purified and communicated through sounds or speech. Prayers, mantras, and chants are, therefore, effective in communicating with divinities and celestial beings or God for help. Hindu scriptures describe the immaterial Atman or the Self as smaller than the smallest and the larger than the largest. It is essentially the same as Brahman, the highest Universal Self. It exists in beings like a flame the size of a thumb in the heart region. It is ungraspable by the mind and the senses and without limits and limitations. It is also described as pure consciousness or witness consciousness, different from impure consciousness of the mind and senses. By meditating upon it and becoming established in it, one attains liberation. Knowledge of the Self is the highest knowledge. By knowing it, one overcomes delusion and egoism.

The Self or Soul and its Affinity with God

The consensus opinion is that the Soul or the Self is a representative aspect of God or the same as God. Hindu scriptures describe it as the Lord (Isvara) of the body and the whole creation. In the body, he is the witness who does not participate in any actions of the mind and body. In creation, he acts as the controller of all. In their essential nature, they are the same and indistinguishable. Some schools of Hinduism believe that the same Universal Self appears in each Jiva as a distinct Self. The reality is that only the Universal Self is real, and the individual Self is an illusion, which disappears when the jiva attains liberation. This concept of the Self (the Person in the body) as a representative aspect of God (the Person in Creation) in Hinduism is a profound and complex one, and it is a key aspect of the spiritual journey for many practitioners.

According to the dualistic school of Hinduism, the Self in each jiva is distinct and at the same from different from the Universal Self. According to them, the individual souls are numerous, but their number may be fixed. The duality between the two exists at all levels and is irreconcilable. Even after liberation, the distinction between them persists. They further hold that the souls are of different types, depending upon their awareness, independence, and nearness to God. Some are eternally free and never suffer from bondage and delusion. Some are liberated souls who escape from samsara. Some remain deluded forever and cannot be liberated. The rest are bound souls stuck in samsara and go through births and deaths until the attain liberation. This is in contrast to Western beliefs, which hold that souls are born on earth only once. After departing from here, they await their fate until Judgment Day, when God will decide whether to grant them heavenly life or condemn them to the fires of hell. Hinduism, Buddhism, and Jainism hold that existence in heaven or hell is temporary and depends upon karma. All jiva have to return eventually to the mortal world and continue their journey until they find a permanent escape from samsara.

The Importance of Spiritual Practice

Is spiritual practice necessary? Many people live on the surface, pursuing worldly goals without ever thinking about them. However, many also believe that we must look within and acknowledge our spiritual nature. It will help us transcend our baser instincts and become better humans with greater awareness, reverence, and sensitivity toward all existence. Spiritual practice means many things to many people. Its essential purpose is to use the knowledge we gain through study and learning to purify the mind and body so that they do not become obstacles to realizing our spiritual goals and strengthening our spiritual nature. It includes a wide range of activities, from the most mundane to the most secretive and from the most moderate to the most intense. Like any other branch of knowledge, spiritual knowledge can be used for selfish and selfless and good and evil purposes. Many people are drawn to it due to curiosity, gain spiritual powers, know themselves, and attain oneness with the Supreme God. Of them, the last two are noble and lead to one's spiritual well-being.

Spiritualism is not ideal for those who want to fulfill their desires or attain worldly goals through them but for those who want to transcend their desires and attachment and work for their liberation, fixing their minds on God with exclusive devotion. It is surely not for those who want to gain powers and use them with evil intentions to control others, influence their actions, or cause pain and suffering. If practiced correctly with the right intentions, it will help us know our essential nature, cultivate discernment, transcend our egos and selfishness, and realize our highest nature or oneness with God. For that, one must be willing to give up everything, perform actions without desires and attachment, and leave their results to God.

Spiritual qualities

When we think of spiritual people, we usually think of gurus, saints, sadhus, tantriks, yogis, babas, rishis, jinas, sufis, fakirs, monks, lamas, friars, and so on. They follow different paths, exemplify simplicity and austerity, follow different dress codes, prefer to avoid the company of worldly people, engage in various spiritual practices, and live mostly secluded lives. However, one should not judge them by their appearance or public conduct since they give up worldly life and may not be interested in impressing others or communicating with them. The following are a few important distinguishing qualities of spiritual people.

1. They believe in their spiritual nature and identify themselves with it.
2. They renounce their physical identities arising from their names and form and identify themselves with the Self in them.
3. They practice mindfulness or remain established in the witness consciousness or the Person (the Self) in them.
4. They overcome desires and attachments and practice dispassion, detachment, and equality.
5. They pursue liberation rather than worldly goals.
6. They remain withdrawn from the world and spend their time in contemplation.
7. They transcend selfishness and egoism and engage in selfless actions.
8. They practice self-control to purity and control their minds and bodies.
9. They are egoless and disinterested in reacting or responding to external events.
10. They exemplify the highest virtues, such as nonviolence, humility, compassion, sameness, etc.

The Bhagavadgita (Ch 16:1-3) lists the following qualities of God-centric people:

Fearlessness, purity of mind, knowledge, concentration, charity, self-control, the study of scriptures, simplicity, truth, non-violence, absence of anger, tranquility, unwillingness to find fault, compassion for all living beings, freedom from greed, amiability, modesty, determination, vigor, forgiveness, fortitude, cleanliness, endurance, and humility.

Jayaram V

According to the Yogasutras (2:3), those who practice yoga to suppress the modifications of their minds and attain self-absorption must overcome ignorance, egoism, aversion, and longing for life. They should excel in virtuous conduct, following rules (yamas) and restraints (niyamas), and cultivating qualities such as non-violence, truthfulness, non-stealing, celibacy, non-covetousness, cleanliness, contentment, austerity, study of scriptures and devotion to God. Classical yoga places great emphasis on observing external and internal purity by cultivating sattva and suppressing rajas and tamas. Spiritual people need not necessarily believe in God. However, they must be virtuous and free from worldliness, desires, and attachments.

Living Like a Lotus Leaf in the Waters of Life

The concept of non-attachment is common to Hinduism, Buddhism, and Jainism. We find its echoes in the renunciant traditions of the world. Non-attachment means not becoming attached to worldly things. It is to live freely like a lotus leaf in the waters of life, untouched or unpolluted by the waters in which it grows. It is living without attraction and aversion towards the dualities of life, without being swayed by the suffering and the weight of the worldly life and without running away from them, but by accepting them, enduing them, and developing equanimity and understanding toward them. Attachment means holding on to things dearly as if one cannot live without them or as if one's life and happiness depend upon them. Attachments (pasas) are the invisible, mental bonds and dependence we develop with the things and objects of the world due to frequent or repeated contact with them, believing that they are essential for our security, peace, and happiness. Our attachments are integral to our essential nature. They limit our vision, thinking, knowledge, and awareness and influence our actions, reactions, and inactions, our joys and sorrows, and our successes and failures. They control our lives, behavior, relationships, and destinies. They also limit our freedom and discernment.

Our suffering arises from our attachments

According to Hinduism, Buddhism, and Jainism, desires and attachments are responsible for our suffering. The Buddha identified desires or cravings as the root cause of all suffering. The Bhagavadgita holds that repeated contact with sense objects produces attachments. Attachments create desires. When desires are thwarted or frustrated, anger manifests. Anger clouds reason and causes delusion or irrational thinking. Delusion results in the confusion of memories and the loss of reason and discrimination. Without the right discrimination, we make mistakes, engage in erroneous thinking and sinful actions, and suffer from their consequences. Thus, desires and attachments are major roadblocks on our path to liberation. Under their influence, we look for sensory gratification rather than salvation and pursue deluded goals, seeking fulfillment and security against the impermanence and uncertainties of life through possessions and relationships. This thinking and attitude become so ingrained in our consciousness that we pursue even spiritual goals for deluded or worldly reasons without realizing it. Desire-ridden actions become a way of life. Attachments are mental habits and habitual thoughts. They make our lives more predictable but, at the same time, keep us bound to the world, produce suffering, and prolong our stay in samsara.

The Buddhist perspective on suffering

According to Buddhism, each being becomes cluttered with desires, attachments, egoism, and other impurities through several births and deaths. As time goes by, these accumulated formations and possessions become a burden, resulting in the jiva's suffering. The Buddha realized that the life of jivas is full of suffering from birth to death because of cravings and the attraction and aversion they induce. Therefore, any solution to resolve our suffering lies in overcoming them. Suffering becomes acute when we lose control, feel helpless, do not get what we want, and fail to resolve our suffering or escape from what we dislike.

Uncertainties of our lives aggravate our suffering. According to Buddhism, desires and attachments which are responsible for our craving and clinging are reinforced by our perceptions and habitual thoughts and actions. They reinforce our selective and preferential thinking and attitude, resulting in unwholesome behavior and sinful karma. It is further aggravated by passions such as fear, anger, greed, lust, and envy. Due to them, we experience mental instability, delusion, ignorance, bondage to the cycle of births and deaths, and the suffering that arises from it.

For the beings who are thus caught in the flux of samsara and mental formations, the only way out of this mess is by cultivating detachment and renunciation, giving up and leaving everything one accumulates from the world and carries as their answer to suffering. In Buddhism, this process is recognized as the emptying of the mind and body of their impurities and accumulations. Peace and stability arise when we are pure and empty, without the clutter we accumulate from the world over several lives. The emptying process begins when one knows the Four Noble Truths about suffering and the Eightfold Path to resolve it.

We can overcome our attachments

The Bhagavadgita identifies attachment as the root cause of our delusion, desires, and bondage. It explains how the triple gunas (modes of Nature), namely sattva (purity), rajas (vitality), and tamas (inertia), induce desires and attachments and influence our actions. According to the scripture, scriptural knowledge or awareness of the true Self by itself does not guarantee liberation. What liberates us eventually is freedom from desires and attachments. When sattva (purity) is predominant, people are attached to virtues and righteous actions that induce happiness and pleasure; when rajas (vitality) predominates, they engage in passions and worldly pursuits that strengthen their egoism and delusion; and when tamas (darkness) is in excess, they become attached to inaction and distorted thinking and engage in self-destructive actions. In truth, the attachments we develop with the world and its objects are responsible for our afflictions and suffering. We experience equanimity only when we practice detachment, renouncing desires and attachments, and cultivate divine virtues.

The world and our actions are not responsible for karma. Karma arises from the desires and attachments hidden in our actions. If you perform actions without desires, karma will not arise. The same is the case if you perform actions without assuming ownership and doership and without desiring the fruit of your actions. One can also escape from karma by surrendering to God and offering him the fruit of one's action. The Bhagavadgita suggests that actions should be performed as a sacrificial offering to God without ownership, doership, egoism, and selfishness to escape from samsara. Knowing that actions arise from the mind and body, the yogi should remain indifferent and mentally detached from his actions. It leads to freedom from karma, sameness, and oneness. Renunciation is traditionally understood as giving up worldly life and living in seclusion, taking vows. The Bhagavadgita imparts a new meaning to it, stating that renunciation of desires is true renunciation, and even a householder who is engaged in his worldly duties may practice it without having to give up the world. By giving up the desires in their actions and offering them to God, householders will attain the same end as the renunciants who give up worldly life and practice austerities and self-control and withdraw into themselves to practice concentration, meditation, and self-absorption.

Jayaram V

Our attachments arise in many ways

Identifying our attachments is the first step towards an unfettered life of peace and stability. With some practice, we can become aware of them, know how to overcome them, and become free from them. The following list enumerates some well-known attachments that we commonly experience. When we suppress them through transformative practices and cultivate sameness toward the pairs of opposites, such as heat and cold or loss and gain, we become free from the modifications and turbulence of our minds and experience peace and equanimity.

- **Physical attachments**: These are attachments to one's body, color, shape, physical fitness, health, and sexual desire. Also included in this category are attachments to material things such as money, house, place, land, nature, clothes, food, people, pets, possessions, luxury, etc.

- **Mental attachments**: These include attachments to particular emotions, one's identity, family name, family status, family background, caste, race, nation, gender, language, color, relationships, social status, power, prestige, fame, habits, hobbies, daily routine, rules, procedures, religion, scriptures, virtue, morality, opinions, judgments, beliefs, prejudices, etc.

- **Spiritual attachments**: These include attachments to one's guru, religious leader, beliefs, God, gods and goddesses, saints, religious tradition, methods of worship, spiritual practices, places of worship, scriptures, ideals, virtue, morality, spiritual life, afterlife, knowledge, symbols, etc.

- **Karmic attachments**: We inherit these attachments from our previous lives in the form of latent impressions and dominant desires. They are difficult to overcome because they arise from our actions in our previous lives, and we may not be able to get rid of them until we neutralize our inherited karma. One such well-known attachment is the longing for life (abhinivesa). Some of these attachments we form with people, things, and places also arise from our past karma. They are also difficult to overcome.

From a spiritual perspective, there are no good or bad attachments. All attachments are binding, create karma, and stand in the way of our liberation. In the early stages of our spiritual journey, we may cultivate detachment by focusing on our simplest desires, such as our preferences for drinks, beverages, tea, coffee, sugar, sweets, or specific food items, and gradually move on to more difficult ones. We may also focus on troublesome relationships that disturb us and consume our time, habitual thought patterns, and emotions that we keep experiencing frequently because of some weakness or vulnerability on our part. Both likes and dislikes arise from attachments. Hence, we should also overcome aversion to things through detachment and learn to tolerate them or endure them. Whether we appreciate it or not, if peace and stability are the aims, we must eventually overcome all attachments to become free from the cycle of births and deaths. Otherwise, we will carry them to the next world and will be compelled by karma to resolve them in our future lives.

Our attachments shape our lives

Our attachments are the cause of our motivated actions, deeply ingrained behavior, learned and conditioned responses, habits, fears, thoughts, decisions, preferences, choices, accumulations, intentional actions, and structured relationships. They are responsible for the actions we perform to gain something, own something, not lose something, survive, succeed, avoid failure, overcome fear, perpetuate our identities, prevail against nature, dominate others, or yield to them. Some of these attachments are also collective in the sense that we share them with others because of shared values or identities. For example, each group, tribe, caste, nation, association, and community upholds certain common beliefs, traditions, likes, dislikes, preferences, and prejudices that are part of their group culture, collective egos, and shared identities. Historically, these attachments played a key role in shaping our civilization and establishing group norms. They also led to suffering, racial inequalities, wars, gender discrimination, slavery, communal violence, social and economic disparities, ideological and political differences, environmental degradation, and indiscriminate exploitation of deprived classes and planet resources.

Attachments produce and perpetuate delusion

Our attachments strengthen our individual and collective identities by reinforcing our selfish desires and interests. They are responsible for our craving and our compulsive actions to accumulate material things to secure our lives against uncertainty and want and experience peace and fulfillment. Under their influence, we pursue our interests and desires as if we have no other option and refuse to let go of things we love, even when they produce pain and suffering and restrict our freedom. Our attachments are the main driving forces of our lives. They are responsible for our happiness and unhappiness and all our emotional, rational, and irrational actions and reactions. We pursue them under the assumption that by fulfilling our desires, we can secure happiness and fulfillment, whereas, in reality, they do the opposite. They increase our involvement with the world and with things that aggravate our suffering and bondage and delay our liberation. Inducing deluded and distorted thinking, they cloud our consciousness and intelligence and interfere without our perceptions, knowledge, and awareness. They prevent us from seeing the truth about our lives and the reality around us, whereby we remain ignorant and develop mistaken notions about ourselves and our essential purpose. We hold on to false beliefs, become limited and self-centered, and pursue selfish goals and wrong ideals.

Non-attachment is the road to freedom

Attachment is, therefore, a fundamental problem. Through innumerable invisible strings, we bind ourselves to the world and limit our thinking, perception, knowledge, and understanding. As we become prisoners of our minds, desires, habits, and habitual thinking, we do not even realize that we are heading in the wrong direction and chasing a mirage in search of happiness. We can resolve these problems by suppressing desires and cultivating detachment, dispassion, and indifference to the world and its objects. Yogis practice it by withdrawing their minds from the world into themselves and remaining focused on the world inside them. They purify their minds and bodies so that the causes (the modes) that induce desire and attachments are fully resolved. It requires firm resolve, faith, and perseverance. To be free from attachments, we must be willing to let go of everything, renounce our attachment to material things, and embrace or endure impermanence without feeling threatened or disturbed by it. We should practice equanimity by not seeking security in things and relationships that are by themselves impermanent, undependable, and unpredictable. We should know ourselves with discernment, without the usual filters of our minds, by becoming mindful of our thoughts, actions, and habits. As the Buddha said, however strong may be our desire to hold on to things and build our lives and dreams around them, all composite things to which we cling so dearly will eventually come to an end.

We should, therefore, establish peace and equanimity within ourselves by cultivating an awareness that is undisturbed by change and impermanence and can survive the vicissitudes of life without being disturbed by them.

Learning to let go of your attachments

From non-attachment comes true freedom. However, how can you arrive at it? How can you set yourself free in a world and from a world that in itself is a web of attachments and relationships? You can make a beginning by becoming aware of what you like and dislike, what drives you into actions and seeking, and what you value most. When you examine your thoughts and actions and the motivation or the desires behind them, you begin to understand how you incur karma and how your thoughts, actions, and desires bind you to your past and future. You realize how your suffering is prolonged by your choices, likes, and dislikes and how your ego spreads its roots in samsara to preserve and perpetuate itself. When you learn to respond peacefully to whatever evokes a habitual response in you, you break the snare of your deluded thoughts and actions and set yourself free from the illusions of your mind. It is not wrong to have things or enjoy them. On the spiritual path, the problem is your attachment to them. Your preferences, prejudices, and distorted thinking prevent you from knowing yourself and experiencing life as it happens without mental blocks.

Overcoming attachments is not a passive process. It requires dedicated effort, determination, and self-discipline. You must become aware of your attachments without confusion or delusion and commit to overcoming them. The following suggestions, proven effective in the past, can guide you in this journey.

1. **Observe the impermanence of life**. Unless you pay attention to the impermanence of life and understand its implications, you will not develop an interest in spiritual life or your salvation. When you meditate upon the nature of the phenomenal world and its impermanence, you will see the impermanence of your existence and the things that you dearly hold. We generally do not pay attention to it because we are not conditioned to dwell on the negative aspects of life. You become aware of the impermanence in your life when you observe the changes that happen to you all the time. For example, your mind is seldom stable. Your body undergoes constant changes. The people

around you behave differently at different times. You can see for yourself how things have changed in your life over a period and how they changed your life and thinking. If you focus on the changes that happen around you and notice their influence upon you, you will gradually awaken to the reality of impermanence that is rooted in your existence and learn from it to cultivate detachment and poise.

2. **Cultivate generosity**. Generosity is not about just giving money. It is giving everything that you have: your love, compassion, time, attention, virtue, knowledge, peace, happiness, and even negativity. You give away your negativity not to others but to God, with feelings of gratitude for the lessons you learned from it. The Buddha included generosity in the seven virtues of a noble person (arya sampatti). By practicing generosity and charity, we can overcome our selfish desires, greed, and the illusion of pride and self-importance. According to Buddhist scriptures, you can practice generosity in three different ways. One, by giving away the material things you love most; two, by giving away the gifts of the Self, such as inspiration, love, compassion, and happiness; and three, by giving away the gifts of knowledge and wisdom, which lead to enlightenment and liberation. By giving away what you dearly love and letting go of your possessiveness and sense of ownership, you disentangle yourself from the seeking and starving mentality of your ego and set in motion the emptying process, which is essential for reaching the state of immutability or no-change.

3. **Contemplate upon death**. Death is the ultimate devourer of everything. Whatever you see in this world will someday end. Everything that you have around you will someday vanish from the face of the earth forever. Death consumes everything, including your body and mind and whatever you dearly accumulate in your life. In spiritual life, you do not ignore death or pretend as if it does not exist or it will not happen to you. You prepare for it as seriously and earnestly as possible. Spiritual people acknowledge the importance of death and spend considerable time thinking about it and trying to accept it with calmness and without fear. They visit graveyards and cremation grounds to see death as closely as possible and deal with the fear, pain, and suffering associated with it. Although we tend to avoid thinking about it, the subject of death deserves our attention

because we cannot experience peace unless we accept it and make peace with it. Contemplation upon death and its various aspects is the most powerful way to cultivate dispassion and detachment.

4. **Relinquish ownership**. God is the ultimate owner of everything in the universe. We exist here as His guests and enjoy what truly belongs to Him. Therefore, the scriptures say that one should live here for a hundred years by renouncing our desire for things and our sense of ownership.

5. **Cultivate sameness**. We tend to react to events and situations habitually according to our likes and dislikes in our effort to stay within our comfort zone and experience peace and happiness instead of pain and suffering. However, we know that this preferential approach does not always guarantee peace or happiness. The panacea to human suffering is not to categorize our experiences to make choices but to accept and tolerate them with equanimity and heroic effort. Although it is difficult, with practice, we can cultivate sameness towards people and things. We can learn to accept things as they are and let go of them at a moment's notice, resisting our tendency to judge the world according to our values and opinions and cultivating tolerance, acceptance, understanding, compassion, forgiveness, and humility.

6. **Practice meditation and contemplation**. As you contemplate the deeper aspects of life, the existence of the soul, and the possibilities that are available to you to work for your salvation, you develop a deeper awareness of your life and the suffering that arises from your attachments. With regular practice of meditation, you gain better control over your thoughts, impulses, and emotions and experience peace and tranquility.

7. **Relinquish the doership**. The Bhagavadgita declares that we should perform all actions in the name of God since He is the controller of the universe, and nothing happens without His will and involvement. When you perform actions, consider God to be your silent partner and the real power behind them. Offer your actions to Him and let Him decide their outcome.

8. **Release everything into the universe**. Whatever we have now comes to us from the universe, and one day, it will return to it. Whether we like it or not, it is the truth. We may think that we own this or own that. However, what we accumulate in the course

of our lives, including our minds and bodies, does not actually belong to us but comes to us from the material universe, just as the air we breathe or the water we drink. We have to relinquish ownership of things upon which we have no real claim and live with the awareness that, eventually, we will them or leave them behind.

9. **Identify your attachments and let them go**. In the course of our existence, we develop many attachments in many different ways. We can group them into physical attachments, mental attachments, spiritual attachments, and obligatory attachments. They do not need any explanation, except perhaps the last one, because we know them by their names. Obligatory attachments are those from which you cannot escape, however hard you may try. Some examples are your attachment to breathing, eating, or sleeping. Some attachments are mild and easy to get rid of, while some are very deep and hard to let go of, such as our attachment to name and form or to life itself. Identify your attachments by contemplating upon them and resolve them gradually, one by one including your attachment to God or the name and form of God.

Detachment vs. indifference

Contrary to the popular notion, a detached life is not a depressing life. Actually, it is a life of freedom from the worries and anxieties that afflict those who are prone to attachments, likes, and dislikes. The very purpose of cultivating non-attachment is to overcome our suffering and mental turmoil. Therefore, to believe that non-attachment makes one's life difficult is in itself a sign of attachment to some deep-seated prejudice. You may have some initial difficulties on the path of liberation as you change your thinking and attitude and subject yourself to rigorous discipline and self-control. But if you persevere, the difficulties will gradually disappear, and you will experience a newfound freedom and live in total peace, responding spontaneously to the events and problems as you begin to let go of your attachments and remove from your life the accumulated weight of your past karmas and latent impressions. A detached person is mentally free from all that holds us in check. He is without obligation and self-inflicted limitations. He lives with faith and conviction in his ideals, preparing himself adequately for his death and his next life.

Non-attachment does not mean that you should not smile, laugh, or experience the joys of life. It means that you have to cultivate sameness towards the dualities of life and accept the pairs of opposites, such as pain and pleasure, unconditionally. It means that you will not seek anything intentionally but accept and experience whatever comes to you on its own as your destiny. The detached mind of a yogi is a mind rooted in freedom from everything and every condition. The life of Lord Krishna is a great example in this regard. He lived a holistic life, enjoyed luxuries, took sides, waged wars, killed several demons, indulged in pleasures and yet remained free from the bonds of life. The transcendental life that we seek as a solution to the impermanence and the suffering of human life is eternally vibrant and yet free from all the limitations to which we are subject. The path that leads to it does not forsake action but attachment to action. It does not forsake enjoyment but attachment to it, does not forsake experience but the desire and expectation of it, and does not forsake morality but attachment to judgment and critical nature.

A detached life is a liberated life in which the notions of a limited self, the boundaries of limited existence, and the idea of limited individuality dissolve. Free from the demands of the self-centered and selfish ego, the seeker transcends these limitations and experiences an expansive vision in which he is not subject to the usual turmoil, anxiety, and uncertainty experienced by others. Because choices or preferences do not bind him, he does not exclude anything or desire to include anything to make himself complete, become a different person, or enjoy a different life. A mind that is detached from the world and oneself is alert, attentive, calm, and spontaneous. It responds to external events, people, and things with compassion and clarity of purpose. It offers us a chance to be who we truly are and experience life without fear and insecurity. He who rises to that level of perfection experiences the true joys of living in the now and here and develops insightful and intuitive awareness.

Those who are detached thus are free from emotional baggage. They do not feel troubled by the memories of their past or the uncertainties of their future. They live without a care, accepting life as it comes. They do not feel the compulsion to plan for their lives defensively or build extensive walls of separation and security around their vulnerabilities. They do not feel the need to defend their interests or assert their opinions in order to find acceptance or approval from others or extend their influence over them. They have the freedom to enjoy their company and avoid them if necessary. They do not mentally depend upon others and do not curtail the independence of anyone. They do not spend their time building their reputation, hiding it, or showing it off. They live without fear, contended with what life has to offer them and what they can do with it, without complaining, without adulation, without judgment, and without striving. They are travelers on a journey of self-discovery who set on their course with complete trust in their faith and their connection with God. They have attained perfection because they have transformed their state of consciousness from having and seeking to "to be."

The Awakened Life

Morality and Spirituality

There is a bridge between time and eternity, and this bridge is Atman, the spirit of man. Neither day nor light crosses that bridge, nor old age, nor death, nor sorrow. Evil or sin cannot cross that bridge because the world of the Spirit is pure. This is why when this bridge has been crossed, the eyes of the blind can see, the wounds of the wounded are healed, and the sick man becomes whole from his sickness. Chandogya Upanishad

May we follow the path of goodness as the sun and the moon follow their path! May we associate again and again with liberal, the non-harming, the knowing. Rig Veda 51.15

May good thoughts come to us from every side, pure, unobstructed, overflowing. Rigveda, 89.1

At each moment in the journey of life, we face a situation where we have to make a choice, consciously or unconsciously, out of multiple options. Whatever you do, or you are, is the result of a choice you make. Thus, our lives are defined and shaped by a constant series of choices we make or let others make, each one shaping our paths, realities, and the fate of our worlds. Whether we are in the pursuit of material success or spiritual enlightenment, what matters most is our commitment to virtue and morality or the good old values of life. We have to choose between good and evil, the right and the wrong, or vice and virtue. Whether in spiritual life or worldly life, our actions should be based on a strong moral foundation, or we will eventually self-destruct. The practice of virtue perfects our character and establishes a certain orderliness, piety, and discipline in our thinking, behavior, awareness, and conduct, without which it is difficult to live peacefully on the earth or secure a good next life. As human beings, we are a mixture of opposites. We have the potential to be good or bad or to be our best examples or the worst. Depending upon what we seek and cherish, we may invite either the gods or the demons into our lives. At each moment in our lives, we are presented with an opportunity to use our intelligence and discretion, make the right or wrong choices, and progress in the right or wrong direction. What we choose at each moment in our lives determines the course of our lives and the fate of our future. Our progress and survival as a species and the fate of this world or our civilization depend upon the simple principle of whether we will uphold virtue and morality and live righteously or ethically for our collective good or succumb to evil thoughts and intentions and self-destruct ourselves through reckless actions.

We cannot act irresponsibly towards others, be they humans or other living beings, and expect our collective good to happen from it. Our interconnectedness with all life on this planet makes it almost impossible to isolate the evil actions of a few from the rest of the world and ignore them or deal with them exclusively in isolation as if they do not produce ripples and touch others or leave their marks on the face of humanity. This interconnectedness should instill in us a sense of responsibility and unity, as our actions affect not only ourselves but also the entire world. The world is now more interconnected than at any time in history. A war does not happen just between two nations or warring factions. Its ripples will be felt all over the world. As the world is increasingly drawn towards materialism, the practice of virtue becomes all the more relevant.

Evil now lurks in our consciousness more than ever as we have become more tolerant and accommodative towards evil people and evil conduct in the name of progress and humanity. As a Saivite guru once remarked, in the days of the Ramayana, the demons used to live in distant lands and enter our world occasionally to cause trouble or disturb people or their spiritual practices. At a later age, they began troubling humans by living amidst them in human form. Nowadays, in the age of Kali, they started living inside our minds and consciousness. If we are not careful, they will take control of our minds and bodies and influence our lives and destinies. This is a sad development, perhaps symbolic, but it sounds true in today's context of declining morality and ethical standards. Evil is now deeply ensconced deep in the minds of many. Those who personify it are also becoming role models and cultural icons for those who lack direction and guidance from their parents. To be free from these developments, the world may have to witness another epic battle in the future between good and evil forces, as portended by many scriptures.

Religion and morality

Every religion and religious scripture tells you that without morality, you cannot reach God. On the surface, it appears as if religion and morality are inseparable, but they are not. A moral person does not have to be a religious person or believe in God to practice his morality. However, a religious person must practice morality to sustain his faith and exemplify the values or the way of life it upholds, although, in real life, we see many people taking liberties with their religious beliefs and moral values and engaging in evil and unethical conduct. Religions may inculcate in us some commitment to morality, but the conviction to be moral or ethical is a personal choice that may arise for any number of reasons. In other words, the practice of any religion does not guarantee the best of human behavior. This is the simple but sad truth. There are as many charlatans in the religious world as there are outside. If you pay attention to the fact that the world's violent crimes have been committed mostly in the name of religion, you will understand why religions may not be the right answer to building human character or establishing an ideal, humane society.

Historically, religion and morality always went hand in hand. In the past, it was inconceivable to look upon any person as moral or pious despite his virtues if he was irreligious or did not believe in God. Many people suffered for their irreligiosity even if they lived virtuously. However, in some parts of the world the correlation was not observed that strictly. For example, in India and China, the emphasis often shifted from mere superficial allegiance to religious conduct and puritanical practices to the spiritual and moral development of human character. Allegiance to God was not considered a strict requirement to practice morality or spirituality or engage in free inquiry. However, people expected religious and spiritual leaders to exemplify virtuous conduct. Buddhism, Jainism, and many philosophical schools of Hinduism do not believe in a creator God. Yet, they commanded widespread following and respect. People were not punished or silenced for their lack of faith in God or for challenging the established beliefs and practices. However, despite these contradictions, we cannot deny the fact that religions have played a significant role throughout the world in inculcating morality and ethical conduct among their followers and have been largely responsible for protecting the world from falling into the hands of evil people or engaging in evil conduct.

Morality in World Religions

In Hinduism, dharma (observation of religious and moral law) comes before everything else. It is the foundation of life. It is the first and foremost duty of every human being. It is also the first of the four chief aims (purusharthas) of human life. The importance of morality in human life is implied in the theory of karma, according to which all beings are responsible for their actions. According to Hinduism, our essential nature and actions arise from three primordial modes, namely sattva (purity or illumination), rajas (vitality or ambition), and tamas (darkness or inertia). People perform their actions according to the predominant qualities and suffer from the consequences. Thus, actions performed out of sattva lead to happiness, actions performed out of rajas lead to stress, and actions performed out of tamas lead to pain, violence, and cruelty. According to tradition, people should cultivate sattva and perform their obligatory duties sincerely to ensure a place in heaven or obtain a better life in the next birth.

Buddhism is founded on the strong foundation of morality. The practice of Right Living is at the center of Buddhist practice. Without inner transformation and purification through virtuous living, it is difficult to be free from suffering or cultivate equanimity. The Buddha suggested the Eightfold Path to overcome suffering, which is about practicing virtues and improving one's conduct (sila). The Eightfold Path consists of the right understanding, right thought, right speech, right action, right livelihood, right effort, right mindfulness, and right concentration. A Buddhist monk practices morality not because of the compulsion to seek the approval or appreciation of others or stand out in society as a pious person but because of the conviction that ethical self-discipline and good character are essential to establish Buddha nature in thought and deed. In the simplest terms, Buddhist morality is based on the two fundamental principles of being good and doing good. Implied in both principles is the underlying theme that one should not indulge in actions to hurt oneself or others intentionally. The Dhammapada declares, "The evil-doer mourns in this world, he mourns in the next, and mourns in both. He mourns and suffers when he sees the evil of his work."

Jainism is a religion of liberation (moksha-marg). It is a very austere religion which declares that without proper conduct, there is no liberation. It recognizes the bondage (bandha) of innumerable eternal souls because of their good (punya) and bad (papa) actions. In Jainism, right faith, right understanding, and right conduct are regarded as the three jewels of the faith. The three jewels are interrelated. Without right faith, there can be no right understanding, and without right understanding, there can be no right conduct. Right conduct is that which leads to liberation and freedom from karma. In

Jainism, both the lay followers and the advanced practitioners have to undertake certain vows and follow a strict code of conduct for their spiritual development and ultimate liberation. Right conduct, along with right beliefs and right knowledge, is what makes life a means to liberation. Right conduct is not superficial or perfunctory obedience to virtue but a natural and spontaneous outcome of inner purification achieved through austerities, self-control, and penances. One can stop (samvara) the entry of karmic substance into the soul, through the purification of the mind and the body, by good conduct and by developing virtues as prescribed in the scriptures.

In Sikhism, there is a great emphasis on the cultivation of virtues and the removal of vices. Guru Nanak, the founder of Sikhism, opposed superstition, ritualism, and social inequalities and laid strong emphasis on good conduct, inner purity, and devotion to God. Speaking against outward religious observances, he said, "Let good conduct be thy fasting." Guru Arjun Dev, one of the notable Sikh Gurus, emphasized self-control and inner discipline. He declared, "Whosoever controls the mind, he is a pilgrim." According to Sikhism, lust, greed, attachment, anger, and pride are regarded as the five cardinal vices that need to be overcome through prayer, service, and charity.

In Islam, good deeds are as important as the five pillars of practice. Prophet Muhammad declared that on Judgment Day, men would be judged by their actions. He said to have remarked, "God does not judge you according to your appearance and your wealth, but he looks at your hearts and looks into your deeds." Regarding morals, he said, "The most perfect of the believers in faith are the best of them in morals, and the best among them are those who are best to their wives." The Quran says, "Whoever does a good deed, he shall be repaid ten-fold; and whoever does evil, he shall be repaid with evil."

If Karma is central to Hinduism, Buddhism, and Jainism, sin is central to Christianity. According to its beliefs, sin is what keeps human beings from reaching God. It arises because of disobeying God's law, turning away from Him and His love, indulging in wrongdoings, and challenging His supremacy. One can absolve oneself from sin by repentance, by declaring faith in Jesus, by confessing one's sins before an ordained priest, and by not repeating them. The Sermon on the Mount contains very valuable moral teachings that are universal. The Bible is not just a book of fables and parables about the life of Jesus and other Prophets, but a book of virtue. Although human beings are born as sinners, virtue is still important and on the Day of Judgment, it comes to the rescue of all virtuous souls. The Ten Commandments of the Old Testament provide a road map for Christians to practice morality and abide by the law of God.

According to Judaism, the world stands upon three things, like the three Jewels of Jainism: Torah (the holy knowledge), Avodah (religious practices), and Gemilut chasadim (loving deeds). Moses had a tough time trying to teach his men to follow the righteous path as chosen by God for the Israelites. Repeatedly, they betrayed him and tested his patience as they wandered in the wilderness in search of their true land. The Ten Commandments of the Old Testament and the 613 commandments found in the Levictus and other books are but long lists of divine laws meant to regulate the lives of Jewish people. They are not meant to secure a heavenly world sometime in the future but a holy and perfect life here and now by protecting them from evil and worldly influences.

Zoroastrianism views the world in terms of an ongoing conflict between good and evil forces. In this conflict between cosmic forces, human beings have an important role to play in keeping evil at bay, which is very difficult because evil has already managed to enter the earth and penetrate various things. In this world, evil forces always wait for an opportunity to enter the beings and the objects of the world and defile them. A great confrontation would take place in the future between the forces of God and the forces of evil in which God would ultimately emerge victorious. He would put an end to all the evil things and consign them eternally to an inescapable hell. Those who support them would also be cast there on the Judgment Day. Zoroastrianism, therefore, urges its followers to practice the right thoughts, right conduct, and right words to safeguard themselves from evil and bid their time until the Day of Judgment.

Norms and values

All religions prescribe a code of conduct for their followers to help them achieve liberation. While there may be wide variations in what they regard as virtue or vice, there are certain norms or standards that they follow to discern right from wrong and enforce order and discipline among their followers. The norms are about what scriptures one should study, how to acquire knowledge, how to ascertain the truth, what to do in the event of doubt and confusion, how to interpret the scriptures, and how to identify the cryptic codes and symbolism hidden in the religious texts. They are also helpful in knowing how to settle disputes among scholars, how to recognize the words of God, how to punish the wicked and sinful, how to protect the poor and the meek, how to regulate the lives of people, how to establish the hierarchy of divinities, celestial beings, and spiritual masters and how to recognize and reward good behavior.

There are norms about rites and rituals, purification and initiation ceremonies, rules of worship, supplications, and prayers. Every religion upholds certain methods of worship and prohibits some. For example, in Hinduism and Buddhism, there are right-hand methods of worship, followed by a majority, and left-hand methods of worship, followed by a few. Some religions encourage direct worship and relationship with God. Some prescribe the assistance of priests and spiritually enlightened masters to mediate on behalf of lay worshippers.

All religions recognize and promote certain qualities as divine and universal, such as detachment, truthfulness, non-violence, non-stealing, devotion, surrender to God, compassion, selflessness, charity, dispassion, self-control, and humility. At the same time, they condemn selfishness, egoism, pride, greed, envy, cruelty, and anger as evil and immortal. They clearly distinguish the difference between the behavior that is conducive to spiritual liberation and that which leads to ignorance, evil, and suffering. They clearly demarcate between moral and immoral behavior and their implications in one's spiritual and religious life. There are also rules for repentance and absolution. These norms have emerged as valid out of historical events, conventions, revelations or popular opinion.

Transcending Morality

On the spiritual path, eventually, we have to overcome all pairs of opposites, including our attitude towards morality and immorality, and cultivate sameness or equality towards both. To be completely free, we have to renounce everything, including our attachment to moral and religious values and our notions of right and wrong, and accept the contradictions of life and the unpleasant truths of human character with tolerance, compassion, understanding, and awareness. We have to withhold our judgment and critical attitude towards every aspect of life, especially what we despise and dislike most, with no particular desire or intention.

Jayaram V

People follow morality for various reasons, such as fear, habit, and expectation of reward, approval, or appreciation. However, at some stage in their progress, spiritual people have to transcend such considerations and make morality an integral and essential aspect of their awareness and thinking. They have to overcome their notions of right and wrong and their judgmental attitude and integrate morality as their essential nature. They should practice it not because they have an obligation to follow the demands and expectations of society or tradition but because they are inherently moral.

A spiritually awakened person practices morality without being aware of it and for no specific reason. For such people morality is not a cultivated habit, but an internal and integrated aspect of their consciousness and their disposition. They do not view it as high or low or good or bad but as the normal state of an enlightened and purified mind. They are moral and commit themselves to a life of purity and righteousness without being conceited about it.

God is essentially righteous, but all contradictions exist in Him. So should be the case with spiritually awakened people. They should uphold morality, renouncing their attachment to it and their preference for it. In many respects, our morals are relative, and our view of morality is this-worldly. Our notions of right and wrong keep changing from time to time and place to place. Child marriages and polygamy were once very common, but today, they are regarded as unethical and immoral. According to our scriptures, actions in themselves are neutral. What makes them right or wrong is the intention or the motive behind the action, and what binds us to this world is our attachment to it. If having the right intentions is helpful in the early stages of spiritual awakening, having no intention and no particular desire become the key factors in the later stages.

Right living for the right reasons

One should come to spiritualism if there is an intense aspiration or yearning to know the truth about one's existence or realize one's essential nature. One should not approach it out of despair or the need to escape from the harsh realities of life. Despair and frustration are the right reasons only if there is a corresponding and matching inner aspiration to know who you really are. In Classical Yoga, it is known as samvega (despair). However, samvega is helpful only when you are ripe for the flowering of your consciousness. You may come to spiritual life for any number of reasons. Still, if you are not mentally and physically ready for it, you will find the whole effort rather meaningless and painful and eventually drop out of it.

You may leave the world for any number of reasons, but how can you escape from the world that exists in you? It is a formation, just like the world outside, and resembles in many respects with the latter. If you want to pursue spiritual life, it is where you have to spend most of your time doing the self-cleansing. On the other hand, if you think that you can use the spiritual platform to further your personal and worldly interests, you may get away with your insincerity and duplicity for some time. However, eventually, your actions will catch up with you, and you will be answerable for the consequences and the pain and suffering that result from it. Scriptures do not condemn halfhearted spiritual measures because some practice is better than no practice. As the Bhagavadgita says, the practice of yoga never goes in vain.

Every tradition recognizes the value and importance of morality and virtue in one's spiritual transformation. Without the right knowledge and right living, one cannot attain salvation. A deeply religious and disciplined life is the most difficult to follow. As a spiritual person, you may renounce the world but not your compassion for it. You may renounce morality along with all worldly desires, but you live and act responsibly so that others may follow you and learn from your example.

Jayaram V

Ten Important Spiritual Truths for Reflection

Spiritual life is not easy to practice. It is a difficult life, where you have to chisel your old self, slowly and painfully, in spiritually acceptable ways to cultivate stability and equanimity. It is a life of innumerable hardships and challenges, where you sacrifice what you love and embrace what you do not. Essentially, it is a self-destructive process in which you aim to transform many aspects of your consciousness, personality, and behavior to make yourself fit for the path, such as your eating, sleeping, and other habits, your dress, identity, and appearance, your relationship with yourself and others, and social engagement, and your attitude towards worldly life and enjoyment. Because of these difficulties, very few people are inclined to turn to spirituality seriously and adhere to the values and discipline it demands. Those who come to it, despite these challenges, find it very discouraging in the initial stages to continue their practice, as they subject themselves to a vigorous process of austerity and self-discipline.

The Buddha recommended ten great reflections for the monks to break free from the old habits of their minds and bodies and overcome undesirable traits and qualities. They serve as powerful motivators for any, especially the early initiates, who want to keep a vigil on their thoughts and actions. He mentioned them in one of his discourses when he was staying at a monastery near Sravasthi in Northern India. The ten reflections are collectively known as the Dasa Dharma Sutra (Dasa Dhamma Sutta) or the Ten Maxims of Dharma. They are generic so that those who are engaged in spiritual discipline, irrespective of their paths, can practice them to protect themselves from minor setbacks and temporary distractions. In the following paragraphs, we will examine their meaning and importance in spiritual life.

1. I am a different person now and follow a different life

On the spiritual path, your world turns upside down as you resolve to live a life of austerity, simplicity, and renunciation, cultivating virtues, restraining your habitual thoughts and desires, and adjusting yourself to a life of discipline and hardship. You face resistance and turmoil as you practice self-effacement and self-denial, letting go of your prevailing relationships, seeking and striving, and your aggrandizing ways of seeking attention and protecting your turf. Having committed to renunciation and not seeking anything that strengthens your ego or gives you a sense of self-importance, you agree to tolerate and absorb every hardship, inconvenience, and obstacle you face without letting your emotions and feelings weaken you or upset you. You consider them useful to know yourself and control your thoughts, actions, feelings, desires, and emotions. You also commit yourself to a life of withdrawal and sacrifice, letting go of your ego as you work for your inner awakening and purification, practicing virtue, devotion, and righteous living, and abstaining from wrongdoings. If you properly enter the spiritual life, you also undertake to observe several vows, which are very difficult to abide by.

Novices who enter spiritual life must live on a seesaw edge of anxiety and uncertainty before they become accustomed to their new way of life. During this turbulent period, they must constantly remind themselves that they are now on a different in life and they must learn to think and live differently. This affirmation will help them stay strong in difficult moments and remain self-motivated. By remembering it, they can boost their morale and persevere on the path despite the challenges.

2. I am dependent upon others

There is interdependence among all the beings who live in this world. There is also a certain interdependence and exchange of energy between all animate and inanimate objects, whether we notice it or not or feel grateful about it. For example, the food we eat, the water we drink, or the air we breathe, besides many other things we use in our daily lives. Many people do not recognize our dependence upon the world or the role it plays in their lives. They attribute their successes and achievements to themselves or their merits. The truth is that we cannot continue here for long without depending upon others or the world. From the time we are born, we receive help from innumerable sources, from our parents, teachers, relations, and all those who help us along the way to be who we are or where we are. Whether you are worldly or spiritual, you cannot deny your dependence upon others. We all are connected to life's innumerable invisible streams in mysterious ways. Whether you admit it or not, numerous people influence your life and destiny. It teaches you lessons, opens your eyes to your faults and failures, shows you the way to forge ahead in difficulties, prevents you from destroying yourself, and stands with you whether you notice or not. Countless people help you in your survival, success, and continuity. You may not even know them personally, but without their help, you would not have come this far or become what you are today.

Think of all those who must have helped you in the past or maybe helping even now: your parents, teachers, friends, relations, well-wishers, enemies, strangers, plants, animals, elements, Nature, gods, invisible forces, and the universe itself. You may not know most of them or remember them. You might have outgrown them, forgotten them, or left them behind. Nevertheless, they all might have helped you grow and become who you are, teaching you valuable lessons, opening your mind to new knowledge and experiences, showing you the ways of the world, and protecting you from harm. They must have stood with you when you were helpless and insecure and taught you the nuances of friendship, betrayal, pain, suffering, enmity, love, generosity, humanity, and so on. They all must have expanded your consciousness in different ways. Therefore, however independent or self-made you may think you maybe, you are indebted to the world and the people in your life.

Your dependence upon the world continues even if you renounce it. In fact, you become even more dependent since your vows may require you to live on others' charity or generosity or the food you collect from them. You may live in isolation and avoid the company of worldly people. However, the world must facilitate your practice and keep you clothed and nourished. Therefore, even as a renunciant, you may practice detachment, dispassion, and indifference but must live in gratitude and reciprocate the help you receive in some way. The world may be an illusion or a difficult place to live, but you must remember that you depend upon it, and it is vital to your practice and continuity. Thus, this sutra is useful to reflect on your dependence upon others and the reason to cultivate humility, gratitude, friendliness, and compassion for all the beings in the world and treat them well without judgment or assuming moral or spiritual superiority.

3. I should now live and behave differently

If the first affirmation is meant to remind you that you have to break away from your past and start a new life, this one is meant to commit you and strengthen your resolve to follow the new way of life you have chosen. It is especially useful in the early stages of your spiritual practice when you begin to adapt yourself to new conditions and practices and face a lot of resistance. You have to remember that you can no longer be the old self you used to be and must now live according to the demands your spiritual practice demands.

In the early stages of their practice, spiritual aspirants, who are not yet accustomed to the new routine, go through a stormy period, dealing with their old habits, memories, desires, and attachments. They must practice discipline, virtue, morality, self-control, equanimity, control over their feelings, passions, and emotions, restraint of the minds and senses, and their natural craving for good food, attention, approval, friendship, luxuries, or a comfortable and eventful life. Until they steady their minds and are accustomed to the new way of life, they must constantly remind themselves of this sutra. It will give them the fortitude to adapt themselves to the new demands and difficulties they must face in the initial stages until they succeed in stabilizing their minds, tempering their expectations, and settling into their practice. If they keep reflecting upon it frequently, the idea becomes entrenched deeply in their consciousness and becomes second nature.

4. Can I find fault with my virtues and my conduct?

However good and ornamental it may appear to the eye, if a water-pitcher has even a tiny crack, it will not hold water or quench anyone's thirst. However pious and good spiritual people may be, if they have even minor faults, they will fail to reach the goal of liberation. In spiritual life, there are no shortcuts. The aspirants must work assiduously to perfect their minds and bodies and make themselves fit for the journey. Even a little vulnerability on their part may throw them out of balance or expose them to danger. Therefore, spiritual aspirants must review their progress objectively to ensure that they are not leaving out anything that may give them trouble at a later stage. Like a night guard on duty, they must keep a vigil on themselves in a world that is filled with spiritual darkness. This affirmation is useful for critical self-evaluation to know where they are heading and where they stand on the path they have chosen. If you are honest with yourself in answering this question, you will find many opportunities to grow, improve your practice, and progress on the path.

Leniency and self-deception have no place in spiritual life. Renunciants cannot compromise their values or take liberties with the vows they take. Moral purity and right conduct are the foundation upon which rests their liberation. Spiritual people must always remain on guard, even after they have spent years in the practice and advanced on the path. They should not feel complacent or take pride in their progress. There will be traps, and they will be tested. Even a minor lapse on their part can bring them down to from where they began. Hence, they must remain guarded and practice self-control, following the instructions given to them strictly, even when they are engaged in the most ordinary tasks, such as eating food or taking a bath. In worldly life, people may take certain liberties with their morality, conduct, or behavior, but in spiritual life, the aspirants should be very disciplined and not let desires and temptations sway them. They must be relentless in their effort, overcome all weaknesses, and achieve perfection to reach the final goal. If it is not done, the mind will bring out all your sleeping demons into the open and subject the aspirants to agonizing conflicts, temptations, and moral failure at the most unexpected moments. This affirmation will help you become self-aware and mindful of your failures and imperfections and rectify them. By paying close attention to your thoughts and actions, improving whatever and wherever necessary, you can quickly overcome the obstacles and make progress.

5. Will the masters approve of my virtues and conduct?

If the previous affirmation is about self-evaluation, about paying attention to yourself, this one is about objective evaluation and about paying attention to what your teachers or others say about you or your practice. Their words carry more weight since they are noble souls, free from bias. They give you the most honest and direct information about you or your practice according to the highest standards of virtue, morality, and discipline. You do not always have to approach them for advice. You may also not always have access to them. You can look at yourself from their perspective, think like them, and see how you may fare in their estimation or measure up to them.

The scope for perceptual bias and selective perception is high in critical self-evaluation. Therefore, one should pay attention to the inputs coming from others, especially the teachers, and whether they approve of one's conduct or actions. We usually judge others from a narrow perspective, according to our limited knowledge, likes and dislikes, interests, and prejudices. Sometimes, we may also evaluate others by projecting our thoughts and feelings upon them. Our opinions and judgments also keep changing from time to time according to our moods and personal agendas. Ignorance is another important factor. If people are ignorant, they will not be able to discern right from wrong or arrive at the right conclusion. Therefore, it is difficult to rely solely upon the opinions of common people or our friends and family to know about ourselves, especially when we know their weaknesses and limitations. The masters of wisdom, on the other hand, are committed to truth. They are free from the impurities of the mind, impartial, and possess an insightful awareness to discern right from wrong. Therefore, we can look at them for the best possible and most reliable advice or opinion and learn a great deal about ourselves. We can also learn by observing them and measuring ourselves against them.

If you want to know about your progress realistically, ask yourself this question frequently to know what the masters may think about you and how they may evaluate your virtue, conduct, and progress. You can do it either by asking them directly or by putting yourself in their shoes and subjecting yourself to critical self-evaluation according to their standards and teachings. The teachers you approach may be alive or departed from the world long ago. If you cannot reach them, you can think of them in your meditation and request them to guide you. You can also use their teachings to evaluate your conduct and your virtues.

6. One day, I will be separated from all that I love dearly

This reflection is useful to contemplate impermanence, cultivate detachment, and withdraw yourself from your entanglements and involvement with the material world. Attachments the most difficult obstacles on the path. They are difficult to overcome because they come in many guises. If you suppress some, they will reappear in

Ten Important Spiritual Truths for Reflection 233

different forms. The world is a transient place where nothing stays forever. We cannot hold on to anything permanently. Things change, people change and everything is eventually swept away by the currents of impermanence. We should, therefore, control our desires and expectations and cultivate sameness toward loss and gain and other dualities.

Outwardly, life may look routine and predictable, especially if you happen to be living a secluded life. However, no one can foretell how our lives may change or what twists and turns may happen in the future. Although we become attached to numerous things in our lives, in the end, we end up with nothing but a few memories. Even they may not survive the death of the body. That is a fact of life. Yet we cling and crave for things and live and act as if things will last forever. In spiritual life, you have to be constantly aware of the transience of life and the emotional disturbances that may arise because of the attachment and the expectations we cultivate. This does not mean that you should not celebrate life or burden yourself with depressing thoughts. It means you must live with wisdom and awareness about the transience of life and accept things as they are without letting yourself fall into emotional turmoil. If you focus on the transience of life and reflect upon it, you will cultivate dispassion, detachment, and sameness towards the pairs of opposites. You will be eventually free from all bonds and entanglements and achieve liberation.

7. I create my experiences, and I am responsible for my actions

This reflection empowers you to control, correct, and improve yourself, not egoistically but responsibly, taking responsibility for your thoughts, actions, and decisions. It makes you responsible and accountable for your life and actions (karma) and gives you a reason to look within yourself to solve your problems and difficulties rather than rely upon others or hold them responsible. It makes you independent, self-aware, and responsive to the pain and suffering you experience when you make mistakes and go through the self-cleansing process. The law of karma is inexorable. We may temporarily rationalize our actions, but our karma will ultimately catch up with us and demand its price. We cannot escape from our past unless we know how to set it right and stop the roots of karma from spreading further and deeper into our lives. Once we are born into this world, we have to face the consequences of our actions and decisions and accept the rewards and punishments that are part of the package. However hard you may try to resist the temptations of life, when you are in a seeking mode, you will continue to push the boundaries of your life, taking chances and finding opportunities, until you realize how your actions and habits are putting you in a bind and how you are the cause and the effect of your experiences.

We are responsible for what happens to us here and hereafter. We may hold God and others responsible for our pain and suffering or our success and happiness, but what shapes them is the law of karma. You create your life largely through your deeds and misdeeds. You precipitate the reality of your life through your mental and physical actions. Even the so-called fate is shaped largely by your past deeds. Others may play some role or influence to some extent. However, they can do so only because you let them. You attract them because of your past or present karma and give them a chance to interfere with you or your actions. When you are deeply involved with the world, you may think that this is the only life you have and the only chance to live happily and you may not concern yourself much with the possibilities of life beyond death. However, death is not the end of it all. There is a life beyond death, which stretches into eternity. When you leave this world, you carry the seed of your next life with you. If the seed is not of good quality, when it eventually germinates and becomes a tree, it will bear bitter fruit and become a source of unpleasantness or suffering for you and others. You must view your life from a wider perspective, in the larger context of your life that spans across several births, and consider the consequences that may arise due to your current actions and lifestyle choices, paying close attention to your habitual thought patterns and your dominant desires because they become the seeds of your future and prepare for the next life.

In spiritual life, you must live responsibly, learning from your mistakes and experiences and correcting yourself. By accepting your pain and analyzing its causes, you can learn from your past and make progress. Every experience in your life is part of a chain of events whose origins or causes remain deeply hidden in your mind and obscured from your surface consciousness. Through meditation, mindfulness, or regression, you can unravel those causes and find solutions. You can understand how your thoughts, desires, and actions precipitate your reality or life's experiences and perpetuate your suffering. Once you realize how you are responsible for your life and suffering through your thoughts and actions and the chain of karma that arises from them, you will live mindfully. You will take responsibility for them and do whatever you can to mitigate them.

8. Am I doing the right things?

This is a continuation of the previous thought process. On the spiritual path, you have to evaluate your actions constantly to know whether you are practicing correctly with the right and approved methods, making the right decisions, and progressing in the right direction. From your teachers or the scriptures, you know which actions are approved, which are optional, and which are prohibited. You can use that knowledge to guide yourself. You need to cultivate discernment since spiritual life is an unchartered territory. You may encounter situations where your knowledge may not be adequate to deal with it. They knowledge you gain from others may not also be adequate. Every situation is different. What worked for them may not work for you. Therefore, at times, you have to rely upon yourself and your discernment to solve your problems. In those circumstances, the best way to decide is by looking at the results. If your actions are producing results, you can consider them effective. If they are not working and you feel you are stuck, it is time to review them and make necessary changes.

It is true that on the spiritual path, you should not be driven by the compulsive desire to be correct. You should not bring your ego into the effort or the judgment. The ego acts according to its preconceived notions, habitual thoughts, likes, and dislikes as a part of its agenda to gain approval, recognition, and attention. It wants to be right at any cost and, if necessary, by rationalizing its actions. Spiritual people should be aware of these thought processes and the involvement of their egos in their spiritual efforts. They must practice humility, detachment, and surrender and cultivate the right views, right thinking, right knowledge, right discernment, and right effort.

9. Am I comfortable with my emptiness?

In worldly life, we are not comfortable being empty or becoming a nobody. We are comfortable with having power, prestige, influence, family, relationships, wealth, status, and recognition. We want to be somebody with a name, status, skills, talents, or some distinction and aim for things that complete us or complement us. We strive to accumulate wealth, power, and prestige so that we will be praised, acknowledged, loved, and accepted, enjoy status and prestige in society, or experience fulfillment. Loneliness, anonymity, or emptiness frightens many. No one likes the idea of being a failure or counted as worthless or empty. The world is conditioned to revere success. It does not forgive those who do not measure up to its standards or meet its expectations. Failures are consigned to the dustbins of history and forgotten quickly.

Worldly life promotes individuality and upholds those who prove their worth through sheer determination and hard work. We admire winners. We worship them. We love to fill our lives with color and action. As a result, we enjoy being competitive and overly active and fill our lives and our minds with excessive clutter, hoping that it will eventually compensate for our insecurities and feelings of inadequacy.

The truth is that all the riches in the world do not fill the void and our craving for them. Our desire for things, achievement, and recognition does not cease even though we have exceeded expectations. You may silence it temporarily with things, but not permanently. With each gain and achievement, it intensifies even more. All the material possessions and accomplishments do not cure our insecurity and our feelings of helplessness against the uncertainties and unpredictability of life. The solution, therefore, does not lie in filling our emptiness and craving with material things or escaping from it through frivolous activity but in accepting it and embracing it with stoical wisdom. We must shift our focus from having to being and gradually withdraw from the clutter and the chaos of our lives. We must empty all that from our consciousness, which creates and perpetuates our hunger and thirst for things.

When we become reflective, the first thing that strikes us most about our lives is the emptiness and the meaninglessness of our whole existence. We will not find one meaningful reason why we are here and why we have to do what we usually do to keep ourselves active, busy, successful, attractive, acceptable, friendly, useful, rich, famous, successful, or simply human. The introspection would either drive us crazy or push us gradually into depths of despair, as it did in the case of the Buddha. If we persist, it may also inspire us to look into the depths of our consciousness to understand what life is all about and how we may deal with it and bring lasting stability and peace into our lives. The wise ones know that all the knowledge, learning, consciousness, and conditioning to which we have been subject from the day we were born are actually obstacles to liberation. They know that all these factors, which we believe are responsible for our success in worldly life, are actually problems in our search for peace and happiness. We cannot resolve them by filling that void with transient things but only by becoming empty through a long and arduous process of unlearning, unwinding, and reconditioning our minds and bodies and freeing them from the shackles of authority and conformity.

In worldly life, your success is measured by your achievements and your accumulation of material things. In spiritual life, your progress is measured by the things you renounce truly and genuinely, and the void that you create within yourself through that renunciation. As a worldly person, you achieve success through goal-oriented actions. You seek people and relationships for your self-preservation. You cherish selfishness as a virtue to accumulate things and fulfill your desires. In spiritual life, that strategy will not work. You must set aside all seeking and striving and lead a selfless, effortless, and unencumbered life. You must shun the company of people and live in seclusion to understand the meaninglessness and the purposelessness of seeking and striving lifestyle. Since the two worlds are so different, when you withdraw from worldly life and turn to spiritualism, you may experience great turmoil, confusion, anxiety, and resistance. This reflection on emptiness will help you understand how comfortable you are with giving up things and living without any hope, desire, security, guarantee, or certainty. If it makes you unhappy, you will know that you are still far away from the goal.

10. Have I attained the superior wisdom that will set me free?

The ultimate purpose of spiritual practice is to gain the right knowledge so that you will overcome your ignorance and delusion and realize who you truly are. By acquiring the right knowledge, you will also be able to discern truth from falsehood and live life the right way without making costly mistakes that may lead to unhappy karmic consequences. The superior knowledge, in most cases, is the knowledge that will help you subdue your desires and attachment, cultivate sameness or oneness, and become free from all the things that disturb you or subject you to dualities and delusion.

This reflection helps you in two ways: first, by letting you know where you stand on the path, and second, by freeing yourself from distractions so that you can remain focused. In spiritual life, as in material life, sometimes you may find yourself moving in circles, indulging in frivolous activities, and losing sight of the very purpose for which you began your journey. With the help of this reflection, you can reset your mind and regroup your attention.

However, at what stage will you know that you have attained the right knowledge? How do you know that you have gained the right knowledge and attained perfection on the path? There are no hard and fast answers to this. Only you will know when and if it happens. Perhaps you may seek the help of the masters who have attained perfection before you and possess the ability to know your situation intuitively or provide you with an insight into your behavior through their wisdom. Alternatively, you may do introspection and see whether your spiritual goals are met. One simple way to do it is by measuring the change you accomplished within yourself or the qualities, nature, and conduct you are supposed to cultivate through your practice.

An equally important factor is what knowledge and wisdom you seek on the path. Our scriptures recognize two types of knowledge: outer knowledge and inner knowledge. Lower knowledge comes from the study of scriptures and the experience of others, and higher knowledge arises in the depths of one's consciousness, in moments of profound silence after years of practice, purification, attentive observation, and self-sacrifice. True knowledge sets you free, while false knowledge binds you to your delusions. Some people are happy with the lower knowledge, and some strive to go beyond it to experience the ultimate state of freedom from suffering.

The ten reflections are useful for cultivating the right attitude and remaining focused and determined. As we have discussed earlier, spiritual life is an uphill battle, where you are constantly tested by your essential nature, primitive instincts, selfish desires, habitual thought patterns, and intrinsic desire for self-preservation. These ten great reflections are very helpful for remaining balanced and focused.

Finding the Right Teachers for Guidance

According to Hinduism and many ascetic and teacher traditions, a guru is an enlightened master, a perfect being who appears among people out of unconditional love to help them return to their source. He is like a Bodhisattva, a selfless being who sets aside his priorities for the spiritual advancement of the world. Those who meet an enlightened master due to curiosity or seek knowledge are deemed ripe for salvation because he gives them a unique opportunity to hasten their liberation partly through their efforts and partly through his blessings. A true master comes to this world rarely. He becomes a guru after prolonged practice over several lives. His mere presence in the world electrifies the atmosphere and inspires millions of people to turn to spiritualism. Slowly but surely, he transforms the people who meet him through his teachings and techniques. Hinduism survived over the centuries because of the selfless service of several teacher traditions and ascetic movements. They protected and preserved their traditions and teachings by passing on their carefully guarded secrets, conventions, knowledge, methods, and practices to a few qualified and trustworthy disciples and successors, who, in turn, continued the practice down the line. Without their commitment and continued effort over these centuries, Hinduism would have been extinct by now.

In today's world, a lot of controversy surrounds the tradition of gurus. As a result, when we hear about them, we do not know whether they are enlightened, genuine, and trustworthy or whether they have questionable pasts, ulterior motives, and hidden secrets. The problem is complicated further by the activities of a few controversial teachers and the scandals erupting occasionally in the news channels about their dubious activities and misconduct. Hindu society is now mature enough to understand the risks involved in following spiritual masters unthinkingly. The connection between a spiritual guru and their disciples is not just spiritual but also deeply emotional and personal, a bond forged in trust, faith, innocence, and the promise of liberation. In the following sections, we will try to explore the mystery and the aura associated with spiritual masters and their relevance and significance in the spiritual progress of the world.

Pros

Those who believe in their spiritual teachers and follow them sincerely defend the institutions of gurus. They speak positively about their life-altering experiences, miraculous events, and association with their gurus and uphold their value and importance in the spiritual progress of humanity. Some well-known arguments put forward by them in favor of the institution of gurus are listed below.

1. Gurus are dispellers of darkness. They play an important role in the spiritual advancement of their disciples by providing them with the right knowledge and guiding them toward their spiritual goals.
2. Gurus are enlightened masters with extraordinary powers, which manifest in them due to their purity, austerity, enlightenment, perfection, and divine grace. They can transform people through their teachings, sometimes with a mere glance or touch.
3. Gurus play a vital role in continuing their teacher traditions (paramparas) and propagating the Eternal Dharma known as Hinduism. They uphold its tenets and act as its protectors and spokespersons.
4. An enlightened guru is God in human form. He has God's permission to speak and act on His behalf. He has no ego because his ego is filled with God's presence. Serving him is, therefore, equal to serving God.
5. Gurus have miraculous powers. Because they are egoless and control their minds and senses, they can easily enter other people's consciousness at will and read their minds. They can receive thought vibrations remotely from others, travel astrally to distant places in meditation or dreams, heal the sick and the disabled with their spiritual powers, and even liberate qualified disciples with their blessings.
6. It is said that a true spiritual master can neutralize the ill effects of sinful karma, transfer spiritual energy to others, or hasten a disciple's spiritual progress with their grace.

7. Gurus often indulge in erratic, outrageous, and abnormal behavior to discourage people from coming to them. One should never judge them based on their appearance or behavior.
8. Gurus promote good values, encourage righteous conduct, and thereby play an important role in the preservation of human values and social norms.

Cons

Those who are opposed to the gurus for religious, personal, or ideological reasons or because they had unpleasant experiences and encounters with them develop a deep distrust in the very institution of gurus, their integrity, and their teachings and methods. They cite the examples of controversial gurus, how they misled their disciplines and caused irreparable damage to the community, the faith and the people who trusted them and wasted their lives. Those who become critical of spiritual teachers and their lifestyles are not necessarily atheistic or irreligious. They may be very religious but do not believe in the need for gurus or dependence on them for one's spiritual progress. They also believe that since knowledge is now freely available, they are not as important for our spiritual development as they used to be in the past. Below are some of the arguments put forward by them in defense of their stand against the institution of gurus.

1. In society, we find many bogus gurus who do immense harm to innocent people through fraud and deception.
2. These bogus gurus misuse their public image, status, power, and influence to amass wealth and live in luxury while they are supposed to renounce worldly life and live austerely, suppressing their desires and attachments and seeking nothing. Some of them exploit children and vulnerable women for personal or worldly reasons by making false promises or offering to grant them spiritual favors.
3. The deceptive gurus indulge in self-promotion, criminal activities, and anti-social behavior. Court cases for murder, violence, molestation, land grabbing, and accounting fraud against them are not unheard of or unknown.
4. Many gurus enjoy personal admiration and worship. They pretend not to notice the personality cult, superstition, myths, and blind following that builds around them due to the activities of

their committed inner circle and even their family members, whom they were supposed to have renounced but continue to be a part of their entourage. They do not clarify the rumors and stories spread by their followers about their miracles, wondrous deeds, and supernatural powers. They cleverly maintain silence and allow people to think of them highly.

5. Most gurus do not seem to speak from their experience but from the knowledge that is already found in the scriptures. They add their personal touch and their brand names and pass it on as if it is their teaching. Some even patent their methods and practices.

6. Some gurus choose successors based on heredity, family ties, or personal loyalty rather than eligibility, knowledge, suitability, or readiness. Once they succeed, they follow in the footsteps of their masters and continue their questionable conduct and deceptive methods.

7. Many gurus seek the company of wealthy and politically influential people to promote themselves or gain their support. They give them undue preference, special treatment, and a private audience, while the common people have to wait in long lines to see them from a distance. They also extend the same courtesy to foreigners who visit them. While this is not a serious violation of ethical conduct, it does show that they do not practice sameness and are not free from attractions and aversion.

8. The movements initiated by the gurus usually decline after their death. Their followers quarrel among themselves and start their movements, each claiming proximity to the departed gurus. This shows that the teachings of their gurus did not prove very effective in their case, and they are still subject to impurities and indiscipline.

Gurus and their significance

Spiritual gurus come in all forms. Some of them are true and enlightened, and some are false and deceptive. It is not easy to distinguish one from the other by their teachings or their appearance because, outwardly, they may follow the beliefs and practices and speak about the same philosophy and code of conduct. With some training and preparation, it is not difficult for an intellectually clever person with erudition and communication skills to pass himself as a spiritual teacher. Therefore, people must be careful in choosing their

Finding the Right Teachers for Guidance

spiritual mentors. A deceptive guru can seriously harm his followers and delay their liberation. Having trust in God is always helpful, but taking certain precautions about one's spiritual well-being is prudence, especially in a world where truth is not what it seems to be. The journey of liberation is riskier and more arduous than crossing the Himalayas. A seeker's progress depends upon whom he selects as his guru and his equation with him. If the guru does not know him and has never met him, he should better look for someone who knows him personally and can give him proper guidance. There is no apparent advantage in going to a spiritual guru if he is too busy to meet you or pay you any attention. The teacher-student relationship is personal. You should know your teacher and what you can expect from him, and your teacher should know whether you are ready for the journey and willing to make the necessary sacrifices. Otherwise, you will be having a delusional and imaginary relationship that will not help you much.

God comes to us in many forms. He especially comes in the form of enlightened masters and teachers to show us the way and help us realize our spiritual goals. He speaks to us through them to give us guidance and inspiration or resolve our suffering. When you are empty, God fills the void in you and makes you complete by awakening his consciousness in you, which is your support and very Self. Gurus are such because they are empty in themselves and are filled with the presence of God. In Kashmiri Saivism, a guru is considered the primary source of liberation. The Shiva Sutras of Abhinavagupta suggest that Shambhavopaya, the method of obtaining Shiva's or a Guru's guidance and intervention, is the most effective compared to the other two methods, namely Shaktopaya (reliance upon the Shaktis) and Anavopaya (reliance upon oneself).

Certain traditions of Hinduism also entertain the belief that gurus can transfer their spiritual energy to their followers and purify them or enlighten them instantly. One such tradition is known as Shaktipatha, the Path of Shaktis, a variation of Shaktopaya. Some gurus in India claim to awaken the Kundalini power in large congregations by holding group meditation sessions or gently touching them on their foreheads or their backs. Since no one truly knows what an awakened Kundalini feels like, there is no way to know whether it truly works and how long the effect will last. Such experiences can arise from self-induced delusion, confirmation bias, or group affect.

The Awakened Life

The importance of discernment (buddhi)

Our world presents us with a complex and ever-changing objective reality where it is difficult to discern truths behind appearances and surface impressions. Just as falsehood can temporarily cloak truth, fake gurus can easily hide in the guises of enlightened teachers and mislead unsuspecting followers. Sometimes, people fall into their trap because of their previous karma. It is as if Maya works through them also to keep people deluded and bound. The false gurus interfere with the spiritual progress of their followers. They create confusion in their minds and lead them astray. They also create doubt and distrust in the minds of others about gurus and spirituality. In this world, things are not what they appear to be and not what they are. The world is created to keep beings distracted and deluded so that they will remain bound to samsara. With our limited knowledge and faculties, it is difficult to see through people's true nature and discern their true character, honesty, and integrity. Hence, charlatans and impostors easily masquerade as virtuous gurus, especially when people are conditioned to respect and honor spiritual gurus, religious scholars, and pious people. One way to catch them is to pay attention to their actions rather than their words and see whether any incongruity exists between them.

Spiritual people should exercise caution and spend more time choosing their paths and gurus than selecting a lawyer, doctor, or tax consultant for help. Choosing a guru requires more effort, especially in today's world, because of the declining moral values and the increasing possibilities of falling into the trap of fake gurus who have now sprung up like mushrooms. The spiritual consequences can also be devastating. A fake doctor endangers the life and health of his patients, but the. The consequences of following a false guru may impact his followers' spiritual progress and well-being for several births. They play upon their gullibility, innocence, and spirituality, give them false hopes and assurances, steal their wealth or honor, and lead them astray. Imagine wasting a whole life with a false master only to realize in the end that, all the while, he had been working for a fraud and chasing a mirage! Those who fall into their trap and surrender to their whims have to endure conflicting feelings of shame, anger, and remorse. Due to delusion and attachment, unfortunately, some gullible followers remain loyal to their false gurus even after they have been exposed as frauds. They live in denial, refuse to see the truth, and even vehemently defend their fake gurus on social media or in public. Sadly, they cannot easily be brought out of their self-induced delusion.

Finding a genuine guru is vital to progress

Salvation involves the difficult process of cultivating purity, self-control, and other virtues that demand many personal sacrifices from the aspirants. To reach their goals, they must undergo a vigorous self-cleansing process, both physically and mentally, without any guarantee, promise, or solace that, in the end, they will be rewarded for their efforts or unharmed. Spiritual transformation is a journey through unchartered territory along a treacherous course of unknown risks and destabilizing forces. As one keeps progressing, the path appears and disappears amidst snares of distraction and demons of deception, which is why we need a guru in the first place. Only a guru can show his disciples the way to the wonderland of immortality through the dense forests of delusion and temptations and protect them from harm by taking responsibility for their lives and actions. He neutralizes their karma and saves them from evil influences. A fake guru does the opposite. He throws them to the demons of doubt and despair and leaves them to their fate. Even if he desires to help them, he cannot since he does not have the purity or the knowledge to lift them out of their suffering and delusion. With his ignorance, insincerity, and incompetence, he compounds their problems by giving them false hopes and leading them astray. According to Hinduism, a guru happens to appear in the lives of his followers by the grace of God, according to their purity, readiness, aspiration, karma, and faith. Just as they are eager to find their gurus and seek their teachings, the gurus are also eager to find their true followers and teach them the right way to escape from samsara. Their coming together is said to have great significance for both and all those who will depend upon them for knowledge or liberation. It happened in the case of Sri Ramakrishna and Swami Vivekananda. Both contributed greatly to the revival and resurgence of Hinduism as a major world religion and spiritual tradition.

The difference between a guru and a teacher

In ancient India, there was a clear distinction between a spiritual master (guru) and an ordinary teacher (adhyapak). A guru commanded more respect in society compared to a teacher because he selected students on merit and assumed responsibility for their lives for the duration of their stay with him. They lived in his household, receiving knowledge from him directly and mastering the scriptures while he took care of them without expecting or insisting on any monetary benefit or rewards in return. He taught them as he pleased, provided they stood up to his standards and expectations. A teacher, on the other hand, taught the students by charging them money without taking responsibility for their care. A guru, in ancient India, was not an ordinary person. He was an enlightened master who lived in a forest, while a teacher was a mere professional who lived among people and helped his students excel in their chosen fields of study. At the end of their education, it was customary for the students to reward their gurus with a gift (Dakshina) without their asking. Teachers, on the other hand, received remuneration regularly for their services. Thus, whatever karmic debt the students owed was paid back. The teachers were mostly worldly people, not renunciants, while the gurus were spiritual people who lived in seclusion and avoided busy places. They taught secular subjects, knowledge of rites and rituals (karmakanda), and various arts and crafts. In contrast, the gurus focused mainly on scriptural and spiritual teaching and the knowledge of the Self (atma-jnanam). Isa Upanishad emphasizes the importance of both types of knowledge for householders to achieve the four aims of human life. Lower knowledge helped them in performing their duties, earning wealth, and fulfilling their desires, while higher knowledge led them to liberation.

Over the centuries, the traditional roles of the gurus and teachers underwent considerable change. Spiritual teachers enjoy more respect and attention in society. Some of them attain celebrity status and act as spokespersons and messengers of faith and Dharma and wield considerable power and authority. Teachers are now a part of the job-holding middle class or working class with diminished status and a limited role in societal affairs. Gurus often run large organizations and manage business empires. Unlike the gurus in ancient times, they live in comfort in their well-guarded Ashrams, are okay with accepting money and donations from their followers, and prefer to live in crowded cities rather than in the forests. We cannot judge them solely for these developments since circumstances have changed, and no one will bother to pay them attention or follow them if they are not distinguished or do not run active social media campaigns. However, this development can have a detrimental effect on the institution of gurus since fake gurus can exploit it for their selfish ends. It also makes genuine gurus vulnerable to excessive scrutiny and attention. At the same time, their increasing popularity gives them the freedom to translate their ideals and vision in the desired direction and establish viable institutions to serve the people and promote the faith. It is also not uncommon nowadays for gurus to face personal attacks from their disgruntled followers who feel scorned, overlooked, or neglected by them and try to belittle their teachers by going public.

Surrendering to God

You can either let things happen or make things happen. One is the way prescribed by our spiritual traditions, and the other is the way of the world. In spiritual life, the former is the recommended option. In worldly life, the latter is the preferred choice. Therefore, if you are drawn to spirituality and looking for an enlightened teacher, you must let him come to you rather than go after him. This is the ideal approach. You must let it happen as a test of your readiness and fitness with aspiration, devotion, and faith in God. Send out an intention into the universe and let him come to you through the will of God as you intended. Often, in our eagerness and impatience, we try to control and regulate our lives. We want to make things happen through organized and planned effort. In worldly life, it is the preferred method. However, in spiritual life, aspirants must renounce egoism, desires, and attachments and perform their actions without expectations. They must also change their attitude toward success and failure and cultivate sameness towards all dualities, overcoming attraction and aversion.

We solve our problems more effectively when we purify our minds and intelligence and cultivate discernment. If you have discernment and if your mind is not clouded by distorted thinking, you will know instantly when you meet a guru whether he is the right one for you. If you do not find one, consider God himself your guru and keep focus on self-study and self-purification. Sometimes, it is better not to have a guru. It gives you the freedom to act according to your best judgment rather than becoming a nameless follower in a guru's gathering.

A genuine guru will not readily accept you. He will not be interested in helping you unless he is satisfied that you are ready for his teaching or the journey and willing to make necessary sacrifices to purify yourself and attain perfection. He may not also put much trust in you until he knows you well and is satisfied that you are not going to be a disruptive force. Therefore, unless one is serious and committed, it is better not to approach a guru in haste and seek initiation. It is not the guru's responsibility to reform his followers. The journey has to be undertaken by the initiates. They should not take for granted their gurus or the guidance they receive.

Know why you need a guru

People seek gurus for various reasons, ranging from purely selfish and materialistic motives to highly spiritual ones. Before you seek one, you should ask yourself why you need a guru, whether you are ready, and whether you need one at all. Is it because you are looking for a mental crutch, a parental figure, friend, or mentor because you feel loneliness or emptiness inside or crave attention? A guru is not a substitute for uncaring parents, children, or spouses. Gurus are not meant to resolve family problems, emotional problems or predict the future. They are not meant for cleansing karma or overcoming past sins. If people approach gurus for these reasons, they should not be upset if the gurus act upon their weaknesses and manipulate them. Gurus are spiritual mentors. People should approach gurus only if they are serious about liberation or spiritual aspiration. At least, they must have serious aspirations for it. They should not treat them as substitutes for shrinks and life coaches or seek them because they are having problems and want them to resolve them by using their powers. They should not be used for distraction or to overcome boredom. A guru may often play different roles as a mentor, parental figure, friend, healer, magician, or fortune teller, but they are not his primary duties, and one must not approach them for these reasons. Spiritual practice requires serious and dedicated effort. It demands an austere approach, an uncompromising attitude, and self-discipline. If one is not ready for it, it is better to engage in household duties, live righteously as a lay follower, and wait for the right time.

One should not approach a guru with a deluded mind, seeking worldly advice. Many people do this, and many gurus are obliged to help them. However, at some point, those relationships fail or generate negativity. Enlightened gurus practice detachment. They remain indifferent to those who approach them. They are not interested in anyone or anything in particular because they are not bound to the world or its ways. In their enlightened minds, they treat everyone equally as aspects or manifestations of a bigger reality. At times, they may show annoyance and deference, but it is mostly to teach the erring ones some important lessons or deliver a strong message. An enlightened master does not let his ego or lower nature interfere with his actions or decisions. He remains equal to the dualities and does not let his problems take precedence. Although he lives amidst the world, he is not part of it.

When you seek a guru, examine your intentions without delusion and with a clear mind. You may seek your guru's help to resolve your problems, but you should not expect that he will always do it. It should not be why anyone should go to him. Gurus are dispellers of illusions, not their perpetrators. They may help others in resolving their worldly problems, not because they want them to remain deluded and worldly but because they may think that it is because of God's will that they sought their help. Whatever may be the case, one should look upon them primarily as spiritual mentors. One should not become addicted to their presence or their speeches because it is a form of delusion only and does not usually end well for those who indulge in it exclusively. We often hear stories about people who act like cult members in the earlier stages but eventually turn against their gurus and end up becoming their betrayers, bitter enemies, and the worst critics. It happens especially if the gurus are dishonest or have not done their job perfectly or if the disciples are deluded and have not learned much from their gurus.

A guru is not a substitute for virtue and purity

Spiritual life is not for those who are not willing to practice virtue and morality or control their minds. Initiates and followers cannot be insincere and impure in their thoughts and actions and expect their gurus to take care of them and their lives despite their failures and weaknesses. Spiritual practice demands a serious commitment. Many spiritual traditions prescribe strict conduct, rules, and restraints (yamas and niyamas) for this very reason. Purity is the foundation for attaining perfection and stabilizing the mind. A half-hearted approach does not work in the spiritual field and often leads to unintended consequences. It is also why the practice of Dharma, or obligatory moral and spiritual duties, is the first of the four chief aims (purusharthas) of a householder. Virtue or righteous conduct is the foundation of spiritual life. Religiosity and morality precede spirituality. Without them one can practice spirituality or enter through doors of liberation. They are necessary to cultivate virtues or divine qualities, suppress desires and attachments, and attain perfection.

Many entertain the false notion that if you worship (pooja) the gods and make them offering, they will help them in their liberation. However, on the spiritual path, rites and rituals are not that important. They can even be renounced since the goal is to establish the mind in oneness and overcome desires and attachments. Spirituality demands an uncompromising commitment to purity, simplicity, austerity, and morality. Without them, the gates of enlightenment will not open. Even devotion (bhakti) is not very helpful unless it is pure, exclusive, and untainted by egoism, desires, and delusion. One must practice exclusive devotion (ananya bhakti) or uninterrupted and undisturbed contemplation on the Self (Isvara-pranidhana) with a pure heart and mind to earn his grace. Even gurus cannot rescue those who do not change their ways or improve their conduct through spiritual practice.

Know the distinction between God and guru

We tend to regard gurus as the living embodiments of God. However, many followers mistake their guru's personality for God, resulting in deluded notions about him and his true role. They look upon him as a savior, forgetting that his primary duty is to teach and enlighten his followers, not to become their God and savior. God is the highest guru. An enlightened guru who attains oneness or pure consciousness embodies God. However, his persona or physical self should not be mistaken for God and should not be worshipped or equated with him. If you do not know the distinction, you will likely get involved with personality worship and begin to venerate your guru as God incarnate or God himself. This is even more serious than the delusion of ignorant people. Hinduism draws a clear distinction between an incarnation (avatar) and a God's manifestation (vibhuti). Every animate and inanimate object in creation is his manifestation only. He is present in them as their innermost Self. An incarnation is different. An incarnation is his direct, active, and conscious manifestation in which he retains all his powers, including his omniscience, omnipresence, and omnipotence. It is, therefore, incorrect to treat gurus as God's incarnations or saviors, build temples for them, or worship them as gods.

One may see God as a guru and treat him like one, but it must be done without delusion. A truly enlightened spiritual master has no ego or no personality of his own. Since he undergoes self-purification, he lets the radiance and the consciousness of his pure Self shine through him. When he speaks to us, it is as if his pure Self is speaking to us and radiating its light. If we have a reason to equate him with God, it is this. Therefore, you may worship the divine nature of the guru because it is pure and the same as God's nature, but it should not be mistaken for his name or form because they are impermanent and do not last forever. A guru is more like a television, or a radio, a communication tool. You are not going to worship them because they deliver great knowledge about spiritual practice or liberation. The same is the case with a guru. Treat them with respect, but do not mistake them for God. The Brihadaranyaka Upanishad points to this distinction. Before renouncing worldly life and taking up sannyasa, Yajnavalkya advises his wife, Maitreyi, in the following words. "It is not for the love of a wife that wife is dear, but for the love of the Self in a wife that wife is dear." He repeats the same analogy using different things. The advice applies to spiritual teachers also. One should worship the guru not because the guru is great but because the Self in the Guru is God, and he has attained oneness with him.

Find a guru who can guide you personally

In the seventh chapter of the Bhagavadgita, Lord Krishna describes four types of people who worship him: men in pain and suffering, curios seekers of knowledge, seekers of wealth, and seekers of enlightenment. Of them, he says the last ones, men of wisdom, are the dearest to him because they identify themselves with him and are forever established in him. Lord Krishna does not undermine the first three. He calls them noble (udara) but considers the last ones the noblest. We may use the same analogy to categorize those who approach gurus and become their followers. Some go to him because they have some problem, a disease, adversity, financial or domestic problems, etc., and want their gurus to help them with their knowledge and spiritual powers. Some people go to them out of curiosity to learn from them the mysteries of life or spiritual knowledge. They are curious about themselves or the metaphysical realm and want to dabble with spirituality intellectually. They spend time listening to his discourses, reading his books, or seeking answers from him to their questions and doubts. Once their curiosity is whetted, they most likely leave them and return to their worldly ways. Then, some people go to them with the expectation that they may help them to improve their financial condition or fulfill their worldly desires, success in business, marriage with a desired partner, or happiness and fulfillment in their personal lives. Finally, some approach them for spiritual guidance with a genuine aspiration for liberation.

If you approach a guru purely for material or personal reasons, such as resolving some business or family problem, it does not matter whether you see him regularly or only occasionally. You can meet him whenever it is convenient for you. If he is busy elsewhere, you can wait for him. Your life will not be disrupted if he is absent for most of your life. The same is the case if you follow him due to curiosity or acquire knowledge. You can continue to read his books, watch his television programs, listen to his recorded speeches, or follow him on social media. That should give you enough opportunities to satisfy your curiosity.

However, if you seek him for enlightenment or liberation and want him to initiate you properly into a spiritual path, you must be careful about whom you choose. You will not go far on the path if you cannot meet him frequently or if he is not readily available or approachable. If you think he can communicate with you remotely with his psychic or supernatural powers across the oceans and continents, make sure your false hopes and expectations do not delude you, and your guru can really do it. Sometimes, spiritual teachers deliberately ignore their students to teach them important lessons or improve their practice. Whatever the nature of your relationship with him, you must never fall into delusion as far as your equation with him. If it is one-sided, certainly, it is not to your advantage.

Conclusion

As the Brihadaranyaka Upanishad states, it is not for the love of a guru that a guru should be dear but for the love of Self in the guru that the guru must be dear. We live in an uncertain world. Our lives are unpredictable. We have limited abilities to cope with our problems or difficulties. The same is the case with our perceptions, knowledge, intelligence, and actions. We also entertain many illusions about ourselves, others, and the world. We do not know clearly what will help us, what will harm us, or how our lives will take turns. We cannot see far into the future or remember everything that happened to us in the past. We are largely a mystery to others and ourselves. Under these circumstances, it is prudent to seek the wisdom of enlightened masters, who may probably have answers to our problems and help us resolve them.

It is comforting to know that we have such enlightened people amidst us who can provide us with knowledge, wisdom, and direction in an uncertain world and watch our backs while we are engaged in our daily battles. We should not misuse our connection with them for selfish or worldly reasons. We should not force ourselves into their lives for attention, egoistic satisfaction, or worldly reasons. If this is the case, we should let them use their energies to help those who are committed to their spirituality and serious about their practice. By doing it, at least you will conserve your energies and focus on your immediate aims.

Jayaram V

The Glossary of Sanskrit Terms

Abhinavagupta: An Indian mystic philosopher of Saivism from Kashmir, India who lived in the 10th or 11th century A.D.

Adhyapak: A teacher.

Adigranth: The most sacred scripture of the Sikhs, literally meaning the first scripture, compiled during the 16th and 17 centuries A.D.

Ahamkar: Egoism or the sense of individuality, which is responsible for delusion and bondage to the cycle of births and deaths

Amedhyam: Impure

Amla: Sour

Anandamaya kosa: The bliss body or the innermost sheath of the human personality.

Anatma: The Buddhist concept of no soul.

Anavopaya: Making egoistic effort to seek liberation.

Anumana: Means inference or suspicion. In Indian philosophy, it is knowledge gained through guesswork or hypothesis based on circumstantial evidence.

Annam: Food

Annamaya kosa: Food body or the physical body formed out of the food we eat.

Arjuna: One of the Pandavas and a principal character in the epic Mahābhārata, known for his skills in archery. He is also the direct recipient of the knowledge of the Bhagavadgita.

Artha: Material wealth. It is one of the chief aims of human life.

Asana: Postures used by the practitioners of yoga to purify and discipline the body.

Ashtanga yoga: The eight-limbed yoga of Patanjali, also known as the classical yoga.

Ati ushna: Very hot.

Atma: The individual Self or the inmost Self, which is said to be the real Self and an aspect of Brahman, the universal Self.

Avidya: Ignorance.

Balam: Physical strength.

Bandha: Bondage of Self.

Bhagavadgita: A sacred scripture of Hinduism, in the form of a long dialogue between Arjuna and Lord Krishna on suffering and salvation. It explains the various ways in which people can attain salvation and freedom from karma.

Bhakti Margam: The devotional path of surrender and unconditional love for God, described in the 12th Chapter of the Bhagavadgita.

Brahmacharya: The practice of celibacy. It is also one of the phases of human life.

Brahmakumaris: Daughters of Brahma. This spiritual organization was founded by Dada Lekharaj, also known as Brahma Baba. Its headquarters is located at Mount Abu, Rajasthan, India, and branches and associate organizations are spread all over the world. The organization is mainly managed by females.

Buddhi: Intellect, also known as the higher mind that gives us reasoning, analytical, and discretionary abilities.

Chaitanyam: Dynamism or activity. It is a quality of animate objects derived from the Self or God, in contrast to the inertial (jada) of lifeless objects.

Charvakas: An ancient Indian sect of atheistic materialists who believed that there was no soul and no afterlife.

Dhammapada: An important text of Buddhism in verse form, based on the teachings of the Buddha. It is regarded as an important text of the Theravada School.

Dharana: Concentration. It is one of the limbs of eight-limbed classical yoga, which deals with techniques and practices of concentration for stabilizing the mind on a material or mental object.

Dharma: A very comprehensive term in Hinduism and Buddhism. It means religious knowledge, religious duty as well as the law of God. It is also considered in Hinduism as one of the chief aims of human life.

The Glossary of Sanskrit Terms

Dhyana: Meditation. It is also another division of the eight-limbed classical yoga.

Ganesha: A popular Hindu deity, with an elephant head. In the Hindu pantheon he is regarded as the leader of the gods and the son of Lord Shiva.

Gata rasam: Not well cooked or partially cooked.

Grihastha: A Householder. It is also one of the phases of human life.

Gunas: Qualities of nature that are present in every aspect of creation. They are responsible for the diversity in the objective world. See also, sattva, rajas and tamas.

Guru: A spiritual teacher who imparts the knowledge of the scriptures and shows the students the means to liberation.

Hanuman: An important Hindu divinity from the epic Ramayana, who is known for his valor, strength, devotion, and purity of mind.

Indra: An important Vedic deity who is extolled in the Vedas as the lord of the heavens and leader of gods. He wields the lightning as his weapon.

Iswara: Lord of the universe. He is the manifest Brahman. In classical yoga the word is used to describe the individual Self, who is hidden in each living being.

Iswara pranidhana: Devotion to the inner Self or to God.

Jina: An awakened Jain monk or an enlightened being

Jnana Margam or Jnana Yoga: The path of knowledge, described in the Bhagavadgita.

Kama: Sexual desire in particular or any desire in general.

Karma Margam: The path of action described in the Bhagavadgita.

Katu: Bitter.

Kosa: Sheath or body. According to Hindu tradition, there are five sheaths or bodies surrounding the Self or the soul.

Krishna: An incarnation of Lord Vishnu, venerated by millions of people all over the world. He imparted the knowledge of the Bhagavadgita to Arjuna on the battlefield of Kurukshetra.

Kshetra: Field. It is also used symbolically to describe the body.

Kundalini: Coiled energy, which, according to Hindu beliefs, remains latent in the human body like a coiled serpent. When it is awakened through spiritual practice, it travels through various energy centers or chakras in the spin region till it reaches the highest chakra present in the head, resulting in enlightenment.

Kurukshetra: The battlefield of the epic Mahabharata, where the Pandavas and Kauravas assembled a huge army and fought for 18 days to gain control of the empire. Out of the millions who participated in the war, in the end only a few warriors survived.

Lalithavistara: A Mahayana Buddhist text that describes miraculous events from the life of the Buddha.

Lavana: Salt or saltiness.

Madhyamika: A Mahayana Buddhist school of ancient India, which rejected extreme views on objective reality and followed a middle course.

Manana: Remembering.

Manomaya kosa: The mental body, one of the five sheaths around the inner Self in the human personality.

Mitra: An important Vedic deity, who is extolled in the Vedas.

Mitrata: Friendliness.

Moksha: Liberation.

Mokshamarg: The path of liberation.

Nibbana: An alternative word for nirvana.

Nirvana: In the Buddhist tradition, it denotes the liberated state or the state of absolute freedom from suffering, births and deaths, impurities, and the impermanence of human life. It is the state in which everything about a person is fully extinguished, including his karma and latent impressions.

Nirvikalpa samadhi: A state of self-absorption described in the Yogasutras of Patanjali, in which one experiences formless self-absorption.

Nidhidhyasana: Contemplation

The Glossary of Sanskrit Terms

Niyamas: Observances or regulations. It is the second limb of the eight-limbed yoga. It consists of observing cleanliness, contentment, austerity, self-study, and devotion or surrender to the Self.

Papam: Sin incurred on account of bad actions

Patanjali: Author of the Yogasutras, who lived around the 2nd or the 3rd century BCE.

Prajna: Wisdom or higher intelligence.

Prakriti: The dynamic energy of God or the primeval energy that manifests in creation as Nature and matter. It is one of the two eternal components of the universe, the other being the universal Self.

Pramana: A term used in Indian philosophy to denote the standard or the method by which one arrives at valid knowledge.

Prana: Life energy or vital energy which manifests in us as breath.

Pranamaya kosa: The breath or the energy body

Pranayama: The practice of controlled breathing to stabilize the mind and energize the body. It is one of the eight limbs of the classical yoga.

Pratyahara: The practice of withdrawing the senses into the mind and the mind to practice concentration and facilitate the inward movement of the mind. It is also one of the eight limbs of the classical yoga.

Pratyaksha: Knowledge gained through direct perception.

Priti: Tasty, sweet, satisfying.

Punyam: Merit accruing from good actions

Puranas: They are books of ancient religious lore regarded in Hinduism as memories of the land's ancient history. They contain stories of creation and the life histories of gods and goddesses and some prominent kings and queens of remote antiquity.

Purusha: A term used in Hindu scriptures to denote the Cosmic Being as well as the individual soul.

Purusharthas: The four aims of human life, according to Hindu tradition, namely religious duty, wealth, physical passions and liberation.

Rajas: One of the three qualities of Nature hidden in every material object. It manifests in us as the seeking and striving quality of the consciousness.

Rama: An important divinity of the Hindus and an incarnation of Lord Vishnu, he is worshipped by millions as God Himself. He is also the hero of the epic Ramayana.

Rasya: Juicy, used in this book to denote juicy and tasty food.

Rta: A very complex Vedic concept that denotes the regularity, orderliness, and hidden patterns of the manifest universe, in contrast to the chaos and disorderliness of the evil spheres. God is said to be the upholder of the universal Rta, and because of that, we have day and night, the hierarchy of gods, social order, seasons, and the orderly movement of celestial spheres and objects.

Ruksa: Dry.

Rupa: Form.

Sadhu: A Hindu ascetic who renounces worldly life in search of liberation.

Samadhi: The state of self-absorption in which one loses sight of all distractions and dualities and becomes completely absorbed in the object of concentration. It is also the last limb of the classical yoga.

Sambavopaya: Seeking the grace of Lord Siva for liberation. It is one of the means used in certain sects of Saivism for self-realization.

Samskaras: The latent impressions that are formed in the consciousness out of our dominant desires, habitual thoughts, and strong memories. They become the seed for the next birth. According to the yoga philosophy, unless they are removed, it is not possible to stabilize the mind or achieve liberation.

Samvega: Desperation and frustration that arise from the meaninglessness of life, from which springs an intense aspiration for liberation.

Samyutta-Nikaya: This is a Buddhist text containing a collection of verses on Buddhist philosophy and practice. In the Buddhist canon, it is grouped under Sutta Pitaka, one of the three baskets of Pali Canon.

Aanyasa Margam: The path of renunciation described in the Bhagavadgita

Sattva: One of the three qualities of Nature. It manifests in us as brilliance and illumination.

Shabda: Word. In Indian philosophy it denotes knowledge that is based on the testimony of scriptures.

Shakti: The energy principles of the universe, worshipped by Hindus as the Universal Mother or Mother Goddess.

Shaktipatha: A special technique used in certain Hindu traditions by enlightened spiritual masters to transfer their spiritual energy to some chosen disciples.

Sila: Good conduct, moral discipline. It is one of the three practices prescribed in some Buddhist traditions to attain perfection on the path.

Skandha: According to Buddhist tradition, aggregates or component parts of human personality

Snigdhah: Oily.

Sravasthi: An ancient Indian city visited by the Buddha during his various travels in the plains of India.

Sravana: Listening

Sthirah: Stable or wholesome, used in this book to describe the quality of food.

Sukham: Happiness or pleasure, used in this book to describe the quality of food.

Svadhyaya: Self-study.

Tamas: One of the three qualities of nature, which represents ignorance, inertia, and darkness in human consciousness.

Tantra: A set of Hindu and Buddhist spiritual practices in which the followers use very unconventional and unusual methods to gain control over their minds and bodies and experience inner peace or attain salvation.

Tirthankaras: An enlightened being in Jain tradition, which recognizes 24 Tirthankaras, of whom Lord Mahavira was the last one.

Tirthankaras played an important role in the revival of Jainism from time to time.

Tikshana: Pungent, used in this book to denote the quality of food.

Ucchistam: Leftover food.

Udara: Gentle, noble.

Upamana: Example or comparison. In Indian philosophy it is knowledge gained by comparing and contrasting things with one another.

Upanishads: These are the end parts of the Vedas, which deal with the metaphysical aspects of the universal and individual souls and passages on creation and liberation.

Vanaprastha: One of the phases of human life in Hindu tradition, during which men are expected to renounce their worldly responsibilities and retire to a forest to prepare for their salvation.

Varuna: A Vedic god extolled in the Vedas as the enforcer of justice.

Vasanas: Strong desires

Vidahina: Overcooked.

Vidya: Knowledge

Vijnanamaya kosa: The intelligence body.

Yajnavalkya: An enlightened Vedic sage whose teachings are found in the Brihadaranyaka Upanishad and Satapatha Brahmana.

Yamas: The first limb of classical yoga, which prescribes five rules for the practitioners for the purification of their minds and bodies. They are non-violence, truthfulness, non-stealing, celibacy and non-covetousness.

Yata yamam: Not fresh, mentioned in the book in relation to food.

Yoga: Interpreted variously as a union, path, one of the six schools of Indian philosophy, state, or condition. In Hindu, Buddhist, and Jain traditions, it is also one of the means to overcome the afflictions and modifications of the mind and stabilize it on the object of concentration.

Yogachara: A Mahayana Buddhist school of ancient Indian origin whose doctrines are based on the different states of perception and consciousness experienced during mindfulness and meditation practices. It is closely related to the Hindu Yoga philosophies and practices.

Recommended Reading

Adiswarananda, Swami. The Four Yogas, A Guide To The Spiritual Paths Of Action, Devotion, Meditation And Knowledge. Ramakrishna-Vivekananda Center of New York, 2006.

B.K.S. Iyengar, with Evans, John J. Abrams and Douglas. Light on Life, The Yoga Journey To Wholeness, Inner Peace, And Ultimate Freedom. Rodale, 2005.

Besant, Annie Wood 1847-1933. The spiritual life. Quest Books, 1991.

Bryant, Edwin F. The Yoga Sutras of Patanjali, With Insights From the Traditional Commentators. North Point Press, 2009.

Cort John E. Jains in the World, Religious Values and Ideology in India. Oxford University Press 2001.

Das, Surya Lama. Buddha is As Buddha Does, the Ten Original Practices for Enlightened Living. HarperSanFransisco, 2007.

Das, Surya.Awakening to the sacred, creating a spiritual life from scratch,Broadway Books, 1999.

Dyer, Wayne W. Your Sacred Self, Making the Decision To Be Free. HarperPaperbacks, 1996.

Feuerstein,Georg. The Shambhala encyclopedia of yoga. Shambhala Publications, 1997.

Foster,Richard J., Helmers Kathryn A. Life with God, Reading the Bible for Spiritual Transformation. HarperOne, 2008.

Harvey, Andrew Edited by. Teachings of the Hindu Mystics, Shambhala: Distributed in the U.S. by Random House, 2001.

His Holiness, The Dalai Lama, translated and edited by Jeffrey Hopkins. Becoming Enlightened. Atria Books, 2009.

Krishnamurti, J. with a foreword by Mary Lutyens. Krishnamurti's Notebook. Krishnamurthi Foundation of India, 1988.

Maharshi, Ramana. The Spiritual Teaching of Ramana Maharshi Foreword by C.G. Jung. Shambhala Dragon Editions, 1988.

McLeod, Melvin. The Best Buddhist Writing. 2006. Edited by McLeod, Melvin and the Editors of the Shambhala Sun. Shambhala, 2006.

Mingyur, Yongey Rinpoche with Eric Swanson. Joyful Wisdom, Embracing Change and Finding Freedom. Harmony Books, 2009.

Muktananda Swami 1908. Play of consciousness, Chitshakti vilas : a spiritual autobiography, with an introduction by Swami Chidvilasananda. SYDA Fdn. 2000.

Poonja, H.W.L. (Papaji). Wake up and Roar, Sounds True, 2007.

Radhakrishnan S. Indian Philosophy, Volume I & II. Oxford University Press, 2000.

Radhakrishnan, S. The Principal Upanishad, Edited with Introduction, Text, Translation and Notes. Harper Collins, 2006.

Rama Swami, 1925. Living with the Himalayan masters. The Himalayan Institute Press, 1999.

Roman Sanaya, Channel for Orin. Spiritual Growth, Book III Earth Life Series. HJ Kramer Inc.1989.

Donald Jay Rothberg, The Engaged Spiritual Life: A Buddhist Approach to Transforming Oneself and the World, Beacon Press, 2006.

Shumsky, Susan G. Exploring Meditation by Susan Shumsky: Master the Ancient Art of Relaxation and Enlightenment. New Page Books, 2002.

Sri Aurobindo, The Integral Yoga: Sri Aurobindo's Teaching and Method of Practice, Selected Letters of Sri Aurobindo Compiled by Sri Aurobindo Ashram Archives and Research Library. Lotus Press, 2000.

Strassfeld, Michael. A Book of Life, Embracing Judaism as a Spiritual Practice. Schocken Books, 2002.

Swami Venakatesananda. Vasistha's Yoga. State University of New York Press, 1993.

Swami Vivekananda 1863-1902. Living at the Source Edited by, Myren, Ann., Madison, Dorothy. Yoga teachings of Vivekananda, Series: Shambhala Dragon Editions, 1993.

Syman, Stefanie. The Subtle Body: The Story of Yoga in America. Farrar, Straus and Giroux, 2010.

Tolle, Eckhart. The Power of Now, A Guide to Spiritual Enlightenment, New World Library, 1999.

Trungpa, Chögyam. Cutting through Spiritual Materialism; Foreword by Mipham, Sakyong; edited by Baker, John and Casper, Marvin; illustrated by Eddy, Glen.

Wallace, Alan B. Buddhism with an Attitude the Tibetan Seven-point Mind-training; edited by Quirolo, Lynn. Snow Lion Publications, 2001.

Welwood, John 1943. Toward a Psychology of Awakening, Buddhism, Psychotherapy, and the Path of Personal and Spiritual Transformation. Shambhala, 2002.

Yoganands, Paramahansa. Journey to self-realization, Discovering the Gifts of the Soul. Self-Realization Fellowship, 1997.

Credits

Cover design by Jayaram V
Images for the cover used under the Pixabay Content License

Jayaram V

Pure Life Vision Books
Selected Upanishads

The selected Upanishads presents original English translations of 14 principal Upanishads, namely, Aitareya, Kausitaki, Kena, Taittariya, Isavasya, Katha, Mundaka, Mandukya, Prasna, Svetasvatara, Paingala, Kaivalya, Vajrasucika, and Jabala Upanishads. This work is a part of our effort to publish the translation of major Upanishads by Jayaram V, including the major Upanishads such as the Chandogya and Brihadaranyaka Upanishads. The last two are published separately and do not form part of the 14 Upanishads included here. This edition features an introduction, original Sanskrit verses in transliterated Devanagari script for each of the 14 Upanishads, their English translation, explanatory notes, a glossary of Sanskrit terms, and recommended reading. The explanatory notes by Jayaram V offer fresh insight into the knowledge, wisdom, and hidden symbolism of important verses. The Upanishads are spiritual texts containing ancient, ritual, spiritual, and esoteric knowledge of the Vedas and constitute the heart of Hinduism. They also served as the principal sources of the Vedanta school of Hindu philosophy, which is currently the most dominant school of Hindu philosophy, and many key concepts of India's spiritual traditions such as Atman, Brahman, Prana, Ahimsa, Karma, Dharma, Moksha, etc. Their influence may have also extended to many philosophical schools of Buddhism in ancient India

Order your copy from https://www.PureLifeVision.com

Pure Life Vision Books
Brihadaranyaka Upanishad

This is a complete translation of the Brihadaranyaka Upanishad, considered one of the most important and voluminous Upanishads of Hinduism, containing some very fundamental concepts that are now an integral part of Hinduism and the Vedanta Philosophy. Through his annotations and introduction, Jayaram V brings out the mystic symbolism and the hidden significance of the Upanishad. This vastly improved and revised edition includes an introduction, original Sanskrit verses in transliterated Devanagari script, a translation of each verse, explanatory notes, and a bibliography. Jayaram has been engaged in the study and understanding of India's religious and spiritual traditions for a long time and has internalized the knowledge. He translated several Upanishads, wrote a comprehensive commentary on the Bhagavadgita twice, and authored several books and articles. His other works include The Awakened Life, Brahman, Introduction to Hinduism, Essays on the Bhagavadgita, Think Success, Chandogya Upanishad, and Selected Upanishads.

Order your copy from https://www.PureLifeVision.com

Pure Life Vision Books
The Bhagavadgita
Unveiling the Gita's Secrets

This is one of the most comprehensive commentaries on the Bhagavadgita in recent times. Jayaram V spent three years working on his previous commentary, published in 2011, and completely revised it. He provides an in-depth analysis of each sloka and chapter, quoting relevant information from classical commentators such as Shankaracharya and Madhavacharya and ancient mystic texts such as the Yogasutras and the Upanishads. He also provides a unique perspective on their historical background, discussing the circumstances, the socio-religious context, and the key influences that might have led to their formulation. In translating the scripture, he adhered to the traditional Vedic interpretation of the slokas without being influenced by any particular school, sect, or teacher tradition. To provide additional clarity and context, he tried to bring out the original intent of each verse and the most plausible meaning of each word in the context of the times in which they were composed. We hope this work will help you under the significance of the ancient wisdom contained in the scripture.

Order your copy from https://www.PureLifeVision.com

Pure Life Vision Books

Order your copies from https://www.PureLifeVision.com.

Pure Life Vision Books
Essays on the Bhagavadgita

In this comprehensive book, you will find a thorough critical analysis of the philosophy, principles, and practice of the Bhagavadgita and its relevance to our actions, character, conduct, and physical, mental, and spiritual well-being. This information will help you develop a deep understanding of the essential philosophy, practice, and basic concepts of the Bhagavadgita and their relevance to your personal and spiritual goals. You will gain insight into the true meaning of karma sannyasa yoga, its relevance to worldly people, and the importance of various other yogas suggested in the scripture, along with other teachings of Lord Krishna about obligatory duties, knowing the Self, performing actions with the right attitude, cultivating discernment, the role of God in the creation and one's life, the journey of souls after death, exclusive devotion, self-control, self-purification and transformation, divine qualities one should cultivate, and so on. You will also learn the essential practices and principles of Hinduism, becoming well-informed and knowledgeable about these profound teachings.

Order your copy from https://www.PureLifeVision.com

www.ingramcontent.com/pod-product-compliance
Lightning Source LLC
Chambersburg PA
CBHW060517080526
44586CB00012B/515